Walter Montagu Kerr

The far interior

A narrative of travel and adventure from the Cape of Good Hope across the Zambesi to the lake regions of Central Africa

Walter Montagu Kerr

The far interior
A narrative of travel and adventure from the Cape of Good Hope across the Zambesi to the lake regions of Central Africa

ISBN/EAN: 9783337257323

Printed in Europe, USA, Canada, Australia, Japan

Cover: Foto ©Andreas Hilbeck / pixelio.de

More available books at **www.hansebooks.com**

THE FAR INTERIOR:

A NARRATIVE

OF

TRAVEL AND ADVENTURE

FROM

THE CAPE OF GOOD HOPE ACROSS THE ZAMBESI

TO THE

LAKE REGIONS OF CENTRAL AFRICA

BY

WALTER MONTAGU KERR, C.E., F.R.G.S.

WITH NUMEROUS ILLUSTRATIONS ENGRAVED BY
MR. J. D. COOPER AND OTHERS

IN TWO VOLUMES.—Vol. II.

BOSTON
HOUGHTON, MIFFLIN AND COMPANY
The Riverside Press, Cambridge
1886

LONDON:
PRINTED BY WILLIAM CLOWES AND SONS, LIMITED,
STAMFORD STREET AND CHARING CROSS.

CONTENTS OF VOL. II.

CHAPTER XIV.

DAYS WITH KING SAKANII.

                                                                                            PAGES

Strangers in town—Prospects of a beer-drinking bout—The great Chibinga dance—Native story-telling—Karemba's tales of the white man and of his own travels—Paying off the Inyota—An unexpected gift—Karemba's pathetic history—Settling with the "faithfuls"—Last glimpse of them—Bargaining with Sakanii, or Senhor Rubero—*Aqua ardiente*—Bewitching the lion—Msenga minstrels, dancers, and jugglers—Social anomalies—Hut teeming with vermin—A lion attack—Number of people killed by lions—Viciousness of wolves—The king tells the history of the town—A great battle—Chuzu's attack—" Well, you did have a lucky escape!"—Settling accounts with Rubero—Characteristics of the country—Working for gold—Msenga slaves—Women's work—Products and industries—Abnormal lips of Msenga women—Teeth-filing—Adieu, Chibinga! 1–23

CHAPTER XV.

THE MARCH TO TETTE.

Manaman, the interpreter—Poor villages—The Dake river—Maranga—Baboons—Incidents of the chase—Sulks—Curing the toothache—"Better halves" and bargains—Daingi—Frightening the water-carriers—A sociable old lady—A piebald Kaffir—Masecha—Occupations of the people—A remarkable exodus—Unsettled tribes—Can goats live in the "fly country"?—My condition after eight months' travel—A useless shot—Nothing to eat—The Fema mountains—"Zambesi! Zambesi! Senhor!"—View of the big river—Tette at last—Received by the governor . . 24–39

CHAPTER XVI.

TETTE, AND ACROSS THE ZAMBESI.

The earliest shower of the season—Mysterious disappearance of a day—Portuguese possessions in Eastern Africa—Zumbo—Tette

PAGES

—Trade in past times—A ruined town—Roman Catholic missions—No understanding of a Supreme Being—Fetichism—The governor of Tette—The garrison and government—Native soldiers—Kanyemba, the black chief—Europeans in Tette—Two hundred years of civilised intercourse—Industries and resources—Prospecting for gold—The rainy season—The Jesuit fathers—Decadence of the Portuguese—Class of steamers for river navigation—Rumours of war—The Makanga tribe—Woman devoured by a crocodile—The tragic story of the Zambesi—Funeral feasts—Recruiting for the advance—A doleful parting—Crossing the Zambesi—A last look at Tette 40-60

CHAPTER XVII.

INTO ANGONI-LAND.

The Revuqwe river—The Caroeira—The new staff—Oppressive heat—Tsetse fly again—Zebra hunting—Salumbidwa mountain—Coal—The Makanga king—A fruitless conversion—Kankune, the murderous chief—Rebellious carriers—Abandoning food—The Landin threaten to leave—Their reasons—Chakundakoro's unpopularity—Night marching—Passing over difficult ground—Awkward tumbles—Mysterious alarm—"Abantu! Abantu!"—Fright of the Landin—Midnight camp of Makanga warriors—A quick retreat—The Mvudzi river—Songless birds—Sugar and provisions stolen—A great native traveller—Sukurumbwe, a warlike tribe—Idea that the English eat people—Difficulties of walking amidst tall grass—An immense grass fire—Devil take the hindmost—The highest altitude of the journey—Landin desertions—Swollen legs, hunger, and sulks—A bad fall—The chronometer smashed—All the Landin desert, and leave their loads—I proceed with a few followers—Buffalo herd—Hunger again—Deuka's town—Coolness of a deserter—"Well, you've got here!"—Misiri's bargains—His culinary art—Maravi discontent—Slave kidnappers appear—Return of the Maravi—A Makololo war—The Maravi desert me—I am alone!—Lucky encounter—Start for the king's kraal—A silent march . . 61-95

CHAPTER XVIII.

TROUBLES AT CHIKUSE'S.

Superstitions about animals — Hippopotamus trenches — Enforced silence—Revelry of rats—A hideous night—The mysterious sentinel—Chikuse—Loneliness—Beer drinking—"Oh, if I could only speak!"—Thoughts of the old "faithfuls"—A shriek and a shot—Queer visitors—One-sided conversation—Lament for the dead—A timely arrival—Eustaquio da Costa—Plans for relief—King Chikuse is satisfied that I can speak—Ring head-dress—Cultivation of tobacco—The Angoni people—Killing a crocodile—Corn stores—Funeral ceremonies—Boy rat-catchers—Hunting reports—Medicines for everything—Quackery—Superstition ineradicable—Worshipping a donkey—The lady and the pombe—Chikuse is splenetic—His cruelties—The Makanga tribe—Food of the Angoni—Their customs—Slave kidnappers—Some aspects of the slave-trade—Horrors of the yoke—Departure of a caravan 96–129

CHAPTER XIX.

DA COSTA, THE ELEPHANT HUNTER.

A visit from Chikuse—The king washes himself—Beads and cloth are products of nature!—No God—Chikuse's wives—Engaging a guide—Music hath charms—The queen mother—A fine old woman—Her love affairs—Bewailing death—Tears and snuff—A scene of murder—Graceful damsels—Looking out for the new moon—Da Costa's kindness—Story of his life—The dreaded Makanga—Cruelty and treachery of the king—Execution of a supposed sorceress—Thrown to the crocodiles—A hunter's life in African wilds. 130–145

CHAPTER XX.

TOWARDS NYASSA.

Departing from Chikuse's—Thoughts of Nyassa—Difficulties—Gifts to slaves—Da Costa's good-bye—Mount Deza—Timidity of women—Mara the Maravi—His fowl-hunts and his wiles—Lying Angoni—Inquisitive blacks—Swarming kraals—Arms of the Assegai—The knobkerry—The Revuqwe—Signs of slave traffic—Slave stampede—"What the devil is the matter?"—Tortures of slavery—Iron smelting furnaces—Arab influence in slavery—Mountain scenery—The land of the rising sun—Nyassa—Salt carriers—"The white man has seen the lake"—How to reach Livingstonia—Crowding natives—The troublesome old men at Pantumbo's—Women at Pantumbo's—Objections to proceed—Look out for the people of Mponda—Distressing march—Fishermen—A disappointing shot—The luckless chronometer—A beautiful scene—"Nyanja senhor!"—Thoughts of the future—Angoni reluctance to go on—Sleep-disturbing hippos—Alarm of the Nyassa people—A hostile reception—"These people are enemies"—The party is surrounded—Explanations—On the shores of the lake—Oppressive heat—My first sickness—A wretched night—Canoeing—Livingstonia at last! . . . 146-183

CHAPTER XXI.

LIVINGSTONIA.

An ill wind again—Desolation—The man with the red umbrella—"All dead; all gone!"—Searching the deserted town—"It was the white man who lied!"—Shattered hopes—A letter to da Costa—Flight of the Angoni—Days of solitude—Mara's pessimism—The races of Nyassa—Fashions—Huts—No tsetse fly—Supplies exhausted—Mara has a full stomach—Teeth filing and tattoo marks—An odd cup of milk—The "look-out" on the lake—Fishes—A sick chief; medicine wanted—Doctoring the invalid—My patient a faithful follower of Livingstone—"All men are liars"—Mara's boon companions—Hard fare—Dysentery—Plucky natives—Stalking a dove—The stomach very near the heart—A sail!—Animal companions—Missionary sacrifice—The spirit of philanthropy—The spirit of the Church—Saddened thoughts—"Mzungo, Mzungo!"—"Steamer ahoy!"—The grasp of a white man's hand 184-208

CHAPTER XXII.

ON LAKE AND RIVER.

Farewell to Livingstonia—On board the *Ilala*—Lieutenant Giraud and the rescuing party—Mara's good-bye—An enticing supper—A hunter shot dead—Eaten by a crocodile—Slave dhows—Routes of slave caravans—Danger of releasing slaves—The road to Tanganyika—Origin of the Makololo war—A tragedy of the Shiré river—The banks of the Upper Shiré—Bird life—Crocodiles and hippos—Matope—Abundance of game—An animated scene—Canoe upset by a hippo—Carriers from Blantyre—Revived strength and hope—Cure for dysentery—Blantyre—The trading station—Comfort at last—Routes to Quillimane—Scarcity of food—Leopard attacks on goats—Death of Captain Foote—The employment of a consul at Blantyre—A bootless expedition—Makoka—Katungas—The significance of *Ilala* and *Blantyre*—Livingstone's tomb in Westminster Abbey—A request for black overalls—A troublesome chief—The incorrigible Fred—Bargaining for a lion's skull—Superstition at Katungas—Ula and Muave—Muave drinking—Ordeals of guilt—Hunting superstitions—Marriage and other domestic customs 209-230

CHAPTER XXIII.

DESCENDING THE SHIRÉ RIVER.

An erratic boat—Mbewe—Chiputula's burial services—The home of the deceased chief—Xopeta people—A rollicking uproar—The *Leviathan*—Canoeing more tiring than walking—Collecting palm wine—Among the water-buck—A good bag—Glad reception—Wet and fever—Approaching the seat of war—Separation of the canoes—Elephant spoor—Enormous ant heaps—Recoil and a tumble—Exciting hunt—The bull charges—Bearing down upon us—A good hollow bullet this time—Hippo attacks—Dangerous moments—Narrow escape of the *Leviathan*—Our new pilot—A welcome supper—News of the death of a chief's wife—Even mourning has a comical side—Ivory laws—Chiroma, Chiputula's town—The story of his quarrel with Fenwick and the tragedy of Chiromo—The sinking of the *Lady Nyassa*—A too well educated savage—Ransom for the steamer—Palm shelters on the *Leviathan*—Scenery on the river—A marvellous scene of the feathered world 240-261

CHAPTER XXIV.

THE PORTUGUESE AND MAZINJIRI WAR.

A scare—Flying natives—Fright of the *Leviathan's* crew—Black Senators in Congress—Bararika, the chief—Anxiety and misfortunes of the people—Expected attack by Portuguese—"Eat and grow fat; we want you next year"—The man with the gun—The challenge and the plunge—A sickening immersion—Hailing the enemy—In the Portuguese camp—Govea, or Don Manuel Antonio de Souza—War at an end—A hostage—"The Mazinjiri will be sure to kill him"—Bararika is enraged—"Why have you brought this man? he is a traitor"—Danger for the hostage—"I want to be killed at once"—A brave fellow—Parrying an arrow thrust—The *Tricolour's* crew rebels—Guarding the hostage—No provisions again—The Portuguese army—Easy discipline—Don Manuel again—He is hospitable—The cause and progress of the war—Example of Portuguese colonisation—An officious official—The scourge of war—Mercenaries of the Portuguese—Defeat of the Mazinjiri—Another horror of the Shiré—The gainers by war—How the mercenaries are rewarded—Under two flags—A fearful storm—Our soaking sleep—Results of the storm—Floating pumpkins, the spoils of war 262-281

CHAPTER XXV.

TO THE INDIAN OCEAN, AND HOME.

PAGES

Devastated shores—Heathen and Christian slavery—Village in flames—Portuguese in our wake—The merry conquerors—Dysentery—The dreaded Morambala—A fusilade—" We thought you were Mazinjiri "—Story of Hooft, the Dutch trader—Scruples of the Wangwana—Putrefying wastes—A heated silent scene—The *Leviathan* becomes unmanageable—An early start—Livingstone's headquarters in 1862—Mrs. Livingstone's grave—Mazaro—Mr. Lindsay—Preparing for the journey to Quillimane—The Kwakwa river—Excellent boatmen—Lovely evening views—Winged tormentors—Malarial atmosphere—Escape from a snake—Piracy on the Kwakwa—Unfortunate fishermen—The river meets the sea—Quillimane—Its appearance—" Oh ! you're not the man "—Hospitality at Quillimane—Fever at the last moment !—On board the S.S. *Dunkeld*—M. Giraud's adieu—Retrospect—Home—The past is sad : is there a bright future ? 282–302

ILLUSTRATIONS.

A Mazinjiri Warrior, Shiré River Valley	*Frontispiece*	
The Great Dance at Chibinga	*To face page*	4
Gold Washing at the Msingua River	,,	18
Msenga Woman	*page*	21
Portrait of the Governor of Tette	,,	45
Camp of the Dreaded Makanga	*To face page*	72
Deserted!	,,	100
Headrings of the Zulu Family	*page*	111
Maravi Hunter	,,	115
Slave Kidnappers	*To face page*	126
Surprising a Slaver	,,	156
Midnight Rescue on the Lake	,,	208
Portrait of Lieut. Giraud	*page*	211
On the Great Elephant Marshes, Shiré Valley	*To face page*	248
Running the Gauntlet	,,	252
Protecting a Hostage	,,	270
"Wo-oh! Ai! Oh!" Singing to the Sea	,,	296

THE FAR INTERIOR.

CHAPTER XIV.

DAYS WITH KING SAKANII.

Strangers in town—Prospects of a beer-drinking bout—The great Chibinga dance—Native story-telling—Karemba's tales of the white man and of his own travels—Paying off the Inyota—An unexpected gift—Karemba's pathetic history—Settling with the " faithfuls "—Last glimpse of them—Bargaining with Sakanii, or Senhor Rubero—*Aqua ardiente*—Bewitching the lion—Msenga minstrels, dancers, and jugglers—Social anomalies — Hut teeming with vermin — A lion attack — Number of people killed by lions—Viciousness of wolves—The king tells the history of the town—A great battle—Chuzu's attack —" Well, you did have a lucky escape !"—Settling accounts with Rubero—Characteristics of the country—Working for gold—Msenga slaves—Women's work—Products and industries—Abnormal lips of Msenga women—Teeth-filing—Adieu, Chibinga !

"WELL, John, weren't we in luck catching the king so soon ? "

" Master looks veree tired.* My gaut, dis is a very beeg man; he got lots of people ! De boys tink de master will them nauting give. Dey say, ' When de king comes he don't care for us.' Dar is lots of peoples here from a town on de Zambesi, and the peoples of dis town is making lots of beer."

Mingling with the regular inhabitants I perceived numbers of people with their hair done up in many fantastic

---

* Judging from appearances, King Sakanii doubled my age in a guess.

shapes and forms, and it was very evident from the prevailing signs that there would soon be a grand beer-drinking bout.

John had been out that morning and had killed a magnificent eland bull with the finest head I ever saw.

The king's boys took possession of the hut which my Inyota men had occupied, who therefore, being turned out, formed a large circle of fires in front of my hut. Shortly after our arrival crowds of people assembled in what I have termed the plaza—that is to say the open space in the centre of the town, between the hut in which I was quartered and the house of Senhor Rubero. Numbers of drums were placed in a row. The feast had evidently begun.

John said that the Inyota or Makorikori, who had accompanied us so far, would be sure to remain until the close of the festivities. One and all the boys seemed beside themselves with joy at the thought of returning home; for I had told them that they would all be paid, and might retrace their steps whenever they wished to do so. Enlivened by this happy news, they threw themselves heart and soul into the convivialities of the hour. Native beer flowed like running water, and koodoo and eland meat were to be had in abundance, for quantities which John and myself had shot had been dried in the sun.

The open centre of the town swarmed with ebonised humanity. Sounds of song and jubilant shouts mingled with the throbbing vibrations of the everlasting drum, breaking with droll and savage harmonies the natural stillness of the forest air. The noise rose and fell like rolling waves of sound, or like the spasmodic drone of a rising gale.

Dark-skinned maidens danced merrily and sang their shrillest notes, keeping time as they stamped the ground, throwing their bodies alternately right and left, and following each other through the snake-like windings of their frolicsome fandango. With more solemnity the older women, bearing upon their backs the young ones, whose little heads would wag in every way, as if they were fixed on the universal joint principle, while their mothers with great flat feet entered upon the dance with a serious earnestness of purpose.

THE CHIBINGA DANCE.

For three days and three nights the drums never ceased to beat. In daytime the fun was fiercest, even when the sun was at its greatest height, and cast down fiery rays upon the sprightly crowd, melting the fat in the glistening locks of their woolly heads, so that it ran in oil all over their bodies, and seemed to give them a zest for further exertion; for the men would vie one with another in the violence of their wild diversion. The dance seemed to partake of the character both of the breakdown and double shuffle. Clouds of dust were raised.

Those men of the mountains who had come with me were by far the best dancers. They stamped upon the ground so wildly that it seemed as though their feet would burst. Their necks, too, appeared to be in danger, as they threw their heads with impetuous force from right to left, and *vice versâ*. The black man never could be happier. For him the world was great and free; or, as John more practically said, " de bellies is full, and dey feel glad,—dey shall all sleep soon."

Groups of the revellers assembled under a small tree near our hut, which afforded shelter during the day, and listened to the stories of Karemba, who was now a man of some importance, for he had been a great traveller, and, by dint of practice, had become an orator and warbler of not a little consequence. Among them were some ancient endunas, who, doubtless, could tell some dreadful stories of the white (?) men's conquests in the great valley. They gave forth long yarns to my boys, telling them how they had travelled, how important they had been as young men, how much they had done, how much they had seen, how the church bells had rung in Kunyungwi on every seventh day; how the white men knelt before a cross surrounded by blazing light to make crops to grow and rain to fall; how the white

THE GREAT DANCE AT CHIBINGA.

soldier blew a bugle at the rising and setting of the sun; how the Portuguese were carried about in easy chairs, and built houses of stone and mud, and never drank water; how the white wives had long flowing hair, and never did any work, and numerous other extraordinary memories.

But Karemba had no idea of being outdone. Not wishing to appear of smaller reputation than his aged rivals, he laid great emphasis upon the relation of his experiences in distant southern lands, where the white man drove oxen in waggons. To describe this with greater effect he gave practical illustrations by shouting and gesticulating in a most violent manner, pantomimically performing all the time the different methods of driving the trek ox. He showed how the white man rode upon the back of animals like zebras, for it must not be forgotten that the people here had never seen a donkey, an ox, nor even a horse. The reality of his description was made more forcible by an action of show of riding a very rough-trotting horse. His mimicry caused great wonder and amusement. My follower also showed how the white man hunted the antelope, firing from the back of a horse when running at full speed.

He also described how the white child was nearly smothered in limbo and beads, and was fed from a bottle, and rolled in a gourd on wheels with its little face hidden from the sun.

One of his most impressive wonders, however, was to count upon his fingers to show how many moons he had travelled with this white man, and how many, many more would pass before he would again reach the land of his birth, the country of Umzila, on the great river Sabia which flowed to the sea through the land of the rising sun.

After a recital of such stories the pipe went socially

round, much snuffling was solemnly indulged in, and copious supplies of beer imbibed.

All things, however—even a Chibinga carnival—must come to an end. Now that the beer was finished the merry-making was stopped, like many another feast in different climes.

I was truly glad when the affair was over, for there had been no peace. During the day I was off hunting for meat, which had to be stored in a small hut set apart as my dwelling, and also as a storehouse for the boys. A horrible effluvium filled the place, and nearly suffocated me. The rats, too, held a high carnival, and made night hideous as they ran with their cold feet over my unprotected face.

The Inyota boys made a most terrific noise in the mornings. They appeared to be testing the powers of the human frame in the production of penetrating sounds, the torment being much aggravated by the effect of the hemp-pipe.

It was with no little pleasure that I paid them off, satisfying them all. One of the company, quite the wildest of the lot, as he was running off to catch his companions who were in advance, suddenly took off his iron and copper bead bracelets and gave them to me. I mention this as an extraordinary incident; for it is most unusual for a Kaffir to make a present without a hope of receiving a better in return. What had actuated him in this generosity I cannot say, but I had at different times looked at his trinkets. This was the man who on my first appearance at Inyota went through such amazing antics, whistling loudly, and throwing himself into threatening attitudes in front of me. He was a beau ideal of the veritable savage, and his every look and action showed that he felt the strongest instincts of savageness. Wild, unfettered, robust, and uncontrolled, he possessed in a marked degree the coveted happiness of a natural life; that happiness which all the multitudes of Christendom are perpetually striving after, and ignominiously fail to achieve. The expression of his emotions was spontaneous and quick, while the noisy clamour of his voice, or the bark of his hemp excited cough, were varied by shrill whistling, or by the music of the wild song of Inyota's saturnalian dance.

The household generally determined that they would not accompany the Inyota men, but would wait until they had a good day's start. John had no confidence in them.

At this point I was able to find out a little about Karemba's history, and consequently ceased to wonder at his serious apprehensions concerning what seemed to him probable dangers in travelling in this part of the country. When he was a little boy he was sold as a slave and taken to Tette on the Zambesi, along with his father and mother, but in a few years they all obtained their freedom, and travelled back to their home in Umzila's country by the waters of the Sabia river.

After the departure of the Inyota men, on the following morning I paid off the "faithfuls," satisfying them all except Karemba, who declared that he wanted a pair of trousers besides the other articles, consisting of some pretty clothes, I had given him. He said I had promised him trousers. I told him there was none to give, but if he came on to Tette with me he would assuredly get them. At the same time I knew well that Karemba wished to adorn his nether man with the corduroy trousers I had on, and although inconvenient under the circumstances, I retired to my den and delivered the unmentionables over to him. As he still craved for something more, I gave him a few pounds of beads, which made him perfectly happy. Karemba had been such a very good boy that his little shortcomings were easily forgotten; they vanished from my mind as though they had never existed, and I was willing to put myself a good deal about in order to satisfy so trusty a follower, and give some evidence of my recollection of his admirable services.

John I could see was busily engaged in picking out some of the sacks that had stood the wear and tear of the journey.

"You won't forget the goat at Shitimba, John," said I.

"No, sir; I take um back to my leetle wife! I like dat de master is coming back mit us too."

"What are the sacks for?"

"I wants dem to take de rice home when I get back to de waggon." The old acquisitiveness still stuck to John.

The faces of Karemba, Sagwam, and Umfana were radiant with delight, showing their innermost feelings of ecstasy at the thought that for them there would be no more wandering. I sincerely hope I succeeded in making them all feel happy. I thought much as I watched the lessening forms of the small party as it faded into the gloom of distance. John's long dream of home and his "leetle wife" would soon be realised. To him and his comrades Chibinga was now fast sinking from view. The small group of faithfuls, after a long farewell, headed towards the south, skirting the banks of the Msingua river, with a fair wind, homeward bound. For some time after they had left I sat on the banks of the river meditating upon the aspects of the situation. Now I was without a single follower.

Returning to the town I found Senhor Rubero, who informed me that he had received news from Chigurindi, his town on the river, which would necessitate his immediate departure. He wanted very much to buy my rifles; but this, of course, was a demand I could never accede to.

When, however, he indicated a liking for my blankets I was very glad to give him one.

The Senhor's supply of goods at this town was dangerously scarce; therefore it was with not a little trepidation that I watched him paying out numerous fathoms of calico for ivory, monkey-skins, and gold. The latter he weighed in a small pair of medicine scales with so much attention as to make it clear that he had a good, if one-sided, idea of its value. What weights he used I could not determine; evidently they were changeable, and conveniently adapted to the appearance and demeanour of his customers. This did not occupy my mind so much as the anxious thoughts about the gradual disbursement of the goods; for all the men who might accompany me to Tette would have to be paid in advance before I could move a step out of Chibinga.

Numbers of superanuated chiefs, grim and time-worn, along with all sorts and sizes of people from the adjacent towns, sat around in a large circle. *Aqua ardiente* was passed freely, and it was almost pitiful to see the simple people, accustomed to nothing stronger than their innocuous beer, drink the stuff—I say it was pitiful to see them shudder from head to foot when they swallowed the fire-water of civilisation.

One evening I witnessed an extraordinary ceremony which happened to be proceeding at the village on the opposite banks of the river. The people were making a great noise. A man dressed in the skin of a lion performed various odd manœuvres around the town's enclosure, his actions being supposed to have some bewitching power over the lion. When first they told me that a lion was near, I thought that surely one of those animals was in the river, as I had often seen the spoor. I ran to fetch a rifle, thereby causing much astonishment and even mirth. The true state of affairs being disclosed, I studied carefully the nature of the curious ceremony; but it was altogether so extraordinary and obscure that I could not quite comprehend its full import. Various presents, however, were laid before the performer, and my observations led to the inference that the mummery was a sort of exorcism of leonine spirits, or a peacemaking with the king of beasts.

In Senhor Rubero's town the Msenga minstrels and conjurers would come before us at intervals, followed by an admiring crowd. Their performances were as varied and remarkable as they were energetic, and that is saying a good deal. I never heard them sing together; their entertainments were usually gone through individually, no matter what fête was proceeding.

Decidedly unique costumes were worn by the minstrels. The principal had his hair in a form resembling a frizzette, passing over the top of the head, shaved on each side, and coloured with red bark, while a wreath from a wild hog's mane encircled his head, giving him a peculiarly savage appearance, as the bristles stood out stiffly all around. Cicatrices covered his face and body. On his neck and wrists he wore a profusion of charms, consisting of crocodile's teeth and wild beast's claws, strung upon gut, and intermingled with porcelain beads, brass wire, and jungle grass. Girding his waist, shells and large red beads alternately skirted many skins of the monkey and baboon, the tails reaching to the ground. The contrast of colours had rather a pleasing effect. Below the knee were leglets of goatskin, white and black, twisted like a spiral spring. Running in a line down the sides of the calves of his legs were rows of bells made from the husks of wild fruit, and loaded with small pebbles. Shells of this description also encircled his ankles.

Altogether, the garb of the Msenga juggler was very passable for a man in his line of business in any country.

His dances before us were of the wildest character, and called forth most powerful exertions. Crossing one foot rapidly in front of the other, he repeated the movement over and over again, keeping time to a hideous noise he made with an instrument consisting of a narrow block of wood, upon which six very strong strings of gut were stretched to their fullest tension, all being firmly fixed upon a large hollow calabash covered with little pieces of bark, shells, and bones, which gave to his song a rattling accompaniment like the clatter of a harsh tambourine. Every now and then he would shake all over, and touch the strings with a master effort, while the perspiration poured down his body like globules of foam.

The snake dance was a singular feat. Lying on his back, and playing all the while, he worked himself through the dust along the ground, making his flexible frame bend in a manner that would have brought applause to any contortionist, even to the "boneless men" whose feats are sometimes advertised.

Best of all, however, was the gorilla dance, in which the performer looked quickly over one shoulder, and then wriggled his body so violently that the numerous monkey tails of his robes were thrown up as high as his head. Then glancing rapidly over his other shoulder he viewed the tails as they rose, being switched up with a dexterity that gave one the impression that they were natural appendages of the man. He then lay flat upon the ground, holding on his chest a wooden mortar in which was some rice. Two powerful men grasped thick poles, and using them as pestles, pounded away with might and main until the admiring audience were perfectly satisfied that the rice was husked.

At every stroke of the enormous pestles the man looked as if he would give way on all sides.

"A savage entertainment indeed!" I think I hear some sympathetic reader exclaim. But, after all, similar amusements may be seen any day in the gilded halls of great cities, and in the lowly booths of villages in the heart of dear old England.

Yes, the people who performed before us typified the minstrels of primitive man, and yet their modes of amusement closely resembled those which I had witnessed far away at home: there were the archaic signs of the "strong man," the musician, and the clown.

Feasting, too, is not essentially different from our own; only the Kaffir never becomes bored with his paint and feathers. If the reader has ever watched the progress of one of our favourite dances—the Highland reel or the popular schottische—from the outside of a thick plate-glass window where not a note of music could be heard, he cannot have failed, consciously or unconsciously, to be much impressed with the universal similarity of human efforts at enjoyment.

Social assemblies present many apt pictures. We see, perhaps, an intensely erudite old gentleman—even a cultured divine—feast, jump, and shout in obedience to all the natural instincts which prompted his naked ancestors to do exactly the same thing two thousand years ago. The old gentleman, possibly, has a polished top to his head, is frozen with pomp, and would think it terribly *infra dig* to run and catch an omnibus; yet there he is jumping up and down, frantically throwing his hands into the air, and opening his mouth to give vent to vehement shouts of exultant savageness, just as the wild tribes inhabiting the virgin forest or roaming over the pathless desert have done ever since the days of Adam.

When evening came I took my blanket and lay down under the tree directly in front of the hut. Efforts to get a little rest were at once interrupted by some women, who made signs that I should not lie there, but should go inside the hut, a den that quite baffles description, through the sickening smell which came from putrifying meat and other unsavoury articles.* But acting on their advice I went in; and as their was no light, I made up a small fire in the centre of the floor. Unluckily it soon went out. Then began a regular night-revel of vermin; they ran or creeped in every direction. The bug's bite was as keen as the tsetse's stab. Rats and white ants were doing their utmost to demolish what little was left of the dilapidated roof. One of the rats giving me a nasty bite on the finger, I struck a match, and immediately the light revealed the teeming life of the place. On the dark mud walls great black and grey spiders were busily exploring, while cockroaches and crickets moved about in whole battalions, the former being especially numerous. This dingy hut reminded me of the den so familiar in Boucicault's half-forgotten drama, "The Streets of London."

Shortly after I had rolled in my blanket on the floor, for there was nothing else to rest upon, I heard a great deal of shouting, varied by shrill and alarming screams. Very soon the town was in a high state of excitement. As was my custom, on occasions such as these, I ran out and discovered Sakanii standing outside his residence, and shouting at the top notes of his voice:

"Bring your guns, guns; quick, bring your guns!"

Could it be an attack? I ran back with all speed and,

* The women's advice was owing to the wolves, which I have spoken of as showing a propensity to run off with people's noses and other portions of their faces.

snatching up C. L. K., went forth quickly to see what was the matter. At a little distance from the town, in the bed of the river, we found a party of panic-stricken women, all shrieking with terror. One of the women having been very badly torn by a lion.

When we returned, I inquired what was the origin of all the excitement. The answer was, that these women were coming back from their gardens, and having missed one of their number, were searching for her, when they heard her piercing screams. She had fallen asleep, and had been attacked by a lion; but through the combined yells of the party, the brute had cleared off. The women said that he had followed them to the river; but that was unlikely, as the feminine noise they were making would have terrified any animal. There was no doubt about the truth of the first portion of their story.

Senhor Rubero told me that between Chibinga and his other town, at least ten men were killed every year by lions. The attacks usually take place during the rainy season, when the people are working at their corn patches, and fall asleep. Some of them are killed *en route* from one town to the other.

Wolves, he also told me, were very vicious here. Many of his people had been bitten on the face. The savage beasts would even enter the houses, if the doors were left open. When I heard this, I fully understood the reason why the people had made such a fuss when I had attempted to go to sleep in peace with the door open; and I have just described how the women objected to my reposing beneath the tree in front of the hut. That they had good reason to dread the exposure was very apparent; for I saw several persons of both sexes, whose faces were very much disfigured by the horrible bites of these ferocious animals.

One afternoon was devoted to walking through the town with the king. He showed me the house, or rather its remains, where his eldest brother had been buried. After the brother's demise, Senhor Rubero had successfully claimed the country; but I heard that he had another brother, who had some pretensions to the leadership, and had caused not a little trouble. The ruined house was enclosed by a fence, through which no native could be induced to pass. The defunct ruler had been left in the home in which he had lived and died, a common custom among many native tribes in Africa.

Beside the remains of the house was a broken flag-staff. The red-tiled roof was sinking amidst a wild profusion of luxuriant vegetation. Tiles in other quarters seemed to be things of a more prosperous past. Nothing but grass-thatch could now be seen on the surrounding huts. Even Senhor Rubero's abode was rather hovel-like, with its walls of mud and grass-thatched roof.

On the west side of the town I was shown a succession of circular mounds, occupying a place where many huts once stood. My royal guide explained with considerable excitement how there had been a great battle on the spot. The people had been surprised by a tribe, living only a few days' march westward from the place, who were under a very powerful chief, and were bitterly hostile to the Mzungo, as his people were designated.

The wild fiends had started suddenly from the forest, in the grey of the early dawn. Ere a stand could be made against them, they succeeded in setting fire to the huts, almost totally destroying the town, for the flames spread with great rapidity.

Sakanii told, with justifiable pride, how gallantly his people had rallied, and although attacked by overwhelming numbers, had repelled the furious onslaught, turning the fate of the fight, and changing doom for victory. He passed on, and pointing to the skull-crowned posts, which stood like grim sentinels at the portals of the town, he said:

"Look, do you see those two heads? They were cut from the bodies of the son and the brother-in-law of the chief who attacked us. They fell to our guns on that memorable day. Ah, *bando de ladrões!* [they are a set of robbers.] Those Makorikori scoundrels dare not come down to this town or to Kanjemba's town on the north of their country."

Hearing the name of a tribe with which I was familiar, I asked the name of the chief, and thought of the strange events which accompanied my wanderings, when he immediately replied:

"Arre! Chuzu!"

"Only eighteen months ago," Senhor Rubero continued, "Chuzu killed two Portuguese traders, who went into his country quite peaceably. They were surrounded, and very few of the boys even got away."

When I told him what my experience had been, he exclaimed, in astonishment:

"Well, you did have a lucky escape!"

Days past, and my longing to leave Chibinga became stronger and stronger. One afternoon Senhor Rubero called to me, as I was returning from making some observations of altitudes; he said:

"In the morning your men will be ready. I have paid them all, thirteen in number."

I was not long in settling accounts with him, and all was then in readiness.

The payment of the illustrious Senhor was a very amusing

performance. The attributes of a keen business man seemed to be born with him, and were seen in every quick glance and anxiously scrutinising gaze with which he accompanied his astutely primitive bargaining. He turned the golden sovereigns many times in his hands, gloating over the chips from the Mammon of the civilised world; for he had evinced not a little curiosity to see some specimens of the English currency, expressing doubts as to its value in reis.

When the time for final settlement arrived, he had fixed to his own satisfaction the relative value of the coins, by the addition of a cypher or two. As he worked at the mysterious form of calculation peculiar to the people of the Zambesi basin, a pang of anxiety passed through me. The paper looked like an ancient Chinese MS., when he passed it over, happily with the words "*dezanove libras*," which, in reis on the paper, looked like an indefinite quantity of pounds.

My stock of provisions was decidedly light, for the king said that six days would see us in Tette, and that it was unnecessary to take much with us. Six days! According to my reckoning, that would be at the rate of about twenty miles a day, very good travelling indeed; just about a half more than I could expect from the Kaffirs, or even from myself, for I was almost bare-footed. An estimate of travel in Africa is like an estimate for building a house in London. You should always begin by doubling the numerals.

This country is about 1,800 feet above the sea. It may be described as a vast forest, extending northward from the foothills of the Makomwe mountains to the Zambesi. The vegetation is as varied and luxuriant as it is abundant. The immense jungles comprise mimosa, acacias, aloes, palms, also thorned creepers and prickly shrubs of almost every description. Throughout the whole basin of the Zambesi, the gigantic *Adansonia*, or baobab, is exceedingly common. Great, coarse reeds, with needle-pointed leaves, fringe the banks of the wide, sandy rivers, which flow in all directions, separating the belts of the forest.

During my stay at Chibinga, I was not at any time idle. If not hunting, I was investigating, and thus gained a good deal of information respecting the various river beds in the vicinity, for many miles around.* In some of the beds I found alluvial deposits, containing a fair quantity of gold.

The principal river was the Msingua, which I have described as being a waterless channel, excepting during the rains.

There may be seen large numbers of the slaves of the Portuguese half-caste who claims this country, engaged in washing the sands in circular wooden troughs, and expertly saving the thin tales of gold, as do the Californians when they " pan out " the gravel in prospecting the value of a " claim."

In other and smaller affluents of the Umzengaizi, such as the Benia and the Mkoma, on the banks of which I found salt efflorescence in abundance, traces of gold may also be found, but not in quantities as in the Msingua.

The women, many of whom carry babies on their backs, dig deep holes in the sand, until the underlying shingle is reached. In these simple wells they wash the sands, and extract its golden treasure. Day after day they steadily work under the scorching sun. The lot of woman is indeed one of toil and suffering in this country.

Doubtless many auriferous quartz veins are exposed in

* The result is embodied in the map which accompanies this book.

GOLD WASHING AT THE MSINGUA RIVER.

the mountains we have just left. Numberless rivulets spring from these mountain slopes. During the rainy season they swell and rush impetuously on their downward course, carrying the gold-charged silt from the water-worn fissures above, to be deposited in the sandy beds of the big rivers flowing through the forest-clad valley. The channels of these rivers, being almost level, act as settlers, and extract all the treasure from the waters long before the Zambesi is reached.

The gold, of which I have many specimens, I found generally free from base metals, and it would likely be easily amalgamated. I have observed, however, in some cases iron-rust on the flakes of the gold.

The natives of this district belong to the Mtande, or Mtavanda tribe. They seem to possess large numbers of slaves, purchased at Msenga, a town on the northern banks of the Zambesi.

The slaves are chiefly women, and they are most industrious, hard-working creatures. From sunrise till sunset they may be seen carrying the heaviest loads of wood, water, and other requisites, including great bundles of grass for thatching purposes. This is the only mode of conveying produce, or transporting goods, that can be seen in the country.

Women, too, do most of the work in the cultivation of the soil. Using an iron hoe, they till small pieces of open ground in the heart of the forest; also plots of land which absorb the water of annual floods. Upon these patches they raise millet, maize, yams, and tomatoes; the latter growing in abundance.

Rice is very scarce. Cotton is indigenous, and is cultivated in small quantities, and spun by hand in a most primitive manner. Weaving is equally primitive, the yarn being usually made into coarse, but very strong blankets. The cotton seemed to be a fine quality.

I watched with great interest some of the operatives making thread in their primeval way. Their spinning-wheels consisted of a thin piece of stick, having at one end a cone of wood with notches, through which the spun thread was passed. A little hook at the apex of the cone held the thread tightly, while the worker spun more, to be added to the spool on the stick. To obtain the required velocity, the spinner would spin the stick between the palm of his right hand and his thigh, feeding the while with his left hand the skein, which he had before partially equalised in thickness.

The men make very neat baskets of palm. The women, as they do in other parts of Africa, prepare the food. The men build the huts and fences, hunt for game, and spin.

The husks of millet and rice are cleaned in mortars, called banda, which are hollowed from the trunks of trees. The meal is ground upon blocks of granite, in a way that reminded me of the method followed by the Mexican tortilla makers.

Msenga women, of whom I have been speaking, are easily distinguished from those of other tribes, particularly by the upper lip, which protrudes excessively, being an artificial growth, in which a ring (*jaja*) is worn. By paying particular attention to her toilet, and yearly enlarging the ring, it is possible for a woman to develop the growth of the upper lip, so as to protrude two and a half inches from the front teeth. Filing the teeth is also a common custom; the usual fashion being the form of crocodiles' teeth, or the saw. Many of them, when approaching middle age, have a thick, yellow tartar coating the teeth; and when they smile, the elongating of the lips sideways turns the ring upwards against the nose, thus disfiguring the face in a most repulsive manner. A European would find it hard to discover the captivation in visages of this description, although with them it is considered a triumph of culture over crude nature. The people generally shave the head.

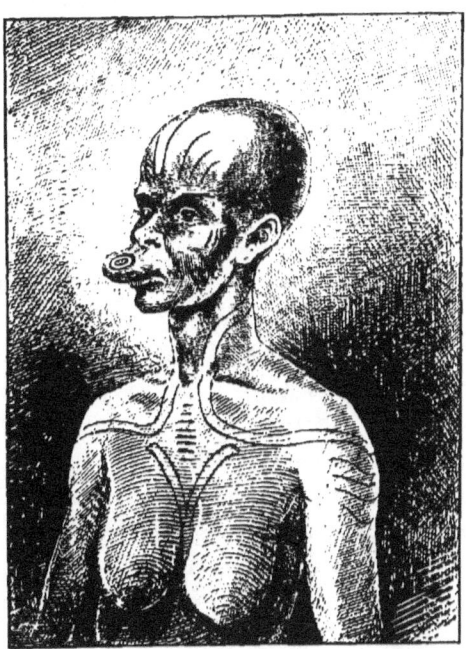

MSENGA WOMAN OF THE MANGANJA TRIBE.

After Senhor Rubero said, "In the morning your men will be ready," I retired, for the last time, to my uneasy couch at Chibinga, longing for the brightening signs of the opening day.

Morning breaks! For some time past the weather has been intensely hot, but the dawn of day brings an easterly wind, sweeping great grey clouds across the heavens, shutting out the fierce rays of the withering sun, and letting us breathe again with refreshing ease.

We leave Chibinga. Our line of march is eastward, across the wide, sandy rivers Msingua and Mkumbura. Onwards we travel, and form our night camp on the verge of some small wells which have been dug in a slow rivulet of muddy silt. Around us is the mopani forest, above which the tall baobab is seen towering high over the stunted growth of other trees. Amid the waving branches and fluttering leaves, the zephyrs of evening sigh and whisper their swelling melody of nature.

Southward the Makomwe mountains, outlined in faintest blue, stand boldly above the forest line. They recall to my memory stirring days passed under the shadows of their rockbound crests. Yes! at last we are well on our way, and the panorama of the eventful past glides its recording pictures vividly and swiftly through my thoughts.

Adieu to thee, Chibinga! The tsetse and the thorn are thy fittest symbols. Adieu to thy ebony damsels! Adieu to they griefs and cares, thy pangs and joys!

I will ever remember the long and toilsome marches over thy parched river beds, moistureless through the fiery breath of the relentless sun. I will ever remember the wild weirdness of the notes of thy free and thoughtless sons reverberating through the stilly night, the rhythmic throb of the tom tom mingling with the harmonious and gleeful shouts of thy people.

Nor shall I forget the great feast. The Msenga jugglers, and their wild, ape-like dance; those long hunts in thy stubborn forests and jungles, amidst whose thorns I strived to find food to keep the wolfish crowd in peace. Above all

I shall not forget those awful nights in thy den with four blackened walls, where utter filth prevailed, and where creatures innumerable and loathsome crawled on the earth, or jumped and played in sportive glee in the noxious air.

Adieu, Chibinga! Gladly, indeed, do I relegate thy pains to the memories of the past!

CHAPTER XV.

THE MARCH TO TETTE.

Manaman, the interpreter—Poor villages—The Dake river—Maranga—Baboons—Incidents of the chase—Sulks—Curing the toothache—"Better halves" and bargains—Daingi—Frightening the water-carriers—A sociable old lady—A piebald Kaffir—Masecha—Occupations of the people—A remarkable exodus—Unsettled tribes—Can goats live in the "fly country"?—My condition after eight months' travel—A useless shot—Nothing to eat—The Fema mountains—"Zambesi! Zambesi! Senhor!"—View of the big river—Tette at last—Received by the governor.

I WILL not attempt to detail to my readers the daily occurrences of the somewhat tedious march to the river, although it was not wanting in vicissitudes and trials of temper.

The interpreter was a young man named Manaman, who had been brought up in Chibinga, and was constantly with Senhor Rubero's children, some of whom could talk a little Portuguese, consequently he could say a few words, sufficient to allow a little conversation.

We had lovely weather for the first few days. Game was sufficiently abundant to enable me to keep the provision department well stocked. The spoor of a great variety of wild beasts could be seen in the sandy river beds which were crossed.

Tsetse fly varied in numbers. Sometimes they were swarming, at other times few were to be seen.

Leaving the Kafua mountains, which we had viewed from the Makomwe summit before descending into the wide valley* to the north, we continued our journey through lands of forest varying in density. The trees became larger as we travelled eastward. Numerous small towns were passed, the inhabitants of which seemed very poor. Their houses were badly constructed. Nothing seemed to be abundant save the tsetse and the clouds of blinding sand. Occasionally herds of antelope and zebra were seen.

Maranga was reached in due time. It is one of a number of towns dotted along the banks of the Dako river (altitude 825 feet), which has its source among the Vunga mountains, and flows to the Zambesi through a deep alluvial soil overlying stratified rocks jutting out here and there in the river bed, and grown over by thorns and stretches of low forest. When we passed, in the dry season, there was no running water here.

A short halt was made at Maranga so that I might hunt a little. With a native of the district as my companion I wandered through glades of high grass, and down to the banks of the river among the thorns. Large troupes of baboons (*cynocephalus babuini*) were soon disporting themselves among the high grass and climbing the forest trees. On the march previously I had shot some of the animals for the sake of their skins—all unfortunately lost.

As we were in search of game I had no intention of firing at these beasts, for there is no pleasure in shooting a baboon or a monkey; but seeing a very large number of them running beside us within sixty yards, some being very large, I raised my rifle and took aim at one of the biggest. At this, my guide seemed beside himself with fright, and frantically signed to me to desist.†

---

* The mountain has a peculiar shape. It forms a low tableland, having a gentle slope of about ten miles running down towards the east.

† The man's anxiety made me think of a little incident which happened

Soon, however, some antelopes appeared, at about two hundred yards off, and attracted us much more than the enormous baboons which were so disagreeably close. A long stalk was necessary, for the antelopes were travelling upwind and the thorns impeded our progress very much. My feet were getting worse day after day. There is nothing in the boot line to be found in this country. After crawling in a breathless state for some time, and every now and then peeping over the rank vegetation, we at last came within range, so that I was able to bring down an eland bull. On the way home I shot some guinea-fowl (*Numida Pucherani*), which were almost as shy as the game. I also brought down a small gazelle.

The game here is so constantly disturbed by the natives shooting with their erratic flint-locks that it is in fact very hard work, requiring not a little dexterity, too, to be successful in the chase. The places where game was

while I was out hunting on another occasion. Observing a couple of baboons squatting on the bough of an acacia, face to face, I fired and brought one of them down, being anxious to see to what variety they belonged. The moment it fell the other jumped from the bough as quickly as possible, and seizing its comrade bounded away into the thicket with surprising strength and agility. Perhaps an occurrence of this kind has led some of the natives to think that there is something human about these animals, although in many districts they do not hesitate to use their skins as aprons before and behind. There is no accounting for the whims of tribes, who show differences even when dwelling in close proximity. I recollect that, while elephant shooting in Southern Africa, when an animal was killed the Zulus, or Hottentots, would devour every morsel of the carcase, and even suck the marrow from the celular bones of the head. The Kaffir in the old Cape colony would not taste such meat, no matter how hungry he was. This I have observed on several occasions, the answer to an inquiry on the subject being, "The elephants are people; we won't eat them." Yet these very people will devour a monkey with avidity, although it resembles them much more closely in figure and action. Possibly the reason they give to the elephant a human connection is that the udder is between the fore legs.

most plentiful were in the young forest-patches, where the grass had been burnt and there was no undergrowth of any description to afford cover to the stalker—not even an ant heap. Antelopes when hunted or disturbed are ever on the alert, and their quickness of vision is most remarkable.

My men had all been paid in advance, as was the custom of the country. This prevented the necessity for my carrying cloth, but then, having nothing to offer them, I would be in an extraordinary fix should they take it into their wonderful heads to walk off, in fact to "bolt." It was a strange experience altogether; for at any moment they might leave me in the veldt or in some small town where the people would give nothing.

Fits of sulks were not of frequent occurrence, and the people evidently had a better idea of such travelling than any tribe I had hitherto encountered. True, they were not without their peculiarities. For example, they were loth to hurry away from the Dake river, where evidently they had numerous friends. The meat, however, was soon finished, and then came my turn. I struck for mileage, and determined not to shoot any more.

We were to have reached the Zambesi in six days. The six days had passed, and we had barely covered half the distance.

One of the men said he had toothache. The whole party was at once in sympathy with him, and every one sulked. To meet the exigencies of the occasion I produced my forceps, which often before had caused fearful shrieks in its work of dismembering the jaw-bone. Much to my amazement he did not seem to fear the dreaded implement of torture, although its appearance had the effect of making him quickly shut his mouth with the evident determination that no white man should run off with any part of his bodily frame. He was a morose creature this. On one occasion I had with difficulty disarmed him, when he had drawn his knife and rushed at one of the boys with the evident intention of killing him. This was the only time in all my experiences in Africa that I saw any attempt at life-taking among the natives, irrespective of their blood-curdling execution scenes.

A south-easterly course was now pursued. For some hours we went down the bed of the Dake river.

Towns were seen at short intervals all along the banks. At one of these we stopped to try and make a trade for pigeons.

A tremendous fuss ensued. The men came out to barter, and the women remained inside, for we were close to the small town with its cane fence. From behind the fence the wives of the traders generally sent out shouts of infuriated remonstrance against the short-sighted bargains of their husbands. The better halves did well in this way. When one of them heard of the arrangement her lord and master was making, she volubly sent to his ears a string of epithets, none of which would have been his choice for a personal description of himself.

The maligned man would then turn round and, looking as angry and as indignant as he possibly could, he would retort in screaming tones that he was doing his utmost to screw another quarter of a yard from the Mzungo; if she would only be quiet he would make a better bargain than she herself was capable of doing. After two or three volleys of dreadful and piercing words from inside the fence, the bargain was at length concluded.

The handling of the birds was a very rough operation. Feathers were torn out and were flying in all directions.

The poor pigeons were dashed roughly into an almost airtight bag, which was immediately closed up. I thought that the place would be a likely outpost for the Society for the Prevention of Cruelty to Animals.

Arriving at the town of Daingi, I stopped to interview a man gorgeously robed in calico of many colours. Properly speaking, he came out to interview me. He inquired where I was bound for, and on being told that I was going to cross the Zambesi and proceed to the Lake regions, he expressed much astonishment, and said:

"Oh, you travel very far. I have never seen a man so white as you."

I asked him how many days he considered the journey from here to Kunyungwi, and he replied about five. Of the Lake regions he knew nothing. Before proceeding on our journey he presented me with a goat.*

Here we left the Dake river. Southward the Vunga hills were visible in the evening light; but it was not until long after dark that we reached a suitable camping-place. Water was very scarce. Since leaving Chibinga we had been blessed with much cooler weather. Relief was found under cloudy skies, very different from the previous incessant and roasting blaze of the torrid sun.

Masecha was the next town we arrived at. It was the dirtiest and most wretched little place which I had yet seen. The inhabitants appeared to be thriftless and slovenly. They wore no ornaments, not even the universal beads, and their whole garb consisted of a very dirty piece of cloth passed over the loins. They seemed poorly fed, and were in very bad condition.

While returning from our evening ramble, during which I had been on the look-out for guinea-fowl, I met a long

* Goats were numerous here, the place not being in a tsetse fly belt.

line of women, about fourteen, all bearing their earthen water-jars poised upon their heads. They were on their way to the river Mudzi, in which they had dug deep holes to get water. No sooner did they catch a glimpse of me than the whole line suddenly broke, and a regular stampede took place, the affrighted women throwing down their gourds and taking to their heels in different directions. Some ran past me, and some ran back. One young woman I noticed making a fine spurt of fifty yards before she disappeared in the bush.

A solitary figure remained standing defiant to the white intruder. This was an old woman whom, from the form of the lip, I could see was a Msenga slave. The appearance of the old lioness was most amusing. Getting up to her I presented her with a few stray beads and an empty cartridge case which I happened to have in my pocket. Her good-will was won at once. Repeating the word "Mzungo" several times, she signed that her companions were afraid of me.

I sat down and pointed to her snuff-box. After a few more pantomimic nods and becks, just as though both were deaf and dumb, we together snuffed the snuff of peace. When I pointed to the fugitives, she laughed most heartily, looking as though she thought, "Ah, you and I are old friends."

Had the old woman and myself been able to converse, there was one subject upon which I am sure we would have agreed. If our thoughts had been read, we should each have been found meditating upon the extreme ugliness of the other. The runaways would not return so long as I stayed, and as I had exhausted all the signs I could think of, I bade good-bye to my new friend and hastened back to the hut, where I found that Manaman, the lieutenant and cook, had ready a plate of millet-meal porridge, most tasteless stuff without salt or milk. He had also cooked a leg of the goat that had been presented to me at the last town we passed. This was to be washed down with the contents of a large gourd (msuko) of pombe, which he had purchased with some of the precious beads, of which there now remained only half a pound.

I observed numbers of women with the thin ring in the upper lip similar to that worn by the Makorikori.

A remarkable curiosity, too, appeared here, in the shape of a piebald Kaffir. A portion of the side of his face was blotched pink, contrasting strongly against the dark skin. On the hands, wrists, and breast the same abnormity was visible. The effect was strikingly ugly. In a slighter degree, I remember seeing a similar monstrosity in the northern regions of Mexico.

The towns through which we were now passing were peopled by the Mtavara tribe. They suffer much from sores and various skin diseases. The man who gave me his hut was in a dreadful condition, his arms and legs being one mass of sores.

At Masecha, the usual town scenes could be witnessed. Lots of men were lounging lazily about the huts; children were busily employed in some unsightly operations on their mothers' head-gear; many of the people, in a kneeling posture, were grinding the corn to meal between the stones used for the purpose; while long lines of women moved about carrying gourds of water upon their heads, looking as erect as though they had been drilled by a military instructor. The constant carrying of weights upon the head tends to give a very erect bearing to most of the native women.

I was informed that these people did not among

themselves buy or sell slaves, but purchased them at Msenga.

Masecha, as I have said before, was very dirty. The street was a litter of débris. Ashes and rubbish of all kinds, the sweepings of years, formed huge piles of abominable filth on all hands. The vile condition of the place must in some measure, if not wholly, account for the odious diseases which prevail among the inhabitants.

The watch and compass surprised the people vastly. When I made the magnetic needle follow my knife, turning it first in one direction and then in another, until the card spun round, the people were beside themselves with unfeigned amazement. No doubt they thought I was a highly-gifted spectre from the ghostly world.

The country we had latterly passed through had a poor and sandy soil, encumbered with thorn bush, wait-a-bit thorns, and other wild shrubs. Birds were scarce.

When we left Masecha, we crossed the watershed, and found all the rivers flowing in a south-easterly direction to the Amazoe. The principal affluent—the Kangudzi—was like most of the other channels we had been crossing: that is to say, a bed of sand where water flowed only during the rainy months.

Throughout all this district our experiences, like the scenery, were monotonous in the extreme. At odd intervals the dismal course of progress was relieved by our meetings with sundry parties of natives *en route* to the Upper Zambesi. One morning we heard the booming of batukas, which, it turned out, heralded the advent of a large party of Mtavara people from a town called Mauntonda, which they were deserting in order to find better land.

The exodus was tolerably large, and its numbers marched along with a merry but tremendous noise. Drum beating throbbed the air, and wild singing sounded high. A motley throng, indeed, they were. Some of them wore ostrich feather caps, others hats and feathers; the old men carrying guns, and the women heavy loads of eatables, neatly packed in palm leaves and grass.

All seemed to be genuinely happy. Probably it has not yet come home to them, what a struggle they have for the privilege of mere existence in a sorrowful life of toil.

The tribes in this locality are constantly changing their towns, migrating from place to place in search of richer lands, as the soil is poor and soon becomes exhausted.

Villages, therefore, are very makeshift affairs. The people generally, whom we saw in the Zambesi valley, seemed to be more indolent than any we had hitherto passed. Skin diseases, such as I have spoken of, were very prevalent, and swellings of the ankles and legs were also noticeable on many occasions.

The country is subject to lengthened and excessive droughts. The tsetse abounds throughout the wide-spread valley. It has been remarked that the goat will live in the "fly country." But to me it was singular that wherever goats were found in any considerable numbers the fly was not observed. Where the fly was prevalent, goats were sometimes kept as pets which had been born in the "fly country" (their mothers having died), and physicked, when very young, by the women.

Large trees, which flourished here, produced a stony, apple-like fruit. These trees, called Mazua by the natives, were dotted here and there through the forest. In flavour, the fruit resembled the apple, and the stone was like that of a large cherry.

Not infrequently a small bush fence encloses this highly-valued tree, showing that some enterprizing individual claims its coveted fruit, which claim suggests forcibly that the pre-emption law exists among these sons of the forest.

Large flocks of grey-winged francolins were seen on the line of march; they were running in the dense underwood with extraordinary swiftness, and did not attempt to take wing until the pursuer was almost upon them. Their clamorous notes were constantly heard, when close by; but the dense cover shielded them from sight, their invisibleness being aided by their speckled grey colour, which matched admirably with the sun-bleached vegetation. Physical torments prevented me from following them up.

Eight weary months had now elapsed since I left the Cape of Good Hope on my northward journey. My condition was miserable; certainly worse than anything I had ever experienced of human ills. The stock of trading articles was completely exhausted, and now I was parting with empty cartridge-cases in exchange for meal. Hardly any game could be found. Even when I did see some impala, zebra, and koodoo, I was quite unable to hunt on account of the wretched condition of my feet.

Otherwise, fortunately, I was perfectly well; but my pedal extremities were blistered and swollen to a degree that defies description. As long as the march continued, healing was out of the question, and stopping meant starvation. The only shoes I had worn for a long time were those—warranted own make—of zebra skins, and they were always full of sand.

Some new mode of travelling was imperative. The carriers' loads were light, so I increased them on ten of the men, by distributing the loads of the four strongest, whom I determined should carry me on their shoulders.

Sensible though it seemed, the change led to a mishap, which was much worse for me. The men were carrying me about two hundred yards each, and while going through this rather circus-like performance, we happened to alight upon some guinea-fowl. My bearer dropped me, like a hot potato, on a very stony piece of ground, and in the effort to save my feet, I gave a severe twist to my left ankle. By a piece of wonderful luck, under the circumstances, I shot one guinea fowl—a godsend, I thought; for I was beginning to yearn for something stronger than turtle dove, and porridge without either salt or sugar.

Fickle fortune again! On examination I found that the bird was a piner, and unfit for food. It seemed as though the spirits of unpropitious fate were hovering around me; but not being particularly prone to superstition, I laughed at the bad fortune, and limped along, buoyed up by the reflection that we were nearing the river, that soon we would see the town of Tette, where I would be able to get a new force of men, and a fresh supply of articles for barter, besides the rest which my flagging frame required before setting out across the big river on the long journey to the lake regions. The men now declared that I was too heavy to carry, so there was nothing for it but to painfully persevere in pedestrian effort.

I have omitted to mention a number of sandy river beds which we passed. There was nothing especially noteworthy about them, and their courses are shown on the accompanying map.

Shidim is the name given by the Portuguese to the country through which we have been passing since leaving Chibinga.

On reaching the Nyansanga river we found a small but fresh stream of water, into which the boys plunged, to bathe during the very hottest hour of the day. The Mufa river was crossed and recrossed.

Then we saw the dark outline of distant hills—the Fema mountains, which the guide said lay within a day's march of Tette. The news cheered us; but Manaman came to me with a most piteous face, saying :

"There is nothing to eat. Can you stand it from here to Tette?"

Truly the whole party looked as though they had not had a "square meal" for at least a month. Hearing that there was a small town in close proximity, I sent a man to it with six strings of beads—positively the very last—in order to buy a chicken, but he returned saying that the people wanted white calico; they would not take beads.

We camped during the following evening on the Fema mountains, which skirt the Zambesi on the south. I told the boys that I was determined to reach the big town by the next night; but they all shook their heads, saying that the distance was far, and that I would not be able to manage it. While saying this they pointed to the sun, and indicated that most of the journey, after crossing the mountains, would be through sand.

"But," said I, "if you work well, I promise that when we drink the waters of the great river I will celebrate the event by giving you some *aqua ardiente*, and if we reach the town before sunset, you will each receive three fathoms of white calico."

This promise evidently met with approval. They had known nothing of the bottle of brandy which I had carefully kept for so long a time, and the prospect of a taste, as well as getting calico, cheered the discontented wanderers mightily, and ensured an early start which I was most anxious to manage. Only another round of the clock's hand, and we get the longed-for glimpse of the Zambesi river, for which I have worked and wearied so long.

The guide, Manaman, and myself left the camp at the first signs of breaking day. We clambered up the southern slopes of the Fema, and ere long stood upon the summit.

The early dawn of opening day was lightened as the heavy clouds were being swept away by a gentle southeasterly breeze. The sun as it ascended in orient sky darted glorious gleams through the grey streaks of clouds, whose frowning folds still hung like a pall in the far horizon.

"Zambesi! Zambesi! Senhor!" was jubilantly and repeatedly vociferated by Manaman and the guide, as though they wished me to thoroughly appreciate the grandeur of the picturesque scene and the triumph of the moment.

I could not help thinking of John. Here was the "big rafeer," but the sight was not for him. How I should have liked to have had some one to whom I might reveal the numerous thoughts that thronged in my mind, recalling the toilsome days, the wanderings, the disappointments and hopes, the reverses and successes of the days that were gone!

Out in the north-eastern expanse was a grand panoramic landscape. Hills and dales, richly wooded ravines, and gentle eminences, forests and brushwood, were gradually revealed by the ascending orb of day, which cast oblique shadows from the rounded hills rising from the river's edge. The bush-covered and broken hillocks gradually sink towards the silent-looking waters of the great arterial stream; fully a thousand yards in width in our line of sight.

High in the air hundreds of storks were flying in sweeping circles, their full, white plumage gleaming brightly against the soft blue sky. On the sandy river brink a few cranes were to be seen disporting in playful mood.

From our standpoint we could see well defined the great bend of the Zambesi, as it swept round in one majestic curve towards the south-east. Thence the winding flow of dark, gloomy-like water, edged with bleached shores of the whitest sand, moved in silent sadness onward, eastward, oceanward.

With the knowledge that I was approaching the great Portuguese trading outpost, I now began to study my personal appearance a little. At best I could only be called a good anatomical subject or study. Bones and muscles showed splendidly. With regard to the outer man, I was miserably tattered and torn: my overalls were in rags; and my feet wrappers were tied up with odd pieces of string.

The *tout ensemble* would have reminded most people of the advanced picket of a caravan of gipsy tramps just arriving after a long journey, and about to lay siege to the sympathy or fear of a credulous public. Appearances, in short, were very far from being what is called "respectable."

The route through the hills was exceedingly rough and stony, carrying us through thick underbrush and scrub.

We soon descended the northern slopes. Striking our way through stunted forest towards the river, we rested at the confluence of the Kapinja. Then, much to the astonishment of all, I produced out of the sack, as if by magic, *the* bottle of brandy, which had been safely carried for over a thousand miles through danger, toil, and trouble. There was enough to give each man a "nip," according to my promise. I was glad, however, to see that a number would not accept the drink. Those who did had been broken in with the *aqua ardiente* of the Portuguese.

A number of small and dry river beds were crossed. In our march the sand was soft and deep, so much so that I felt as though I were performing the feat of the circus strong man, that is tugging half-hundred weights on each foot, with a very small amount of the essential to do it on.

The hardest five hours and forty minutes that I ever spent were passed in that harassing march along the sandy shores of the river. At the end of that time we reached a small ridge near the fort, west of the town.

I took in my belt here up to the last hole, as if bent upon the pursuit of some fleet-footed animal; for I was determined not to hobble dejected-looking and exhausted into the town. Appearances otherwise were bad enough, and much depended upon my making a good impression, so as to get quarters as comfortable as possible.

Braced to the occasion, but with mingled feelings of relief, satisfaction, and anticipation, I in a little time found myself standing in the pillared porch of the governor's house at Tette. To him I presented a letter which I had with difficulty procured from the Portuguese consul at the Diamond Fields, South Africa, and with these credentials I was received most courteously, a room being set apart for the accommodation of myself and my men.

CHAPTER XVI.

TETTE, AND ACROSS THE ZAMBESI.

The earliest shower of the season—Mysterious disappearance of a day—Portuguese possessions in Eastern Africa—Zumbo—Tette—Trade in past times—A ruined town—Roman Catholic missions—No understanding of a Supreme Being—Fetichism—The governor of Tette—The garrison and government—Native soldiers—Kanyemba, the black chief—Europeans in Tette—Two hundred years of civilised intercourse—Industries and resources—Prospecting for gold—The rainy season—The Jesuit fathers—Decadence of the Portuguese—Class of steamers for river navigation—Rumours of war—The Makanga tribe—Woman devoured by a crocodile—The tragic story of the Zambesi—Funeral feasts—Recruiting for the advance—A doleful parting—Crossing the Zambesi—A last look at Tette.

ON the morning of the 1st of September, 1884, a fierce wind scoured through the silent streets of Tette, raising clouds of dust and afterwards bringing down a heavy shower of rain, the earliest of the season.

An examination and comparison of my journals showed that a day had been lost somewhere, for I was one day behind in date. How could this have occurred? Every day I had, to the best of my knowledge, written in the pocket journal. Finally, I came to the conclusion that the loss had occurred during the excitement of the forced marches in the Makorikori country; for in respect to time the nights there had been as lively as the days. On questioning the governor about the matter he replied:

"We have heard nothing of the outer world for many months; but I think we are right as to the date."

The Portuguese possessions of Eastern Africa are divided into nine districts ruled by governors, under the control of the governor-general at Mozambique, which is the Portuguese headquarters on the east coast.

The district of Tette extends from a point a short distance west of Sena to somewhere eight days' journey to the west of Zumbo. This definition of boundaries can hardly satisfy the exacting topographer, but it is the only one I could get.

Zumbo is the farthest Portuguese station inland on the Zambesi, being about 500 miles from the sea. Its foundation dates from 1740. The native tribe which inhabits its belt of country gets the name of Wazezuro from the Portuguese.

The town of Tette is situated on the southern banks of the river, on a series of sandstone spurs running in ridges, gently sloping towards the water, to which they are parallel. On these ridges the houses have been erected, while the intervening spaces form the wide streets. The steep slopes of these ridges quickly carry off the surface water during heavy rains.

If the observer stands on the right bank of the river and looks towards the south, he can see at a glance the extent of the town. In the foreground, close to the stream, he will remark the governor's house (Palacio do Governador) above the esplanade; its bright white walls, red tiled roof, and pillared entrance being the chief architectural feature in the crumbling city of ancient slavedom. The receding ridges rise gradually. On right and left numerous native huts may be observed, with their short hedges of cactus intervening. A few broken lines of houses, an hospital and barracks, and a few merchants' dwellings, form the principal buildings.

On the summit of the gentle eminence stands the fort, with whitewashed walls, over which the colours of the nation float. Farther to the south-west the Carocira mountain tops cut into the sky, forming a pleasing background to the picturesque scene.

Let us saunter through the streets of this African settlement, which has existed for close upon a century and a-half. In the days when Livingstone described the place, as he saw it on his westward journey of exploration over twenty years ago, Tette was a tolerably lively city. Many Europeans, mostly Portuguese, helped to swell the commercial population, which lined the streets, and bartered with the black man for his treasures. Ivory, gold, as well as "God's image done in ebony," were the saleable commodities drawn from the heart of the land.

With the times, the scene has changed, and the men too! Forgetting for a moment that much of the old prosperity of the place was built by inhuman slavery, one cannot help having a feeling of melancholy in wandering through the streets of the now desolate town. Had it been the abode of devils in times past, there would be a difficulty in triumphing over its decaying walls; for men can never look with pleasure upon the evidences of Nature's destructive powers.

Solitude reigns supreme. On every side you see the wasting work of Time's relentless hand. You see it in the crumbling ruins of houses, at one time inhabited by prosperous merchants. Indigo and other weeds now rise rank amid the falling walls, and upon spots where houses once stood. You see it in the church, which has now crumbled to the ground. Departed glory is knelled to you by the bells which toll from the slight structure—a sorry substitute for a church—where the Jesuit Fathers and their small flock now perform the holy rites of their creed.

Earnest though these fathers be, they must view with sadness the failure of the work of their predecessors, who, centuries before (for they were evidently among the first to set forth in these wilds), wandered amid the savage aborigines and courted martyrdom. Have both the labour of love and the sacrifice of life been fruitless? To-day, if you make inquiries of a native grown to manhood within the sound of the mission bells, and familiar with the inside of its church, he will tell you an extraordinary story regarding his ideas of the meanings of religious ceremonies.

Were you to build an immense church, with a spire as high as that of Canterbury Cathedral, the only effect would be that the people would worship the spire. They would have little or nothing to do with the words of sacred teaching. Crucifixes, pictures, and all such aids to the fervour of devotional life, are only looked upon as fetich. The superstition of the people seems to be ineradicable; and at Tette this is especially noticeable, owing to the mixed character of its population; the distributing influence of the slave trade having given great variety to the races. With no knowledge of a Supreme Being, they had no religion, no thoughts of immortality.

A volume might be written upon the fetichism of Tette alone, taking into account the various grades of the superstition common to the inhabitants, who are called Teteiros, and chiefly belong to the Maravi and Wanhungwe. To heartless bewitchment by human beings are ascribed the adverse freaks of the weather, the failure of the crops, and other disasters. For every premeditated action there is a medicine. Not to speak of bodily sickness, there are medicines for success in hunting, for fair weather, for rain, for peace, and for triumph in war. They dance, sing, feast, and beat their drums in war, or peace, in grief or joy.

The god they look up to is the king, or the master, who rules them by terror. When any one dies of disease the body is thrown into the river, except in the immediate vicinity of the town. The bodies of those who have been killed by order of the chief are invariably given to the crocodile.

Among almost all the tribes in the vast valley a fandango follows in the wake of every fate, whether it be a birth, marriage, or death. Every birth has its omen: at every death a man is bewitched. The native's measure of day is in the sun; his months are in the moons; and his years are in the chronologies of kings.

Senhor Luis Joaquin Vieira Braga, the governor, treated me with great kindness and unvarying courtesy, giving all the information he possibly could give with regard to the contiguous tribes, the character of the country, its prospects and past history.

The governor is a man of moderate stature, and erect bearing. His complexion is bronzed, and he has, or had, a long, black moustache.

Holding rank as a major in the army, his career had been full of successes. He had served in various native campaigns and had acquitted himself in a manner which had won the favourable notice of the authorities at Lisbon; a fact which was evidenced by the number of decorations that had been conferred upon him. He was well liked by the Portuguese both at Tette and at Quillimane.*

Senhor Braga seemed to understand most thoroughly the native character, and there was no doubt that he ruled them with the indispensable rod of menace. Between him and the natives there seemed to be no love lost. Afterwards I learned that the natives called him Chakundakoro, which

* Recently Senhor Braga has resigned his appointment as governor.

meant all the unutterable things that could be thought or dreamt of.

I found him a most energetic man, doing everything he possibly could to check the ravages of time, by rebuilding, so far as was in his power, the dismantled fabrics of the town. The barracks, hospital, and governor's house, had been rebuilt by him, and under his directions the promenade

SENHOR LUIS JOAQUIN VIEIRA BRAGA—GOVERNOR OF TETTE.

had also been constructed. It runs parallel with the river bank from the front of his house to the barracks, a distance of about 800 yards.

All this was done by native labour. The artizans work on the weekly system, and are paid in goods, consisting of articles of merchandise, principally *algodon*—white cotton.

The soldiers were blacks, armed with muskets and

bayonets, and wearing clothes of cotton and shakoes. It is generally assumed that there were some Portuguese among them: but I saw only two sergeants and one officer. The military department is doubtless faulty, for it leaves the white people in the town entirely at the mercy of the natives should a rising occur. Throughout the whole of the Portuguese territory of the Zambesi—a territory, by the way, which has never been clearly defined —the rulers have little power in a military sense. Government is wholly a question of price and purchase, should they require to enforce their laws or to prosecute a campaign.

From Zumbo down the Zambesi to the sea the Portuguese Government has to rely entirely upon native soldiers, of whom there are very few. Strictly speaking, however, it depends upon the half-castes, who have in the course of time, and by force of circumstances, gathered large followings of natives, who look up to them as kings, and under whose banner they will fight and die.

These kings are the people who hold the Zambesi. Without their co-operation the Portuguese could not hold the river for a day. At Tette the garrison is just sufficient for temporary defence. The most trifling campaign could not be prosecuted by the force. On the other hand, if the native force is considered we find a fair array. Kanyemba, the black chief at Zumbo, whose district extends to the northern bank of the Zambesi, has at least 10,000 armed men at his disposal. This body has been armed by the Portuguese Government, which has also conferred upon Kanyemba the honourable appellation "Sergento Mor." Presents, likewise, are given every year to keep the people under a sense of obligation to help in warfare when called upon. Lobo, another black chief, who married Kanyemba's daughter, gets the distinction "Capitao Mor." He has

3,000 armed men. Thus the Portuguese have actually armed a force sufficient to overwhelm them in a day. I do not prophesy that a massacre of this description will take place, but judging from present appearances the probability is strong—supposing that the natives think, as other natives have thought, of the glories of regaining their conquered country.

About thirty Europeans still reside in Tette; but the main portion of the trade of the place is in the hands of three or four merchants. They complain that the tide of prosperity is ebbing away. The elephant has trekked to the far interior, carrying with him the precious ivory which —excepting the slave trade—has formed the chief support of commerce in these parts since the conquest by the Portuguese.

Thousands of native hunters still leave Tette every year; and with their flintlocks and spears go very far afield in search of the much-coveted animal. Success in hunting, however, is slight, and year by year the results are diminishing.

At Tette we stand in the city of a dominion. Two centuries have passed away since its conquest, and the concurrent introduction of civilisation to its unimpressionable people.

What is the outcome of this two hundred years' intercourse upon the moral or social status of the inhabitants? Slavery, it is true, does not flourish in the same open way that was shown in days gone by; nevertheless it is yet carried on to a considerable extent. To find out how it could be utterly eradicated without seriously injuring those who are now in bondage is an inscrutable problem. The people have been brought up in the atmosphere of slavery, and cannot understand any other form of existence.

Money, as a medium of exchange, is but little known even at the present time; mercantile transactions being usually carried out through the barter of cloth, beads, and *aqua ardiente*, the latter forming a highly-important article of commerce.

Industries are few. The people manufacture rings of gold, and out of hard wood—*lignum vitæ*, of which there is abundance, and ebony—they fashion various forms of cups, bowls, and ornaments. They make pipes of clay, which have not changed their form or improved from time immemorial. The rough clothes they wear were to some extent made from indigenous cotton; but the trifling industry in this department is on the wane through the introduction of Manchester goods.

They till the soil with the hoe. These implements are made by tribes away up in the mountains, who bring their blacksmithing products to the dwellers of the great valley in exchange for cloth and fossil stones. The tsetse fly being so close to the town makes it impossible to employ cattle for the purposes of agriculture; and for this reason a plough is an unseen article throughout the length and breadth of the Zambesi valley.

In the heart of the town I never saw the tsetse fly. Therefore a few poor-looking cows were kept, but were not allowed to wander far. With reference to the tsetse, I should mention that when game, such as the buffalo, elephant, &c., become scarce, as was the case recently in the neighbourhood of Delagoa Bay, the fly in a great measure disappears, it being said, with good authority, that the little pest breeds upon the buffalo dung. Doubtless when the game, at present plentiful, disappears from the Zambesi valley, a like result will follow.

Near Tette the soil yields very good crops, although they

are somewhat uncertain, on account of the frequent droughts. Greater certainty exists with regard to produce of the lands farther down the stream than in the immediate vicinity of the town, because the frequent inundations of the river between the months of November and June ensure the requisite irrigation of the land in which the people sow and secure good crops.

The governor informed me that in the previous year two strangers—white men—had come from Quillimane with a view to prospect the gold resources of the Amazoe river (numerous affluents of which we crossed on our journey), which flows into the Luenha, and thence to the Zambesi, about twenty miles below Tette. Unhappily, disaster followed them. One died of the fever, and the other was forced to return to the coast in a lamentably sickly condition.

Intensely hot weather followed our arrival in Tette, the thermometer registering 89° to 90° in the shade, that is to say, in my chronometer-box, lying in a well-sheltered and apparently cool place. Little or no idea can be formed of the terrible strength of the heat. Out in the sun it was unbearable.

The rainy season was approaching, although as yet we had only had a few slight showers. There are seldom any severe rains until the end of November. In April they cease, but slight showers are known to have fallen as late as June. From what I could learn, the biggest floods occur during January and March. Vast tracts of land are then submerged. Some districts depend upon these floods for the essential fertilisation of the soil, similar to what occurs in the great Nile valley.

Tette is subject to intense droughts, which, indeed, often prevail throughout the whole of the lower valley of the

Zambesi. Such droughts in all probability are due to the influence of the distant mountains north and south of the river basin.

The great scourge of all the great river basins of Africa is the malarial fever. It is very prevalent in Tette, but much more so nearer the sea. The changes of season are usually the most deadly periods. Many men and women were in the hospital when I was in the town.

Personally, I got on well, improving in condition every day. The resting was thorough, and I had an ample supply of cooked food. A pair of shoes, just like dancing-masters' slippers (being the only articles of my size to be found in the town), tended to work wonders in comfort and returning vigour.

I paid a visit to the Jesuit fathers, of whom two were French and one Hungarian. Fever seemed to have affected them greatly, their ghost-like forms being very unpleasant to look upon, the result, probably, of the exceedingly sedentary life they led, coupled with the circumstance of their being stationed so long in one place. Their companions were a few very unhealthy-looking little boys—orphans—evidently half-castes.

Should any one desire to have a relative buried with a service by the priests, the Jesuit father, bearing a cross, leads the funeral procession, with a number of little boys robed in white. One of these funerals I witnessed, and was astonished to remark how very few people followed; none, in fact, save the relatives of the deceased. No crowd was attracted. This may be looked upon as another example of the slowness of the native to imitate the customs of the white man. A more commonplace, but perhaps more significant, instance is that neither coffee, tea nor sugar have ever pleased the palates of the native inhabitants of Tette, who still prefer to imbibe their unvarying beverage, the simply-concocted beer.

The races of the Zambesi valley are very dark-skinned, much more so than the people I have encountered on the high lands. Possibly this is what impressed Livingstone, who in one of his books has remarked that moisture and heat produced the blackest types of man.

The vitality of the people is wonderful. On the morning after a birth the happy mother may be seen again in the fields, seated under the shade of a tree, with the new arrival swathed in cloths and slung on her back, showing that she herself is ready and willing again to begin work.

Marriage customs are simple. When a man becomes enamoured, his usual course is to plead his suit either through his eldest aunt, or one of the girl's sisters. The medium is designated *buia*. To this person he presents his petition, handing her at the same time a string of white beads, while with many urgent entreaties he begs that she will lay his proposal before the young girl's family. The medium then lodges the application in due form, and receives from the family several strings of beads of the same colour, with the assurance that the offer is provisionally accepted. The young man then enters the service of his prospective father-in-law, in the capacity of a domestic servant, so that the family may learn something of his disposition. After a service of two months, the plea is again placed before the father of the intended bride by the same medium, who receives the presents that are to be distributed among all the members of the family, to the extent of twenty strings of white porcelains and a few yards of calico. White only is accepted, as coloured cloth would betoken evil.

Accompanied by an escort of relatives and friends, the

bride-elect proceeds to the kraal of the bridegroom, the company carrying various articles of food, such as a plucked hen, and an egg resting on a plate piled with meal, the latter being considered symbolical of the innocence of the bride. Musical instruments are played in the procession, and the people shout and dance in testimony of their joy.

During all this ceremony, the bridegroom is not permitted to appear outside of his hut. He is dressed in his best, decorated with beads, and anointed with the oil of almonds. No sooner is the first part of the ceremony over than he comes to the threshold of the hut and shows himself to the assemblage, the chief of the bride's family receiving presents from them. After this he is taken back to his hut. The ceremony of giving away the bride follows, and then she is introduced to the hut of the bridegroom.

When kings desire to marry, they merely issue an order to the father to present his daughter, and the request is immediately complied with. The king looks upon his subjects as being slaves. He may have as many as fifty, or even a hundred wives. Should it suit his humour to put any of them to death, he does so without further ado. Executions are carried out sometimes in the presence of the woman's father, who, through fear of giving offence to the king, will exhibit satisfaction rather than sorrow. Any appearance of grief would be fatal to him. Occasionally the king may order the father to be the executioner, and even then the horribly unnatural command is obeyed with apparent satisfaction.

When deaths occur they have to be reported to the king, the bereaved ones beseeching his majesty that they may be allowed to mourn for the departed. On the request being granted, lamentations and wailings are lustily uttered by a crowd of relatives and friends assembled in front of the deceased's hut. The burial rites being concluded, a number of slaves are left to watch the grave, day and night, guarding it from the ravages of wild beasts and the baneful incantations of sorcerers. Peace-offerings of food are given to appease the wrath of spirits, while words of exorcism are muttered, the talkers striking their breast as they address themselves to the unknown. Funeral obsequies are terminated some time afterwards by a feast.

But burial ceremonies differ among the various tribes. Of the Muzimba people, and the Makanga, it is asserted that it is customary for them, among other barbarities, generally to bury, along with a defunct monarch, two or four male slaves and two female slaves, who have previously been suffocated. The bodies are placed in the same tomb with the king, and a short distance off another slave is strangled and his body fastened to a tree, in a sitting posture. This is a custom very similar to that described by Mr. O'Neil as being practised by the Makua people at Mozambique.

At Tette, white ants are troublesome beyond description to the householder. They get into the roof and quickly destroy the rafters; they are equally destructive on clothes, furniture, and household goods.

From what I have seen of the Portuguese, they are good masters, and possessed of great patience.

How often must we think of the strange vicissitudes of nations; of their changes from puissance to impotence, from enterprise to indolence, from opulence to poverty, from courage to timidity, from conquest to subjection! Is it possible to think, without pity, of the decadence of the Portuguese, the great explorers and colonisers of so many vast regions of the world? Their tide of progress and prosperity has turned for many years, and is ebbing fast from the sands of time.

Notwithstanding this, it cannot be said that the absence of progress and prosperity in the valley of the Zambesi is due entirely to want of energy on the part of the Portuguese, for the country is by no means inviting, or adapted for advantageous development.

Tsetse fly abounds on the southern side, and there is also a belt of it on the northern lands contiguous to the river. Through the shifting, sandy bank the channel of the so-called navigable portion of the river (reaching to near the Kebrabasa rapids, 334 miles inland from the mouth of the river, and 50 miles above Tette), is so shallow in parts that, during dry months, it is with no little difficulty that the merchants of Tette can get their goods up from Quillimane, the transit being still effected by means of canoes and small keel boats.

There can be no doubt that the kind of vessel most suitable for steady work on a river of this nature is the flat-bottomed, stern-wheel steamer, such as may be seen on the shoal-bedded rivers of North America. A steamer of this description would be particularly serviceable, for on different occasions when the river is blockaded on account of war, the accumulations of months have to be sent down stream. Canoes are not procurable in sufficient numbers, and, besides, the time they take, especially if the river is in flood, in making the return trip is a serious consideration. Such a block occurred during my stay. For three months before they had had no communication with Quillimane, a circumstance which was due to the existence of difficulties with a chief called Inhamessinga, successor to the notorious Bonga, after whom the chief town was named: it is situated at the confluence of the Luenha river with the Zambesi, twenty miles down stream from Tette. Inhamessinga is a very consequential man, who at any time can blockade the river.

Intelligence was also received of a war between the Portuguese and the Mazinjiri on the Shiré river, while day after day the wildest rumours were brought to the governor to the effect that the Makololo, also on the Shiré river, had been fighting with the missionaries, and that the chief Chiputula had been killed by an Englishman.

Altogether, the state of affairs was decidedly adverse to the prospects of obtaining men to follow me from this place to the north.

The Makanga tribe, whose attitude lately had been very defiant, dwelt on the north. If I proceeded in a direct line to the lake, I would have to pass through their country. My friend the governor was very reluctant to let me depart.

But what could be done? Clearly I could not stay for ever at Tette. The Makanga people had already robbed some parties bringing ivory to Tette, and they were in no way to be trusted. Despite this, however, I persuaded the governor to assist me in procuring some men.

Every day the heat was becoming intensified, and it seemed to inflame my anxiety to move onwards.

A report was brought in to the effect that a woman had been taken by a crocodile. I learned that this was a very frequent disaster, it being estimated that between Sena and Zumbo, a distance of 360 miles, there are over a hundred persons devoured by these monsters in the course of a year. Water-carriers, who approach the edge of the river to fill their gourds, are the chief victims of the sly reptiles. The river is literally alive with them. Great numbers of hippopotami may be seen a few miles below the town of Tette.

During the evening Senhor Braga, the governor, and myself used to walk through the solitary streets and visit the two principal merchants, Senhor Martinez and Senhor Pereira. One of these nights was very lovely, and I lingered upon the river banks long after the tattoo had echoed away across the expanse of the quiet waters.

Reposing life has left the air in a mute calmness. Above, the pale moon floats gently through the illimitable vault of gloom, out of whose darkness occasionally come fleecy clouds—the harbingers of coming floods—to pass fitfully across the light which garnishes their edges with a bright and silvery gleam. The beauty of the heavens is reflected on the glassy surface of the great river as I watch the rippling waters flow onward to mingle with the distant sea.

Sealed is thy tragic story, oh, mighty Zambesi! Thy woes of a thousand ages are untold. Smoothly and silently though thy waters run, the storms of human warfare and the miseries of human cruelty have cursed the varied scenes through which thou flowest. Silence beseems thee best. Flow onward, then, in peace, and let thy waters be broken only by the hideous monsters which rise to the surface from thy living mysterious depths. Upon thy banks the hand of time hath imprinted indelibly the epochs of the primeval world, but the dread story of the centuries of man's life in thy land of sorrow shall ever be unknown. Thy countless branches stretch far away through a vast region to draw the moisture from thousands of leagues of mountain, plain and forest, where as yet the white man hath not planted his foot, and knows not the sequestered mountain-spring which gives thee birth. Like thyself, year after year, these add new horrors to their history, to be for ever silent as the tomb; they carry their burdens of woe towards thy dark, unwritten waters, ever flowing onward to the vast ocean of sorrow.

My reverie is broken. Awakening the stillness of midnight, I hear the booming of drums. At first they beat slowly and with distinct pauses. Then again more quickly, boom, boom, boom! These re-echoing sounds vibrate from the villages which environ the town. They tell that the feast which follows a funeral is proceeding, and accompanying the beat of the drum I hear the chant of the people, as they sing of the good deeds of the departed. Louder and louder grows the sound, until it becomes a vociferous clamour of countless voices, mingled with the clangour of batuka and marimba, inharmonic, wild and sad, breaking the silence which had fallen upon the slumbering town.

Such were the weird notes, which more than once lulled me to sleep during my stay at Kunyungwi.

After a week's residence my physical condition changed very much for the better. By that time I was in a state of thorough repair, although my feet were not yet healed. The governor kindly offered me quarters, should I wish to remain in Tette, until news had arrived from the outer world, as well as some more definite information as to the state of the contiguous tribes. Time was an object, however, and therefore I was unable to accept his hospitable offer.

The old spirit of adventure was aflame. The star of hope was in the ascendant. It was a case of, Ho, for the north! the land of doubt, the country of the Angoni, the home of the Landin. I must push on.

The work of recruiting had been placed in the hands of one of the governor's subordinates, who assured me that he had all the party in readiness. From Senhor Martinez I then made a few purchases of cloth and other necessaries for the road, and on the following morning was ready to make a fresh start.

Although anxious to visit the hot springs which lay on the north bank of the Zambesi, a few miles up-water, I had to abandon the idea, as it was with the greatest difficulty that even a few men could be induced to go with me northwards, on account of the extraordinary rumours of hostilities on every side; some of the reports being true. However, I was informed that my men had all been paid, and that among the party the principals, acting as guides, were some Landin, whose country lies on the high flats to the west of Lake Nyassa. They had brought ivory to Tette, and as they were now on their way home, they would guide me, and carry light loads.

The bugle from the fort sounded the *reveille* very early on the morning of our departure. I sprung from my bed full of energy for the fresh start, and looking out at the window could see that some of the Maravi had already arrived.

A few delays took place, and much to my disgust the *palmero* was brought into requisition.

The loads, principally sacks of rice and meal, were piled on the sandy beach below the governor's residence. Two boats were in readiness to ferry the party over.

I had been in Tette for only eight days, yet I felt as though I had been in the place for years. Happy, indeed, has been my fortune! Generally speaking, wherever my wandering footsteps have taken me in different parts of the world, it has been my lot to find good, kind, and hospitable people.

One of the Jesuit fathers bade me a most doleful adieu.

"Oh, I am afraid you will be killed!" were his parting words. "You will never see your home and England again!"

Senhor Braga and some others came down to the shore, and watched the mixed crew as they tumbled into the boats one after the other, with their assegais, bundles, bags, gourds, wooden troughs, and some with flintlocks, besides their loads. A number of people, who evidently did not belong to the party, also crowded in, bringing the boat's gunwale down to the water's edge. The shore party wished us good luck. The boats swung out into the moving stream, bright with the reflected blue of the sky; the short paddles broke the waters into foam, and we soon were ploughing our way with good speed across the mighty river.

On our left we passed the tiny, picturesque island, which faces the town, with its numerous green shrubs, and silvery sands glistening in the glare of the sun. In a short time we landed on the northern shore.

Even now my men were entirely unknown to me; for it had been a very difficult matter to get them to leave the town. I calculated that I would soon know each individual when on the north side of the river; but numerous stragglers made it difficult to select the men.

Chibanga, however, was the individual who was to have charge of the Maravi men. The Landin were very independent, they did not wish to carry anything, save their shields of buffalo-hide (shaped exactly like those of the Zulu), and their own provisions. Misiri—a Portuguese slave, and rather an old-looking boy, more, I think, from wear and tear than from a weight of years—was to be cook, companion, and interpreter.

The Landin showed unbounded delight at getting out of the town, quickly divesting themselves of their skin sporrans and the bits of calico that covered their nakedness.

Taking a last look at the lovely landscape which formed the background of Tette, its detached hills towering up here and there from amidst the woodland, graced in the centre by the bold form of the Carocira mountain, I bade farewell to Southern Africa.

CHAPTER XVII.

INTO ANGONI-LAND.

The Revuqwe river—The Carocira—The new staff—Oppressive heat—Tsetse fly again—Zebra hunting—Salumbidwa mountain—Coal—The Makanga king—A fruitless conversion—Kankune, the murderous chief—Rebellious carriers—Abandoning food—The Landin threaten to leave—Their reasons—Chakundakoro's unpopularity—Night marching—Passing over difficult ground—Awkward tumbles—Mysterious alarm—"Abantu! Abantu!"—Fright of the Landin—Midnight camp of Makanga warriors—A quick retreat—The Mvudzi river—Songless birds—Sugar and provisions stolen—A great native traveller—Sukurumbwe, a warlike tribe—Idea that the English eat people—Difficulties of walking amidst tall grass—An immense grass fire—Devil take the hindmost—The highest altitude of the journey—Landin desertions—Swollen legs, hunger, and sulks—A bad fall—The chronometer smashed—All the Landin desert, and leave their loads—I proceed with a few followers—Buffalo herd—Hunger again—Deuka's town—Coolness of a deserter—"Well, you've got here!"—Misiri's bargains—His culinary art—Maravi discontent—Slave kidnappers appear—Return of the Maravi—A Makololo war—The Maravi desert me—I am alone!—Lucky encounter—Start for the king's kraal—A silent march.

DEAR Reader, if you have patiently borne thus far the burden of my story, I pray you to accompany me yet farther. We will move onwards, and passing through a few more villages and jungles, will climb the southern heights of the wide Zambesi basin, to roam over the vast and wild plateaus of Angoni-land, and together view from Manganja's rugged range the first glimpse of Nyassa's crystal sea!

A short march brought the party to the banks of the Revuqwe river, one of the most considerable branches of the Zambesi, the confluence being about three miles below Tette. The Revuqwe evidently drains a very large area, and traces of great floods were apparent in its channel, which was between 400 or 500 yards wide at this point. The freshets had broken the banks, leaving grass-covered islands, with ridges of loose rock and sand rising between the various channels, which now carried away the fallen waters.

Towards the north, the view was picturesque in the extreme. The outlines of the blue mountains in the distance were softened by the evening shades. Away at the utmost limit of view sombre mountains, cañons and jagged cliffs mingled with the tops of the forest trees. From amidst these gloomy shadows of rude nature comes the swift streaming waters of the Revuqwe, whose winding course is skirted with spear grass and various species of palms.

Our camp was close to a lovely scene, where we had the shelter of a large tropical tree. We halted just as the sun was declining in the western horizon, sending a blaze of glowing crimson across the sky. I could still see the tips of the Carocira mountains, and they powerfully reminded me of the days when, with longing eyes, I had watched them from the south. With the dying light such thoughts faded away, leaving to memory the miseries of the toilsome days of the past.

"Well there can be no more bother about men; that's one comfort!" and with that consolation in my thoughts, I rolled over on a cane mat, which was lent me by one of the village dons. Excepting the Landin, the boys with me had all been selected, and by the governor's secretary, too. Heaven knows! they looked about as wild as any mortals could look, without going out of the category of human beings. What about the Maravi, or Tette men? Well, there could be no doubt about them surely. That little difficulty, when they laid down the bundles of rice on this side of the river, as we disembarked, meant nothing; of course not! What, although they did leave the stuff lying all over the beach? I supposed they knew what they were going to eat. Not for a moment could it be thought that savages would forget their insides.

A sharp prick at this time made me renew my acquaintance with the tsetse; after sundown, too, which was rather alarming. I wondered what luck awaited us now, and ruminating upon present signs and future prospects, passed an excessively hot night. The heat had not been so oppressive at any period during the journey.

Neighbouring natives informed me that the Makanga tribe had attacked a train of ivory, and robbed the carriers.

Forests of varying density were penetrated in our route during the next few days. Mopani, thorny jungle, long coarse grasses and clusters of bamboo were the principal growths. River beds of dry sand such as the Matizi, Nyamtara, and Nyabzigo ran through the country.

The tsetse swarmed in certain localities, but altogether they were not so bad as we had found them here and there farther south.

Now we were gradually — very gradually — ascending. Until the course was altered, however, we could not reach the mountains, for we were heading E.S.E. This low, monotonous country tired me dreadfully, and the excessive heat was painfully exhausting: every day I felt it becoming worse, walled in as we were by jungle grasses, in which, as a matter of fact, we were hidden for the greater portion of the journey in these parts.

The flat belts of jungle held the heat closely, and a welcome freshness invigorated us when we reached any open spot, or the small course of a river. Meat would not keep, so it had to be eaten immediately on being killed. Flies gathered round it in myriads. I observed particularly a green fly, which gave an exceedingly painful sting.

Early one morning, after passing the night on the banks of the Nyabzigo river, I espied a large herd of zebras. As they were bearing down in our direction, I signalled to the boys to stop. All responded effectively by at once squatting on their haunches, so that their bodies were immediately lost to view in the thick cover. Unobserved, I stalked to within sixty yards of the advancing herd, and bowled over a very fat specimen, wounding a second, which gave a hard run of over half a mile before I managed to send home the fatal shot. Abundance of meat was secured by this morning's sport.

I am positive that the great amount of exercise which I was compelled to take throughout my journey greatly helped to keep me free from fever and from other ailments peculiar to tropical climates. But in this zone of unbearably torturing heat I felt these running spurts after game were anything but desirable.

Pursuing our course for two days through an uninteresting country, covered with tropical vegetation, we crossed the Shikambe and Mjobva rivers, both of which give their waters to the Zambesi above Lupata gorge, and pitched a camp at a place which I have designated the Palm Wells, 800 feet above the sea.

High and lovely trees, in all the natural glory of their plume-shaped leaves, surrounded the new camp. The broken outline of the Salumbidwa mountain loomed up in the eastern sky. The Maravi and Landin soon kindled a fire with the unfailing couple of sticks. Hastily, then, they set up the crude frame of forked sticks on each side of the flames, and soon on the supported pole were dangling long strips of dark-looking flesh, which had been kept far too long to be sweet. Rice was cooked in the roughest earthenware pots.

All being ready, the human vultures began a most voracious revelry, not only gorging themselves, but sleeping, snuffing, and sneezing, besides smoking dried hemp, which made them cough in a most violent manner.

Every now and then the tsetse would alight upon our thinly-clad bodies, making us jump again as though twitched with the fine lash of a whip.

Coal exists in this region. Some pieces which the natives brought to Tette seemed, in my opinion, to be of fairly good quality.

From our position at Palm Wells a range of high mountains was visible above the dense forest on our left. The inhabitants of this land are called Mwendapezi, the country being termed Chuwe. Still farther to the west, on the banks of the Revuqwe, live the Makanga and Muzimba, under an aggressive and arbitrary king, who, when a boy, and in view of his advent to power, the Portuguese captured and conveyed to Tette, where he received some tuition.

Upon his brow was sprinkled the holy water of the Christian font, and he was named Cipriano Gaetano Pereira. Notwithstanding these endeavours at conversion, it was soon seen how deeply savage instincts were implanted in his breast. Returning to his own country he came to the throne in 1876, and now rules with the rod of a tyrant and the lust of a fiend. Gratifying the grossest appetites of his inhuman disposition, the shedding of blood and the sacrifice of his fellow-beings form his chief delights. Brandy is his master, and cruelty his ruling passion.*

* Brandy may be procured at Tette; parties being sent for it with ivory, &c., in exchange.

Every year Kankune, or Sakakaka, as the natives call him, kills numbers of his people. I became acquainted with a man who had been an eye-witness of one of his murderous freaks, when, in a malignant fit of rage, he threw his favourite wife as food for the crocodile.

Kankune carries on perpetual wars of rapine and murder, having under his sway many thousands of warriors armed with flint-locks, assegais, battle-axes, bows and arrows, and shields. Firearms have been introduced principally by Arab caravans from the east coast. Traders passing this neighbourhood are frequently robbed; for the people pay little or no heed to the Portuguese authorities at Tette.

When we set out upon the march from the Palm Wells, it became evident that something had to be cleared up among my staff; some trouble that evidently thickened the minds of the Landin and the Maravi. Not only was there a reluctance to move, but an absolute indifference. On the previous day I had noticed that some of the Landin had thrown down the rice bags, just as they had done when leaving the banks of the river, when we were opposite Tette, on the very day of our departure.

At that time I had been positively compelled to look as threatening as I could, and with angry words force them to pick up the bundles. At first they refused, but after shaking one of them, and giving a volley of good round words in Spanish, Portuguese, English, and Zulu, we managed to proceed. My readers may imagine how grievously I was pressed before I could bring myself to adopt such a course of coercion towards those in whose hands I was.

Besides, it was a risky game to play with these savage Landin, and I was not slow to attribute the second signs of disaffection to my own conduct on the previous occasion.

Already half of the supply of rice was abandoned. From this I inferred that there was something radically wrong among the Maravi as well as the Landin, else they would not have been so careless about the commissariat department. To cogitate upon the evil appearances, I sat down under the imperfect shade of a tall palm. In all likelihood I would have dozed off to sleep, but the inevitable and industrious tsetse kept me fully awake by its incisive powers of puncture.

For some time no one came near. The company sat in groups at some distance from my retreat. Had we remained a week in this state I was determined to say nothing. I could not have enforced any action, but knew that the pangs of hunger would compel the Maravi to stick by me; for it is extraordinary to notice the rapid subsidence of provisions when there is no way of replenishing the supply. The Landin were, of course, perfectly independent.

I awaited the result. Soon Chibanga, the head man of the Maravi, accompanied by Misiri, approached. The latter, poor creature, was afraid of me, and also of the Landin: he evidently was a man long accustomed to hard usage. Chibanga's news was far from encouraging.

"The Landin are going to leave the white man and his things here!"

I insisted upon learning what their grievances were. Some time elapsed before an answer was vouchsafed; for, with the exception of one man, the Landin were a very surly lot. The man I refer to was evidently the leader, a "grande," as Misiri called him, meaning a headman among them.

A very good-looking fellow he was. His features had more of the Arab type than I had yet seen in Africa. Advancing towards me he lodged the complaint of his men, which amounted to this: that the press-gang at Tette, acting under the orders of Chakundakoro, had compelled them to enlist in my party against their inclinations: giving them only two fathoms of wretched, flimsy cotton instead of four, which was what they asked and what the governor's subordinate had assured them they would receive.

Chibanga corroborated this statement, saying that the Maravi had all received four "bracos," but the Landin only two, just as had been stated. When I inquired why they did not refuse to move until they were paid, they said that the deputy of the governor had threatened to throw them into jail if they refused. Exclamations, of a far from friendly character, broke out when the name of Chakundakoro was mentioned; making me think that if he undertook a journey such as mine his prospects of returning would be far from healthy, especially if he went among the Landin, with whom he was a man something worse than notorious.

I thought a great deal more than I cared to say about this treatment of the men. To my friend the governor I attached no blame. His knowledge of the Kaffir character was far too thorough to allow him to use compulsory measures with men whom he knew would have my life in their hands.

From my journal written on that day, I copy the following:—"I do not blame them. I would have done the same myself, and perhaps not given my man the chance to arrange matters."

To the Landin, however, I had to make good the difference, which was a heavy draught upon the limited stock.

This matter being adjusted, inquiries were made respecting the route, for it occurred to me that we were holding too much to the eastward. They pointed N.N.E., remarking that it would be in that direction we would proceed; but added that it would be impossible to advance during daytime, as there was no water, consequently we would have to make the distance between the heats.

Another obstacle was the fact that the Makanga claimed the country, a trouble I could not comprehend at the time, but afterwards found out what it meant. A Landin to a Makanga is of the "red rag to a bull" sort of provocation.

Throughout the weary length of a tiring and trying day we sat, half suffocated by the heated atmosphere, awaiting anxiously the signs of the setting sun, at which time it had been arranged we should make another move. Progress was quite different now; we used to anticipate the rising sun, now we longed for the gloom of night. Oh, for the mountain air once more! What a blessing it would be to have just one whiff of the morning breeze as it kissed the hill-tops far above the sweltering plains and valleys!

Partridges were seen in close proximity to the camp, but only two, and at most four, in a covey.

Evening was close at hand, and as I had been asleep most of the day I found it hard to tell at a glance whether I was witnessing the sunset or sunrise. The similarity of appearances was remarkable. In the morning, a faint crimson haze hung over the horizon like a veil of tinted vapour, behind which the sun's disc was strongly defined, presaging the tremendous heat of the day. These appearances are repeated in the evening; but the western sky assumes richer hues when old Sol is lowering behind the misty curtain, and the shades of night are falling upon the earth.

We are again *en route*. Six hours have passed since we left the Palm Wells. With the exception of two very short halts—only a few minutes—we had continued to march with a good, cheery swing.

The night was dark, some angry-looking clouds obscuring the gleam of the white-faced moon. The result was that we had a good many awkward falls, as we passed among dry cuts and yawning gaps overgrown with wait-a-bits, cat's-claws, and other thorny creepers which tore the hands. Through this cause my hands were in a most unsightly condition for some time.

Some of the crevices were like water cuts, through which we had to creep on hands and knees, for the heavy foliage shut out what little light there was. At odd times I listened with pangs to the thumps which my chronometer and sextant box were getting.

I always kept well to the front with the Landin; the Maravi often loitering miles behind.

Emerging from the thicker bush, the party now entered a sun-parched forest in which large sycamore trees were scattered, and where prairie fires had swept away with an irresistible strength the thick undergrowth of rank grass.

Hardly had we entered the forest when, quick as lightning, and without a word of warning, one of the Landin, who was ahead, turned round and caught me by the shoulders, pressing me to the ground as he uttered in an excited undertone:

"Abantu! Abantu!"

The word was spoken with great emphasis. What could be the matter? What was going to happen? Where, in the devil's name, was that loiterer Misiri? I could not speak!

A mysterious performance then took place. The Landin hastily looked to their flint-locks, and taking off all the things they carried, laid them down close to the tree beside which I had been deposited. One comfort I certainly had. That was the trusty "Express," now my only reliable companion.

Absolute ignorance of the circumstances was maddening. I was determined in my wish to get up; but no sooner did I attempt to rise to my feet than the Landin, who were quivering with nervous excitement, and anxiously looking ahead, pressed me down with all sorts of signs, at the same time repeating impetuously and earnestly the mysterious warning, "Abantu!"

One of the Landin turned back with a rush, vanishing like a swarthy sprite into the gloom of the forest. Those who remained were full of apprehension. When the rest of the party came up they immediately put down their loads and disappeared in the forest.

More and more I wondered what devilish thing was about to happen. Was I to be offered up as a sacrifice to some wild fetich as a new eatable, or what?

Misiri at last arrived—he was always last. Comprehending the situation immediately, he told me that a camp of Makanga was ahead. I responded by saying that I would go with the Landin to them. On our hands and knees we slowly and stealthily stalked through the forest, beneath the glimmering light of the moon, which now and then cast our shadows clear upon the blackened, fire-baked earth.

For some time nothing especial could be distinguished. But at length the ruddy reflection of rising flames dancing amidst the forest trees could be discerned, and showing the trunk of one of the monarchs of the woods which had fallen.

What the Landin meant to do when the object of our cunning stalk had been reached, I could not conjecture.

My mind was busy with thoughts that at this juncture some of the party, which had lingered far in the rear, would inevitably pass the man whom I had left with orders to stop them. Should that happen, and if they innocently made the slightest noise they would soon attract the attention of the wild Makanga.

Nearer and nearer we drew, until we could see the fires blazing. For me the scene was one of the most intense excitement. I could perceive the bronzed figures of numerous men stark and clear in the flickering light of the merry flames. Some of the men were eating, others were grouped indifferently about.

No sooner did the Landin observe the position of affairs than they turned round and beat a rapid retreat. Away we sped at a good pace farther towards the east. Now I could understand why the Landin were averse to day travelling in this country—there was something else besides the water difficulty and the heat.

After threading our way through stubborn jungle, over a low, flat country, covered with high forests, in the midst of which noxious gases rose from the heated soil with sickening effect, we reached the foothills of the Kapirizange mountains, where, after a halt, we gladly began the ascent.

Before advancing farther I asked Misiri for the little kettle of water which I had given him to carry. This was a trust I rarely allowed, but on this occasion he had suggested it. Guilt was in his face when I asked him for the kettle of water. "There is none," he said sheepishly. Poor Misiri, the temptation had been too much for him.

The slopes were climbed and we reached the backbone of a rugged spur. From this elevation we looked back, and for the last time viewed the great basin of the Zambesi.

Towards the north lay a great mountainous region.

CAMP OF THE DREADED MAKANGA.

Mountains with cone-shaped summits were seen on the left. One, of pyramid form, was called Bonamarungo.

Our descent brought us to the Mvudzi river, which is a large and very clear stream, shaded by two mountain ridges. It was quite a glad and refreshing sight to see the waters tumbling and splashing in silvery sprays around the polished boulders; and it was music to the ear to listen to the merry rippling and gurgling as the stream danced on its way, sometimes broken by sudden and pretty falls. On the banks, the long grass droops and quivers with the stroke of the flashing mountain stream, which flows in a westerly direction onwards to the Revuqwe river, just above the chief town of the Makanga king.

Palms and a great variety of large forest trees clothe the steep slopes which rise from the river's banks.

Kingfishers, spoonbills, divers, and other water birds swooped past, alighting gracefully upon the boughs which in fantastic beauty overhung the happy waters. No song of birds, however, enlivened the ear.

Fish might be seen in every pool. In shape they seemed to resemble perch.

By this flowing waterside I was quite ready and even glad to make a halt. All the party were in need of rest.

The sun was a quarter high, and we had been on the march sixteen hours since leaving the Palm Wells.

During the whole of that time we had not eaten anything, neither had we moistened our lips. It was one of the longest and most exciting nights I have ever spent.

After a long sleep I awoke and shouted out for Misiri. I told him that I would like some coffee, and asked him for the sugar, of which I had a fairly good supply when we started. At this request Misiri's expression became as uneasy as it had been in the morning, when I had asked for the water. He said nothing in reply; so I examined the tin box. It was empty!

There could not be the slightest doubt that this awkward peculation accounted for the Maravi men staying behind on the previous night before the alarm. I more than half expected that all the biscuits had also been demolished, when I next told him to bring the biscuit box. Bread I never had on the march during all my journey.

Now there were positively no provisions for me, excepting a small bag of beans. As it would be premature to complain, I was silent. So long as the delinquents confined themselves to eatables, their larcenies were of little account, and up to the present they had not taken anything else.

My luxuries were gone. But, as on previous occasions, I comforted myself with rougher fare, devouring a piece of a small antelope, which I had shot in the early morning, also a dish of maize-meal porridge.

The Landin are by far the most indecent people I ever travelled with, or encountered in any way. They are worse than nude, for they decorate their naked bodies in a grossly offensive fashion.

One of the Maravi men had been a great traveller. As we sat in camp, he related how, when a young man, he had been taken far to the north-west of the country we were then travelling through, and had lived with a very warlike tribe of people, who, when babies, had the scalp pressed up towards the back and top of the head, and tied so as to keep it in that position. As the child grew, its mother continued to press up the scalp, until finally the hair, which grew from this lump or knot of flesh, could be pulled up, and drawn to a point, with pieces of stick and bark. When this had been done, the resultant decoration was saturated with grease.

These people, the Maravi said, were called Sukurumbwe. Naturally, I cannot vouch for the authenticity of such information; but, notwithstanding this, it is interesting to repeat such tales.

He also told me of a tribe, which he called Shimbamwuneni. This people lived still farther to the west. The Maravi, his own tribesmen, he said, could not understand them. For example, he spoke of them saying *mema* for water, the Maravi word being *madzi*.

Further he related how he had travelled on the northern side of the great valley of the Zambesi; north of Zumbo, among two tribes, called, respectively, Siankope and Siamwenda. Not the least interesting portion of this wanderer's intelligence was the news that, when boys were being recruited, the Tette people said:

"Ah, don't go with the Igrezi [English], they eat people!"

I tried to explain, as best as I could, to the man and his friends that the white race—the Igrezi—were the first to repress the traffic of slavery, which existed in his country; they were the liberators of the black slave, and his best friends among all the nations of the world.

Just before beginning the ascent of the Kapirizange range, I had seen tsetse fly; but in the mountains none were to be found.

Oh, beloved mountains, where the wind blows fresh and free, laden with no poison from the miasma of swamp rotting in the great river valleys! Most intense was my feeling of delight, while listening to the gentle zephyrs rustling through the branches which waved beside our new camp, and making the leaves of the tall palms tremble like restless pennants. Although we had ascended only about 600 feet, that is to say, but one step of the rugged ladder that leads to the great plateau, what a contrast the place was to our previous camp!

Necessity, including scarcity of provisions, compelled early starts. The men said that, even on the mountains, marching during the daytime would be too hot.

So about 2 A.M. saw the small party shouldering the loads, and quitting the pleasant camp.

We struck out in a northerly course, under the glimmering of a splendid starlit sky, passing through a country claimed by the brother of the Makanga king. His name was Shagwadera, and from what was said, I judged that his acquaintance was by no means desirable to cultivate.

The features of the country changed but little. We still ascended, and soon were lost in the thick belts of coarse, reed-like grass, which waved high above our heads. Walking in such circumstances is very laborious, a sort of swimming action having to be maintained with the arms, in order to prevent the sharp, prickly seeds from getting into the eyes. Notwithstanding all endeavours, however, these seeds stick all over the body, giving great pain, as their subtle points pierce like the tsetse, and have the additional discomfort of leaving their ends in the flesh. Burrs, too, cling to the clothed parts of the body.

A slight dew falls during the night, causing a sensation of chilliness when the slightest pause occurs in our stemming the bending waves of the high grass.

The stars have faded from the wakening sky. Darkness lifts, leaving the faintest tint of blue in the brightening heavens. White, fleecy clouds move swiftly westwards.

The wind has risen to half a gale. Above its tempestuous voice we suddenly hear a deafening noise, like the mighty peals of thunder, or of great waters falling over a vast precipice. Nearer and nearer comes the ominous sound, borne towards us by the rush of the impetuous wind.

The air becomes darkened with charred straws, which are whirled about in waving clouds, and fall on every hand like winter's withered leaves.

They are a sign of an immense grass fire. Soon bright and blood-red tongues of flame can be seen darting skyward, and swaying and waving before the gale. The conflagation rages directly across our path; its devouring tongues sweeping fiercely through the dense cover.

Among the company, it is at once a case of every man for himself, and devil take the hindmost. With the greatest difficulty the wild flames are avoided; but at length in safety we hear their crackling, and see their fantastic wreaths angrily coiling around the stems of the great trees, which lift their crowns high above the destroying sea of fire.

> . . . "the palms, canes, brakes you see
> Wrapped in one agony
> Of lurid death."

Still ascending, we pressed on in a northerly direction for some days. Nothing could be seen to relieve a sort of dumb monotony in the surroundings. Game seemed to be very scant. Winged songsters were unknown. No human habitation met the eye. Much of this poverty of prospect must be attributed to the miserable character of the soil; the land of the country consisting mostly of barren mountains and rocks, the surface of the lowlands being covered by heavy forests.

Difficulties with the carriers increased, as lessening provisions made it necessary to live entirely upon meat.

On each side of our path the mountains rise up; the Kapirizange chain on the left, and the Manganja range far away on our right, the latter forming a continuous rocky line northwards to Lake Nyassa, and hemming in the high tableland of eastern equatorial Africa.

The Landin call these mountains Makurungwe or Makungwa. We crossed the well-watered rivers, the Mkondozi and Mauni. The steep alluvial banks of the former are clothed with mopani and tropical shrubs.

Mounting the tortuous path that winds up the southern slopes of the Jandani mountain, we reached a point which was 5,200 feet above the sea-level, this being the highest altitude attained during the whole journey, and viewed towards the south and east the crowns of a thousand hills. Floating in the heavens were countless nebulæ, wafted by the prevailing winds from the distant Indian Ocean, and bearing their rain-charged vapours on to the mountain regions.

In a little time we descended the grass-covered slopes. The Gutambo mountain rose up close on our right. We made our camp amid large rocks, which were piled in the centre of the Rumbuni river.

Recent marches had been accomplished almost wholly during the night. A much greater distance can be covered in this way, and with less fatigue, than by pursuing the journey during the heat of the day. Near to the Mkondozi river, which we were approaching, five of the Landin deserted; but their loads in the first instance having been rice, now almost entirely consumed, the disaffection was not altogether to be regretted. Much, however, depended upon the loyalty of the few who remained, for they were the guides. The Maravi hunters, as a rule, know the country; but unfortunately those who were with me were quite ignorant of the routes.

The camping-place we had pitched upon was decidedly

novel; for we were in the middle of the channel, lodging among huge boulders, about which the waters dashed furiously on every side. Although the Mkondozi is not a wide stream, it carries a large volume of water, and the current is very swift.

When we had settled down for a little, the Maravi men came before me in couples, shuffling their feet, and clapping their abdomens, as they asked for food.

"We must go back," said they, "we cannot go farther with 'Igrezi.' We will die for want. We cannot walk without food."

To me it seemed irrational, even for savages, to force these endless supplications for food in a country where it was absolutely impossible to procure it. At that especial time I felt that my turn for complaint had arrived.

"Why have you loitered on the way," I asked, "until the food has almost disappeared? I warned you that we must hurry to some country where we could buy food. I have done my best to shoot game for you, and you still have some dried meat left."

I saw one of their number carrying a goatskin full of meal which had been brought for me. This I divided equally amongst the Maravi, at the same time cautioning them on the imperative necessity of economy, and showing the thoughtless folly of their proposal to return to Tette, as they would assuredly starve long ere they reached the river.

Nothing was said in reply. A very unlucky thing was that Chibanga, the headman of the Maravi, was suffering from swollen legs, an extraordinary infirmity for one of his race; it had the effect of making him very sulky.

I continued expostulating with the people. One question I would ask before they decided to leave me.

"What are you going to live on while on the road back?"

When they heard this question they looked more sulky and, if possible, more idiotic than before; and the answer came slowly and without spirit:

"We will go back to Kunyungwi in the morning!"

"All right," I replied. "Go; but remember that Chakundakoro will hear of this!"

The mention of the ogreish name produced much murmuring. Poor old Misiri looked much as he usually did, comical but greatly worried; he, no doubt, had his conscience pricked by the knowledge that he had eaten most of the food which had been brought on for me. Possibly, however, his melancholy humour was due to the fact that the supplies had "given out." Be this as it may, he declared that he was ready to stay with me whatever happened. In my small bag of valuables I had reserved two packets of maizina, which now came in very opportunely.

The five Landin who had remained with me now came forward without any ceremony, and said they wanted cloth, otherwise they would leave. The trouble of this demand was that I could not give to one without giving to all, and my supply was very limited. At the same time, I had an idea that should I give the Landin cloth, they would go off to their country, leaving me all the sooner to my own resources.

I inquired how far it was to a town or village. The reply intimated that it was a long way to the king's town; but after a considerable amount of questioning, I extracted the information that there was an Angoni village a good day's march from where we then were. We could not reach the place, however, until late in the evening.

Having learned this much, I announced that to all who would continue with me I would give an extra fathom of cloth on our arrival at the village, but not an inch before that time.

"As for your hunger," I continued, "you have yourselves to blame. Enough was provided for you, but by your own choice you threw it down, and left it to rot in the valley of the Zambesi!"

Delay would be positively disastrous now. One course only could be pursued, and I would have to use all the energy I possessed in order to get the Maravi to obey commands.

What would have happened if they had all disappeared, and left me solitary in this strange land, without the means of carrying the few valuables—a better term would be "indispensables"—which I had with me would be difficult to imagine. Should the worst come, I determined that the struggle to avert catastrophe should be a hard one.

Three o'clock in the morning saw me up and stirring about the camp. The Maravi to the last refused to go. The Landin had started ahead, so it became absolutely necessary to use very forcible language, backed up by a good deal of threatening, before the reluctant Maravi could be got off. I had to lift each individual's load, and literally drive them all out of the camp.

Even when they were on the road the troublesome people would not move at anything like a good pace; for at the best their rate of progress was a miserably worn-out sort of travel, under which circumstances the Landin were soon entirely lost to view. I poured out maledictions upon the whole race, telling them that should they fail to reach the town upon that night, wherever the place was, I would give them no cloth, buy them no food, and so let them starve.

Poor souls! they were perhaps weakened by hunger; but there are times with the black people when you are compelled to show the savage side of your nature. A little of it, however, goes a long way.

On such occasions as these I felt the want of a good, faithful follower, a man who could assist; for now I wished to keep up with the Landin, who were by this time some distance ahead. An uncomfortable suspicion disturbed my mind, that if I left the Maravi they would drop the things and bolt.

We had to climb a steep mountain-slope, on which broken stones were strewn in vast quantities on every hand, making walking very disagreeable as well as toilsome.

While making the descent towards the Vilange river, one of the boys fell over a ledge of rock and rolled over the "side-hill." By this accident my chronometer got its *coup de grâce*, because the stumbler was carrying it at the time. I rushed up and examined the indispensable instrument; its life was extinct. It had stopped, and I remember that I looked with not a little animosity at the boy who had been caressing the rugged slopes, thinking from my heart that his injuries were far from being sufficiently severe.

Having crossed the narrow river, another affluent of the Revuqwe, I observed lying on the other side of the trail the baggage which the Landin had gone on with!

What did this mean? Where were the men? The bushes and every hidden nook for some distance up and down were searched, but all to no purpose. The missing Landin could nowhere be seen. They had fled, leaving us to find our way as best we could, and introduce ourselves to the Angoni king!

However, they had said on the previous night, when they were questioned, that the town could be reached that same evening by hard marching. Now what would the Maravi men do?

I sat down to await the coming of the stragglers of the party. There they came, looking utterly forlorn and careless. Chibanga, their so-called leader, was hobbling along bearing his weight on a tall stick. He was the only one who seemed fairly " done up."

The others were averse to entering Angoni-land; that was clearly evident. They sat down in a ring around me and said they wanted to rest. Chibanga and Misiri spoke:

"The Landin have left us! What is the white man going to do? We cannot carry the things."

I was not long in telling them what was to be done.

" You cannot," I said, " go back to your own country in this condition. You are footsore and hungry. The Landin said that we could reach a town to-night, and we are now on a trail which must lead to it. I will leave half of your number here, while the rest will go on with me. Then I will send you back food as soon as we reach the town."

Chibanga, I knew, would be quite unable to proceed with his swollen legs. We had come so slowly in the morning that we would have to proceed at a rapid rate if we intended to reach the town upon that night, assuming that such a place was within any reasonable distance.

The provisions were then collected and given in charge of the men who were to remain as guardians of the valuables. Of course they protested, saying that there was not enough for them to subsist upon should I not return upon the next day.

This was an awkward fix. To overcome difficulties I told off the men who were to remain with Chibanga, piling up the few things to be left under their care, and seeing a skerm hastily completed, in the centre of which the few dejected-looking creatures were huddled.

Then we started off. The pathway which we followed was very narrow but clear. I led the way.

Excepting a few pounds of rice, which Misiri had stuffed into the cook box, a wonderful receptacle of confusion, we had no provisions left, but we moved along at a good brisk rate. When the stomach depends upon activity, lassitude is soon displaced by energy even among the Kaffirs. In this particular, it appears, human nature is alike all the world over.

Our way took us out of the small forest which fringed the river's banks. As we stepped out a new freshness seemed to invigorate us. The view opened out on all sides showing a vast wilderness; for now we had climbed the heights and reached the great plateau of Angoni-land.

Much cooler weather prevailed. Recent rains had vitalised the young and succulent grasses which clothed the stretching prairie with a verdure of varying tints of blending shades. Far away to the north-east, in the horizon, could be seen various stony peaks rising up to salute the sunlight.

Five miles, a rough guess, to the north were two low hills. On reaching the nearer of the two we surprised a herd of buffalo, which dashed off at headlong speed, sweeping round in a remarkable curve, until they struck a small clump of young machabele forest, in which their living mass of black was soon lost to view.

It is wonderful what a sense of exhilaration is raised by a sight of this description, all the better if it is unexpected. You are assured that game exists, and that so long as the ammunition lasts you cannot starve. Ascending a gentle rise in the undulations of the plains, we carefully scanned the landscape for beacons in the shape of the tops of village huts.

The light of day was fading, so we pressed onward with unflagging energy. As the sun declined our hopes of reaching the town fell also. I had caused a serious delay by attempting to bag a buffalo; but the brute had seen me, and was too keenly on the alert through the start we had given him. The scantiness of the cover for stalking was a great drawback, for I could not approach near enough to get a good shot.

The shades of night descended, and disappointment was the destiny of the day, our unavailing march seeming to be mocked by the ruddy globe of fire, which bathed with blood-red light the waste of undulating hill and vale.

Cheerless, indeed, was the evening; for without food the black man is silent. Long ere the new morning broke we were again up and away, and soon after following the winding pathway, trending a gentle slope, we viewed with gladdened eyes numerous tops of huts.

There was the town! Now we would soon see what sort of reception the Angoni would give us. Brimful of curiosity I walked on, and soon found myself close to the outskirts of a town environed by fields of harvested maize. That the people had heard of the coming man was evident from the large crowds assembled outside. Anxiety had made me quite forget my party, and I had walked on wholly unconscious of the fact that they were in no hurry to proceed. Now I was compelled to await their arrival before we entered the town.

The whole population turned out *en masse*—with dogs and children in swarms—to take the measure of the intruders. We all seated ourselves under a baobab tree, which evidently was the column around which the tribunals of justice assembled; for under the same shelter sat numbers of old men smoking and snuffing, who looked upon us with countenances expressive of much curiosity and gravity. For hours we sat in this position gazed upon all the time by the surrounding masses; certainly the dirtiest and most uncouth set of savages I had yet seen in Africa.

On our right the two mountain tops broke the waving line of distant country, called by the natives the Zenza mountains.

My conjecture regarding the decamping of the Landin proved to be correct, for I remarked amidst the crowd the unconcerned visage of one of the deserters who left us on the Mkondozi river. I immediately told Misiri to collar him and bring him to me. This done, the fellow coolly squatted, and looked as though he had never seen me in his life.

I had no intention of raking up past delinquencies, or in any way anticipating his merited judgment day, but I was really anxious to know whether we were to remain seated under the baobab tree for any protracted term of life. More practically, I wanted a hut in which to place the goods, also men to go back immediately with food and bring along the things from the Vilange river.

This was a most important matter. I could not trust the Maravi, and so long as I could secure my effects in a hut I might be able to do something. Without the goods, I would be still more at the mercy of these suspicious-looking people.

After much deliberation, the worthy deserter answered that the headman of the town must be seen—his name was Deuka. Determined not to disclose the contents of my packages before the mob, I said that first of all I must have a hut, and when that was given I would speak.

And so another hour passed silently away. Not a word was spoken, not a syllable addressed to any one of the party. Misiri at last broke the silence in a most comical manner, as with a half-suppressed smile he said to me:

" Well, you've got here."

There was something exceedingly funny about the remark, for it meant so much. True, I had " got here," but what a struggle we had had to reach the place! Now the situation seemed little better than when we were on the march.

As we had of a surety been long enough seated to decide to the people that our intentions were far from being warlike, I then said that Misiri had better go on a foraging tour through the town. He immediately went and took up his position beside a very fat and ancient old lady, whose thick coating of grimy dirt told that her occupation lay in the agricultural line.

Good Misiri had an eye to business: he was trying to effect a purchase. The conversation was slow, but ultimately they both vanished together. My follower soon returned holding two squalling hens. I noticed that his waist-cloth was almost gone; only a very small portion remaining as a sort of apology for an apron.

" Where are your clothes, Misiri?" I inquired.

" Buying!" was his laconic answer.

While he had thought of me he had not altogether forgotten his own half-famished condition, for behind him walked a young girl carrying a large gourd of native beer. Misiri's interview with the earth-encrusted old lady was productive of further good, as the lower portion of a hut was set aside for me and mine.

The place was very filthy, having been used as a chicken and goat house. But here there was no choice. I was bound to get a corner somewhere, no matter what was its condition, so we scraped out the goat pen, after which the dirty savages filed in and squatted about until every available inch of space was occupied.

Smoking was greatly indulged in, a fire being lit in the centre of the circle; a fire of this kind being indispensable for Kaffir comfort, no matter what degree of heat may be generated. Now and then on those occasions when the atmosphere savoured too much of Kaffir, I would go out, and soon all would follow and sit around me, so that it was impossible to be alone.

All this time I sat in silence, watching Misiri preparing the supper, and first depriving the two hens of their cackling lives. This he did in a most expeditious manner, whipping their heads off and stripping the feathers with marvellous celerity and in the most dexterous fashion, suggesting the idea that on more than one occasion he had found it necessary to deprive a bird of its identity.

Misiri was excessively dirty, and especially fond of hot nut oil, or venison fat, for sauce. I never failed to have a qualm of inward emotion, a dread, as it were, of what was coming as I watched this doughty *chef* of the culinary art working himself into a pouring perspiration over the mysterious compound, burning his fingers as he attempted to hold the edge of the clay pot, while the smoke of the root fire rose in clouds, choking and blinding him. When at length his operations were over he would place the pot before me, along with a tin plate and a spoon, the latter being the only feeding tool left in the outfit. Squatting before me he would then await results, or rather his share.

The Maravi who were with me now demanded their cloth,

I having taken the precaution to bring that on with the advance guard. When in the act of giving it them, second thoughts passed quickly through my mind.

Was I to pay the cloth promised? If I did, I would most likely never see them again. If I refused, I would be accused of deceiving them. I concluded, however, that the latter was the only plan to ensure the bringing of the things which were left on the road; therefore I declared that I could not give them anything but food until their comrades were here, and all the remaining things were safely housed.

Great disatisfaction was the result of this decision, but by dint of unwavering diplomacy I persuaded the refractory crowd to leave long before daybreak, so that at eventide they would be back.

A restless and utterly wretched night was passed in our revoltingly dirty hut, literally teeming with vermin, and reeking with sickening smells. The place was only eight feet across, and the blacks crowded in around the smoky fire which nestled in a small hole in the centre.

Long ere day had dawned the Maravi had left, taking with them the necessary provisions. It was three days since we left the unfortunate Chibanga, so I felt that he and his companions were by that time knowing something more than usual of the pangs of hunger.

During the day some hunting parties arrived, bringing with them large bundles of dried buffalo meat. I perceived that these Angoni had not a good show of flint-locks, being mostly equipped with bows and arrows.

To be ready for any emergencies, I thought it would be wise to at once interview the headman. After making my presence tolerable by means of the inevitable gift, I told him I wished to place all my goods in his hut, as there was no room in mine. In reality my object was the safety of the stores. The thought of losing the rifles occasioned real dread, although I had taken the precaution to disconnect them, butts from barrels, rolling them in rags.

Inquiries about the lake met with no satisfactory reply. He said Chikuse was the king of the country, and that his town lay to the north; from all I could gather about two days' march.

I then inquired who formed the parties which had been arriving, but could get no trustworthy answer. Large parties had been coming in from the east. They were armed with bows and arrows, assegais, and shields. Misiri pointed out the direction from which they came. It was only afterwards that I found out that they were undoubtedly slave kidnappers, who had been down in the Shiré valley.

I had not seen Misiri since early morning. The sun had just sunk to the back of Mboma mountain, which lay to the west of the town, its low, pyramid form being visible from the plains eight miles south, when my valuable intrepreter appeared.

He was most affectionately drunk. All he was able to stutter was:

"Senhor, tem fome" (you are hungry).

He had sold every atom of his waist-cloth in order to procure the native beer, which causes a drowsy inebriety with intermittent stages of excited action.

The Maravi arrived with the goods. The quantity was all right, but the condition was not. Although the chronometer had received an almost fatal blow during the eventful night march from the Palm Wells, still it had not been quite destroyed. Now the outer box was completely smashed. The thermometers, too, in metal cases, were broken, while everything else seemed to be in a state of irreparable dissolution, the sight stirring my breast with inexpressible feelings of grief.

After the cloth promised to the Maravi had been paid, they made a demand for more, remarking how tired they were, and how other miseries afflicted them sorely.

My intention was to postpone further conversation until the morning, preferring to speak only when it was absolutely necessary, and at seemingly opportune times. But here Chibanga, as spokesman for the whole party, addressed me, saying that the Maravi had concluded to return to their homes. My contention in answer to this surprise was to the effect that we were still far from the lake; but seeing that the king's town was only two days' journey they should accompany me so far, when their trouble would be compensated just as it had been in this town, according to my promise.

No, they were going home. Would no one go on with me until I could get other men at the king's to take me to the lake? Not one would go any further.

About that time, it is only fair to say, there were a great number of rumours about a Makololo war raging near the shores of the lake.* Africa has no exception to the general rule of rumour, which, as in England, France, America, or any other country, rolls on like an avalanche, gaining in volume as it proceeds.

Had these rumours terrified my stubborn staff? I could not tell. I thought, however, that the morning might bring a flame of hope, for now there was not the slightest spark. Come what might, I was pretty sure that the condition of affairs could not be worse; for the slender thread

---

* The Makololo has been used as the designation of the broken tribes over whom Livingstone placed Makololo people as chiefs. Strictly speaking, the races are not Makololo, but Manganja and Ajawa.

upon which my prospects hung was solely the possibility of being able to converse in broken Portuguese through the interpreters Chibanga and Misiri, who could make themselves understood by the natives. Of course, they could say whatever they pleased, and in the same way they would tell me whatever suited their own purpose.

Acting on the new determination, I on the following morning made most strenuous efforts to recruit among the Maravi—a barren and dispiriting effort, any description of which would assuredly weary the reader.

Yet, in the dilemma, I reaped benefit from having given largess to Mtande, the head man, who had stowed my things in his hut.

By this time I was beginning to realise thoroughly the utter loneliness of my position. One man left upon whom I could rely would have made me feel comfortable, but at present I could not foresee what might happen at any moment. Fateful positions inevitably lay in the future of my progress.

I completely banished from my mind all the hopes I ever had of the Maravi accompanying me farther, and the distrust seemed justified when some of them came forward to loiter about and laugh derisively as I struggled to effect a start, and to make the Landin (or Angoni) comprehend my wishes by signs, and by the measures of cloth which I laid beside each load.

The Maravi disappeared—where I could not tell. I was deserted in this strange country, left amidst new surroundings and unknown, and seemingly far from friendly faces. Not a word could I interchange with a living mortal. I was alone!

The task seemed quite hopeless. There was no one to help me now, so I was thrown upon my own resources and ingenuity to steer as best I could out of the strange quandary. I had almost succeeded in effecting a start, having paid six Landin, but through being unable to make them understand my intentions another day was lost.

As any one can fancy, the position was now far from being conducive to blissful repose. The mind was too much occupied by thoughtful studies of every plan which promised to better the prospects of advance. The over-recurring mishaps of carriers had always been the worst difficulty.

On this occasion various payments in cloth had again made the stock run very short. In fact, if ever I reached the king's town I would not have anything to offer him; and then how was I to reach the lake?

Tired of making efforts to sleep I got up, and, seeing no one about, strolled to the outskirts of the town, and through the furrows of the maize fields, talking to my shadow, which was distinctly pictured by the bright moon. The voice, however, in such experiments becomes monotonous, no matter how you contradict yourself in the effort to be two. I can imagine a prolonged existence of this kind causing madness.

There stood the baobab tree like a small grey tower, with a black cavity gouged in one side. Under the pale light it looked like the goblin's tree so familiar in pantomimes.

A man was walking after me. What on earth did he want? I paid no heed to his presence, but continued my ramble for a little, until I saw that he was evidently bent upon making up to me. Then I halted. The man had a black calico sheet (dyed by the natives) wrapped carelessly around his person, and, perhaps through the time and place of meeting, he seemed to me a strange mortal.

"Señoro!"

The word surprised me. It is the way which some natives have of addressing the Portuguese. I was not long in airing a little of what I knew of the language, and found to my great delight that the midnight stranger proved to be a man from the east coast, from Mozambique. He said he had seen me going out alone and without any weapons, and remarked that it was not safe to do so, as there were Makololo about. What he meant by this I never could make out, because then we were very far from the locality where the Makololo war was said to be raging.

I tried to induce him to accompany me to the king's kraal; but he said that he had a number of comrades encamped some distance off, and he could not leave them. The comrades were a party of hunters. A promise of a present, however, brought him to agree that he would help me to get Angoni men as an escort to the king's town.

Notwithstanding the fact that I had considerable difficulty in conversing with my new friend, his appearance at that emergency proved a blessing. His name was Frasincho.

Time seemed to fly at a furious rate whenever the occasion for moving arrived. Frasincho was true to his word, but it became evident that he was rather frightened of the Angoni. I stood with the fragments of cloth, trying to make bargains that were perforce curbed by economy as well as by unhappy dreams—too well conjured by experience—of the trying days in store. In matters of bargain Frasincho was silent, and not infrequently his dumbness was very aggravating. Three of the six Angoni men who had been paid on the previous day again came forward, but three more were again paid.

Once when the three men who had been paid refused their loads I indiscreetly, in a moment of haste, shouted out to them in Zulu the word thieves. At this Frasincho quickly and wisely said:

"Don't say anything more; you are alone in this people's country."

I made Frasincho explain to the Angoni that they should say to the king, whenever we arrived, that I wished boys to go to the lake to my white brothers. Frasincho, although calling these people very bad names, said the king would be sure to give me boys.

A lunch on fresh air and on recollections of the past sufficed me, as shortly afterwards I sat watching the six savages plunging and sporting in the deep waters that eddied round the jagged rocks of the Kameo river. We were six miles north of Deuka's town, at the place where I looked upon the sparkling volume of swift flowing waters which flowed westward to the Revuqwe river.

As we moved on, for the halt was of brief duration, the country became more open. The waves of treeless land in the small river valley looked flat, so that the eye's vision was extended, the small grass-covered hills sinking into the prevailing plains. In the uneven horizon were still seen the Manganja peaks, rearing up against the blue of the eastern sky.

It struck me strangely during this part of the northward march that my life was entirely in the hands of these wild Angoni. No doubt they were imbued with all sorts of ideas as to the hidden powers which the white man had. Necessity compelled silence upon my part. Among themselves they had had several disputes, and then for many miles we marched along without a syllable being uttered.

CHAPTER XVIII.

TROUBLES AT CHIKUSE'S.

Superstitions about animals—Hippopotamus trenches—Enforced silence—Revelry of rats—A hideous night—The mysterious sentinel—Chikuse—Loneliness—Beer drinking—"Oh, if I could only speak!"—Thoughts of the old "faithfuls"—A shriek and a shot—Queer visitors—One-sided conversation—Lament for the dead—A timely arrival—Eustaquio da Costa—Plans for relief—King Chikuse is satisfied that I can speak—Ring head-dress—Cultivation of tobacco—The Angoni people—Killing a crocodile—Corn stores—Funeral ceremonies—Boy rat-catchers—Hunting reports—Medicines for everything—Quackery—Superstition ineradicable—Worshipping a donkey—The lady and the pombe—Chikuse is splenetic—His cruelties—The Makanga tribe—Food of the Angoni—Their customs—Slave kidnappers—Some aspects of the slave-trade—Horrors of the yoke—Departure of a caravan.

On approaching the Revuqwe river a herd of hippos was seen, but not being aware what the superstitions of the people might be, I refrained from trying some very inviting shots. Not a few tribes, as I have already stated, have an idea that departed spirits go into these animals.

I had crossed this river at a point where it was hundreds of yards in width, that is to say, at its confluence with the Zambesi. All the tributaries which flow to it from the eastern watershed I had also crossed. Where we stood now the distance from bank to bank did not exceed seventy yards. Further up it rapidly narrowed. The banks rose steeply on each side, and in many places might be seen the paths or deep trenches dug by the hippopotamus during the time of torrents. The animals crouch in these watery retreats, some of which are so well defined that they might have been shaped by the spade of a dexterous digger.

About four o'clock in the afternoon, after surmounting another dividing ridge, we could see numerous depressed ravines converging into one wide valley, which was studded, at intervals of, say, half a mile, with the villages of the Angoni. At this point I made a wild attempt to get in a word in Zulu, asking where Chikuse's town lay; but my vocabulary was not sufficient to make the people understand the question. Therefore I confined my attempt to a repetition of the word Chikuse, all the time waving my hand vaguely towards the north. They pointed to a town almost at the top of the western slope in the far distance.

A pretty cool breeze was blowing from the east, and, as the ground was bare, walking became tolerably easy. When we arrived at a village I had to pass through a most trying ordeal. I wanted to say, "Where is the king?" but found that I was powerless, speechless, while likewise I was becoming a little anxious because my talk brought no response, although it evidently was a source of a little amusement to those who stood around.

Often enough it is disagreeable to know everything that is going on; but it is infinitely worse to know nothing, and at the same time to be quite unable to give utterance to a single word that can convey a meaning.

I had not forgotten that Mtande had spoken of Chikuse's being a two days' journey. Frasincho had said that the town was not very far from the Revuqwe, and now we had advanced nearly seven miles north-west of the river. Thinking was of no avail now; for I felt myself in the hand of fate, and decided to be patient.*

* This village is marked on the map, but I was unable to find out the name.

After being seated for some time, the headman of my Landin escort conveyed me to a hut, which by all appearances had not been occupied for some time.

One of the six men who had accompanied me had disappeared at an early period of our march. He was now seen approaching accompanied by a number of men armed with clubs and shields. They sat around and seemed to be in earnest conversation with the headman and people of the village.

I took up a position outside the hut set apart for me, and sat musing and speculating upon the probable upshot of all this palaver. In no very cheerful mood, I remained here until the evening star had sunk, and the southern cross uprose in the star-jewelled firmament, and, touching its zenith, went on its endless empyrean way.

Wearied with looking at the passers-by, I at length retired to the den, a turmoil of voices in high dispute seeming to follow me in my dreams. Twice I was awakened by a man trying to close the grass-formed door of the hut; but on both occasions I shoved it down again.

Rats! rats! rats! What a high revel they held! Again my abode was alive with these detestable tenants of the damp dungeon and the drain. The small umbrella which, by advice, I had procured at Tette as a means of protection against the fierce rays of the sun, was here found useful for another purpose. I put it over my head as a shelter, because the vermin in the straw-thatch roof continued to send down straw, sticks and mud, until they sounded like hail upon my gingham, only it was a hail of dirt.

Sleep, as may be imagined, came only in snatches. I fairly shudder at the memory of the horrors of that hideous night. I did not know whether I could effect a start on the following day. Surely I could never spend another night there.

I thought of the miserable nights I had spent at Chibinga, but the new state of affairs beat them to shivers.

What did that man want at the door? My mind was tortured, my body was fatigued, and my inside seemed torn with the bad food, consisting of half-husked rice which formed my only sustenance. I copy from my pocket-journal, written about that time: "Such is the life of an explorer who sets out without great resources!"

In course of time I became so restless that I went out of the hut for a change, and to take a look about. The pale moon cast clear shadows upon the footworn streets, pencilling with its truthful beams the numerous forms of hut and hovel, and the shaggy lines of rough fence and straw-thatched roof.

Again I saw the figure of the man. The thought that occurred to me was that he had been placed there to watch the movements of the strange being who had visited them.

There was something dramatic in the appearance of this ghostly visitant. Dreaming and waking, the sight of him haunted me like a "familiar," and aroused ogreish thoughts. His figure appeared grim and gaunt, shadowed upon the glimmering street.

Imagination being fevered, I could fancy him saying:

"Shadow of the departed, whose material form has been dead a thousand years; white rover of the desert, why come you alone into the land of the black man, to stop the rain and poison the earth? Away! Away! back to your den, and keep to yourself the baneful influence of your evil spirits who dance to the rattle of dead men's bones!"

"Demon of a legendless race!" I thought. "What

mission can yours be that you stand there immovable, the bodily reality of the vision of my hideous dreams?"

Again I lay upon the ground seeking repose, and thinking with all my heart that I would rather, a thousand times, be in the old den in Chibinga's sun-parched lands. Curiously enough, on this occasion, being wearied in body and mind, I fell into a deep sleep.

Bright sunbeams were streaming through the chinks in the cane sides of the old hut when I awoke. I had slept as I had not slept for a very long time.

Concerning the journey to the king's town, I shall not weary the reader by recounting its many details. Let it suffice for me to say that I shall never forget the eventful march, with all its halts and tedious parleys. I longed to ask these men where the king was. I certainly could not be accused of warlike intentions; but long afterwards I found out that in my solitariness all the trouble was centred.

Two villages were passed before we reached the outskirts of the town; but ultimately I found myself in its centre, which was a large open spot surrounded by huts on every side, some being of much larger dimensions than any I had previously seen.

My followers again and again repeated the name "Chikuse, Chikuse," making me wonder what sort of preparation was necessary to meet this great mogul.

Where was he? I was wide awake, as any one may imagine, at such a moment. At the same time I was much troubled at having to become what a reporter would call the "cynosure of all eyes" under my present disadvantageous circumstances.

Armed warriors approached until they came within disagreeable proximity. I was seated on a rock, close to

DESERTED!

which sat the six men who had accompanied me. Soon I heard a buzz of noisy excitement at my back, and turning round to see from whence the sound proceeded, I observed a considerable crowd descending the gentle slope of the town's site. In the thick of the crowd was a very broad, fat man, robed in a mantle, or rather a sheet of a deep blue colour. The people wore nothing upon their heads, and very little upon their bodies—no Kaffir does excepting when he has become a degenerate civilised Kaffir.

The Angoni despot approached. I arose, but was immediately pressed down on the rock by my followers, who appeared to be awe-stricken. There I sat, he and his people also sitting, the distance between us being about fifteen yards.

There could be little doubt as to which of the crowd was Chikuse, for the whole demeanour and bearing of the fat man told me that he was the monarch. Few words were exchanged, and those were between the headman who had come with me and himself. I wonder what was said!

Chikuse laughed, and seemed rather to scoff at my dejected appearance; and when he laughed all his courtiers chimed in. I was convinced that I had given them a big surprise, if nothing else.

Nevertheless it was a great relief when the ordeal was over, for I had been bathed in perspiration through the steep ascent to the town, and now, under a stiff breeze from the eastward, I was becoming chilled.

The king rose and pointed, standing in his place, while I followed the men to the hut which had been granted to me—a very small one, only seven feet in diameter.

A description of the utter loneliness of my condition at this time would be an impossibility in narration. Everything was different from what I had expected, for Frasincho had said that the king would treat me well, and help me onwards. From all I could see, however, I had fallen into very bad hands; but there was now no remedy excepting to await the decision of fate. The Landin must have told Chikuse that I was *en route* to the lake.

Beer drinking seemed to be going on to some extent in the huts immediately adjacent to that which I occupied.

I have had a good deal of reflective comparison during the quieter moments of my travels, and at this time I began to think that the climax of awkward experiences had been attained. We are but creatures of a moment in action and in life, so that we are often impelled to meditate upon the past and compare it with the present. This seemed the worst of all the vicissitudes which had yet disturbed me.

The doubt as to what was going to happen was as bad as staring pale death in the face. What would the king do with me? There was but one thing, should he suspect me of being a spy. I soon resigned myself to fate. Oh, if I could only speak to the people!

Disturbed nights were passed, and in the daytime I had many moments of terrible suspense. One night as I sat in that wild place my thoughts wandered to John, to Taroman and the few " faithfuls " who had left me many, many miles to the south. Had they ever arrived at the " New Valhalla," at Buluwayo, to tell my old friends where and how I had been deserted? How strong was the yearning to know what had happened! It was now long since I had bidden adieu to my old followers.

During this reverie I had been oblivious to surrounding noises of passers-by. All at once, however, I was startled by a piercing shriek as of some one in dire distress, the cry being instantaneously followed by the sharp report of a gun in close proximity. Springing to my feet I was outside the small enclosure in a moment. Not a soul was to be seen, not a sound heard; the place was as silent as the tomb.

Much impressed by this mystery, and cogitating upon its possible meaning, I returned to the hut, and, closing the small grass-thatched door, lay down to try and sleep away the uneasy night. The effort was useless, for in a little time arose the noise of many disputing voices, while the people in crowds surged past the hut talking as though their lives depended upon their words. I wondered if all the hubbub was about me, and if so what might be the next move. Attributing the whole uproar to the influence of their accursed beer, I once more rolled over in the endeavour to forget myself and the world.

I certainly fell asleep, but was again awakened. I heard as though whispered from without some words of a language which to me was perfectly strange. On hearing the sound I sat up, for drowsiness was easily thrown off.

At the door were two dark figures. They turned out to be two women, who had evidently been stimulated to approach by copious indulgence in the favourite beverage. The pair did not move from the door until they were captivated by the sight of some blue beads, a small packet of which I had with me, which made them bolder, so that they entered the hut and sat down. I needed company very much, and was not particular. One of my unexpected visitors was a very old and withered woman, and from former experience I judged her to be a slave. The other was a young and fat dame, with skin the colour of a cigar. She resembled the type that I had seen in Matabeli-land, and was evidently a good-natured girl, although she seemed to be in an anxiously watchful and timid state, not in fear of me, but apparently in case of being discovered in my hut. On two occasions after listening a little they made haste to get out, but returned bringing in a gourd of pombe, most of which the younger lady imbibed herself, and with evident gusto, for she would smack her lips heartily after every copious draught; and then continued her conversation in a manner which seemed to show that she was intent upon weighing every syllable she uttered.

In whispered tones she continued to talk for hours, constantly repeating the name Chikuse with impressive awe, while she shook her head and drew deep sighs. I, of course, could not understand a single word she said, whether she was warning, consoling, or encouraging me. But there was something very discomforting in her manner, for after placing great stress upon some words she would sigh heavily, ever and anon turning to her old companion evidently for a verification of what she was telling me. Seeing that she came in the night to whisper about the king, I inferred that mischief was brewing, but I continued to nod assent at the end of her long sentences, until the strange visitors took their departure.

With the first faint flush of the morning light the air was rent with wild shouts and cries from an assemblage of men and women, the voices of the latter mingling shrilly with the hoarse roar of their smoke-inhaling husbands and brothers, a combination which gave a doleful tone to the mournful morning chant.

I knew well what that meant, for I had often heard it before. They were wailers who in lamentation cried for one who was gone. The weird song of woe was kept up until the sun stood high in the heavens, and then it died slowly away.

Afterwards a long line of people could be seen filing out of the town, and near to the leaders were two men who bore suspended between them the dead body of a woman, wrapped in the cane mat upon which she was accustomed to sleep. There was no wailing on the line of march. All was silent. The hut from whence the body was taken was adjacent to mine, and on the return of the burial party a large crowd stood in front of it, shouting with greater vigour than before.

The circumstances of these surroundings were far from being inspiring, and thousands of anxious thoughts flashed through my mind at the time, when I felt that I was so completely at the mercy of these most heartless fiends, who look upon killing as a pleasure, and only await the word of their king to give them a human life for sport.

I had said to myself, " This town cannot hold me another night;" but, again, there fell the shadows of the opposite huts cast by the rays of the lowering sun. To the east I saw the imposing Manganja crags rising two thousand feet above the plain, and the crimson and gold of their glowing granite slopes told of another night.

Having still a few pounds of rice left, I boiled a little for supper; and after partaking of this frugal repast, studied the small chart by the faint light coming from the smouldering embers of a root fire. I desired to fix my position, an experiment I did not dare to make in the daytime, being particularly careful not to show the sextant, watch, and papers, in case they might excite the suspicions of these fetich worshippers. On the sign of one error of judgment I might be despatched without grace or ceremony.

I then began to turn over in my mind what course should be pursued. I remembered having been told in Tette that numbers of Maravi men had left on elephant hunting expeditions through this country, and that a month before my departure a Portuguese had started with a large escort of Maravi to hunt in the north. No sign of any hunting party had come under my notice since we left Deuka's. The country was so vast, and as I had seen no elephant spoor, I came to the conclusion that any or all of such parties must be much farther north—nearer the lake perhaps.

Long reveries and meditations upon future plans only intensified the dispiriting sense of helplessness. The spell was suddenly broken.

"Amigo!"

At the door of my hut, as though he had risen from the earth, stood a man. I heard his salutation, but the darkness prevented me from seeing his face.

What stroke of fortune was this? At once I tore out some loose straw thatch, and kindling up the fire invited the stranger to enter.

He was a small man, with a somewhat dark complexion, and proved to be Eustaquio da Costa, a Portuguese elephant hunter, who had just returned from a hunt, and having heard of my arrival came immediately to see me.

The elephant hunter was astounded to find a white man in such a solitary state, and told me he never travelled without a strongly-armed escort. He had just arrived from another town of Chikuse's, about half a day's journey further north. Elephants were scarce, and therefore the members of his party were ranging far inland and northward.

When I told da Costa of the course I had travelled, he said I had run a great risk, especially as the Makanga people were a bad and treacherous race, who robbed and murdered parties with ivory and other produce. As he advanced through a country he sent men ahead, while he followed in rear with a hundred armed retainers.

Then I explained to him my extraordinary position, and described what I had gone through at the other towns in this country, telling also of the alarming experiences of the previous night, of the beer-drinking turmoil, of the start I had got by the report of a gun in the next hut, followed by the carrying out of a dead body in the morning, and of the visit of the fat dame. Why did she come to me? was a natural question. Last of all, I told of my reverie upon plans to reach the lake alone.

The arrangement now made was that I was to remain in my quarters until he could hear what was going on.

"Once," he said, "their suspicions are aroused, it is almost an impossibility to remove them, or convince the people of good intentions. I will get some men to bring on the things you have left at Deuka's with the headman."

After this marvellous encounter, all past troubles vanished from my mind like a flash. Surely I would now manage to get on, seeing that I could speak!

On the following day my friend told me what had transpired. The king said that on the day I had come I had brought clouds. I was accused of being a spy. My presence was ominous of evil. They insisted that I was not a man; that the race from which I had sprung had no home, and no country, but were wanderers on the face of the earth. Illusion has nothing too extravagant for these people's conjectures as to the existence of the white man.

One thing which they could not understand was that I came without a following of men. This was thought a marvel.

During the following days my friend da Costa did everything that lay in his power to help and explain away the many suspicions and awkward surmises which filled the king's mind with regard to me.

My friend the fat lady, who turned out to be the king's

sister, continued her visits, but she always shook her finger and nodded her head, as she spoke by the hour.

At last the king sent for me, saying to da Costa, "I want to see him speak. I do not believe he is your brother." *

Hearsay had made me acquainted with the sort of man with whom I was about to deal. Had an execution been in order it could not have caused more excitement than the circumstance of my approaching the sanctified enclosure of his majesty did among those who were present. Truly mine was a strange case.

We found the king in a circular hut, and surrounded by courtiers and slaves. The walls and roof of the hut were formed of bamboo, thatched with long coarse grass. The plastered floor was of blackened, polished mud.

There, on a cane mat, sat Chikuse, the despot in whose hands lay the destinies of thousands of human lives. He was apparelled in a blue calico sheet, which had been a gift from da Costa. I had a better opportunity of scanning the man than I had on the first ill-starred interview, for I was now quite close to him.

Chikuse was a young man of enormous dimensions, and with a light, reddish-brown complexion. Although his expression had a vacant look, the appearance was deceptive, for I noticed on different occasions that he was of a very observant nature, and as easily impressed by trifles as children are in many cases. That he was fully conscious of his power was easily seen. In that country he was the great "I am!" and his every action and look betrayed that he was quite wrapped up in the grandeur of his personal importance. Vanity beamed out in every line of his fat and sensual countenance. Nearly all African

* Among natives "brother" means one of the same kraal.

potentates, however, are imbued with the weakness of vanity, in fact it is their chief characteristic.

His old and corpulent mother sat in front of him, a picture of obesity. With her, Chikuse had indeed a heavy score of debts; for he had killed six of her lovers, and the seventh, a young and rather a good-featured man, on whom she lavished a profusion of cloth and beads with which he might decorate himself, stands in daily danger of having his earthly career cut short.

A number of questions were asked, but never, not even once, could I catch the eye of Chikuse, who was careful that such glances should not bewitch him.

Many personal and rather funny remarks were passed upon nearly every movement I made.

"Why does he wear such a queer hat?" was one of the curious inquiries. The king was himself the best of all, for while looking round upon his apprehensive and obsequious circle, the expression of his face seemed to say as distinctly as possible:

"Now, I ask you all plainly and fairly, did you ever see such a remarkable individual as this in all your lives?"

I thought, judging from her ways, that the old mother stood up for me, and this I afterwards learned was really the case.

Chikuse was determined that I should speak; nothing less than a conversation with da Costa would satisfy him. To satisfy the people, da Costa made a few remarks, to which I replied briefly. This performance drew forth a deep and long-drawn sigh from the old woman, gradually breaking into a gentle and pitying laugh.

She was satisfied the poor thing could speak. The witch-doctors, no doubt, had decreed that "it" was harmless. However, I could see by the grimaces of his majesty that he did not trust his eyes and ears on this occasion; he evidently thought himself the victim of an illusion, and was determined to have further oral testimony of my earthliness. The main questions asked were:

"What has brought you here?"

"What are you going to do?"

"Do you wish to buy people?"

On being informed that I did not wish to buy slaves, but desired to have men to take me to Nyanja (as the lake is called), Chikuse grunted; but I was unable to get an answer as to whether, or when, I could get carriers or guides to go with me. There could be no doubt that the fact of my having put in an unlooked-for appearance without any men of my own was the real cause of so much suspicion.

The king is much feared by his people, for his power is absolute.

The headmen who rule the outlying villages dress their hair in the form of a skull-cap, trimmed neatly round, and coped with a ring composed of wax. The latter is found deposited by a small insect upon the bark of trees. This ring or cap is a gift of the king, and the practice of presentation and wearing, in some respects, resembles a Matabeli custom. It is a sign of distinction, and gives a great lift to the headmen in the eyes of the people. The ring headgear of Chikuse's people was different from that worn by the Zulus.

It is noteworthy that the ring adornment is worn only by Zulu tribes and their descendants.

Chikuse does not wear the ring. He anoints his hair with nut-oil, and wears a very neat, small bladder on the top of his head.

The soil about here was very poor, consisting of dis-

GROWTH OF TOBACCO. 111

integrated granite. Abundant moisture, however, ensured good crops.

Tobacco was largely grown. All the men and women take kindly to the weed in some form. Generally, however, it is used in the form of snuff, the people being more inveterate snuffers than any tribe I had yet come across. Perhaps some African enthusiast might see how the whole of this vast plateau could be utilised for the production of tobacco. This would be a splendid subject for a speech,

Matabeli.   Zulu.   Angoni.
HEADRINGS OF THE ZULU FAMILY.

although the mode of transportation might not be touched upon. And yet, as a matter of sober fact, this land is not so badly situated for the conveyance of goods.

Small, humped cattle, and flocks of goats could be seen grazing quietly upon the green, grassy banks of the little rivers. Cattle, as a rule, however, were very scarce, but goats were plentiful.

The inhabitants are known as Angoni, Mangoni, or Landin, the latter name being often spelled Landeen, and they are undoubtedly of Zulu origin, although in the country which I am now speaking of they were a very mixed people.

When the Zulus from the south side of the Zambesi, below Senna, swept like a storm-cloud over this country, conquering all before them, the race of inhabitants were Xopetta, who, as a matter of course, became the slaves of the victorious impi. By the mixture of peoples the language has become corrupted, or rather hybrid in its character.

The Angoni, when entering or leaving a hut while you are there, salute you with the words "Sikomo bambo," which means, "Give me leave to come into your house." I observed that they used the word sikomo on all occasions when anything was given them. At such times, too, they frequently clapped their breasts with the palm of their hands. In Xopetta language they say "éko," which is intended to convey the same meaning as "sikomo." "Bambo" is the word used by sons to their fathers, and by inferiors to superiors. "Tekuone" is a word used in salutation; it means, "I see you," being equivalent to the "sagu-bona" of the Zulus. Should a visitor come from a distance, and happen to be acquainted with the people, they clap their hands.

Peoples and languages seem to be mixed. Every now and then I heard Zulu words. One night a man coming into the kraal accidentally struck a bystander with his rifle, and he instantly said "pepa," as do the Zulus, the word signifying sympathy, or a polite pardon me.

While awaiting the king's pleasure, da Costa and myself sometimes went out on short hunting expeditions; but game was hardly to be found, on account of the numerous villages which dotted the land in every direction. Hippos abounded in the Revuqwe or Revubwe river, even at places where the stream was but a stone's throw wide.

One afternoon I succeeded in startling a very large crocodile, which we saw on our return journey homewards. While walking along the banks of the river, we came very near to the reptile, as he lay close to a pile of drifted reeds. The first thought that struck me was whether the people would be like the Matabeli in their superstitions, in which case the dispatch of a crocodile by the ruthless hand of man would be a dreadful crime. Ignoring all superstition, however, I thought I would risk the attack, especially as the villagers hard by had said that they had lost a number of goats lately through these obnoxious monsters.

Having come to this conclusion, I stalked up on all-fours, until I got within a few yards of the ugly customer, when I gave him the benefit of six ounces of lead, driven by sixteen drachms of the best powder, that being the contents of both barrels of the elephant rifle. The two balls passed clean through the head.

A few of the Angoni from the village soon came to the spot, and seemed very much pleased at the result, so that I was satisfied that whatever might be their particular persuasion, it did not lie in the reptile direction.

Here and there along the banks of the river might be seen the Angoni larders, or properly speaking, corn stores. They resemble small huts perched upon poles, sometimes seven feet above the ground, the store-room being thickly covered with mud. By this means the ravages of rats and other vermin are frustrated.

Upon the day that I killed the crocodile we met a large party of men and women going out to perform their ceremonies at the grave of a man who had been buried a month before on some sacred hill near by. The women were carrying large gourds of native beer, which were to be placed at the grave, as the company included all the relatives and friends from other towns. The final ceremony of mourning would thus be gone through effectively, and on the return to the town a great beer-drinking feast would take place.

As the long line was coming towards us, I could not imagine what could be the cause of the very queer and tipsyfied-looking antics of the man who led the train of mourners. He grasped in his hands a long stick, bearing his weight upon it, while he would stagger to and fro, drooping his head and swaying his body as though he would fall within the next few paces. I was told that this was a customary performance when such groups met others on the line of march, the intention being to show fatigue as well as grief. Whether or not this is a practice among other tribes, I cannot say, but I had never seen it before.

Shooting a beautiful crested crane on the banks of the little tributary stream called the Kapambazi, within a mile and a half of the town, we carried it back and presented it to the king, who was much pleased, as he values the feathers very highly.

The sun was low, and the evening delightfully cool, so after supper we sauntered up the gentle slope at the back of the town to while away an hour or two. We were much amused by watching a troop of little boys, armed with torches, in keen pursuit of my old enemies the rats, which positively swarm among the loose rocks in the hills. It was curious to notice the ardour with which they entered into the spirit of the chase. They might be seen day and night at the sport. From all I could see it was a bad time for rats, for their hunters seemed to be bagging at every moment.

On returning to the town we found that a number of da Costa's men had arrived. They reported buffalo to be plentiful towards the west, but elephants were few in number. Among the trophies they had brought were the tusks of two elephants, and an abundance of dried buffalo meat; but the latter was in a deplorably filthy condition. So far as we were concerned, our tastes inclined in the direction of the

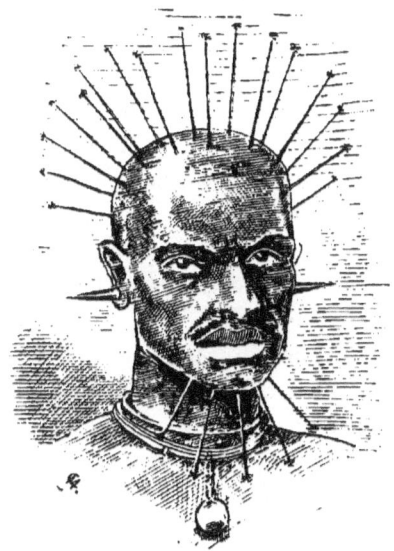

MARAVI HUNTER.

small fowls of the country, which we could readily procure in exchange. Strangely enough, poultry was by no means abundant.

One by one the various Maravi hunters came and clapped their hands to their master, some of them remaining to relate exciting narratives. At last there came a very solemn-looking man, whose *ensemble* was most peculiar. Going through the short ceremony of salute, he seated himself in a most decorous fashion. The head-dress of this new arrival was a perfect work of art, sufficient to discourage the most devoted coiffeur in the Rue de la Paix or Regent Street.

On his chin were five stalks, each about six inches in length. These radiated, and each had a rosette of black hair blossoming at the end, and artistically bound with fine yellow bark, reminding me of the top of a new fishing-rod. Similar long-stemmed flowers of jet-like blackness were to be seen all over his head.

After a lengthened silence this splendid dandy deigned to speak, telling a most amusing story much too long to repeat, but all in praise of his master's medicine. I must here explain that these people must have medicine for every external freak of nature, and these medicines are specially made by the doctors, of whom there is by no means a dearth. The doctors play upon the credulity of the natives, much in the same way as do the medical charlatans of civilisation, with this difference: that the medicine supplied to savages merely stimulates the superstitious mind, leaving no injurious effects upon the stomach or constitution.

There are medicines for hunting, for war, for peace, for love, and for every other inclination of the human mind. Doctors of reputation attend to each distinct description of luck that is required. Nothing can be too outrageous or extraordinary in the concoction of such medicines, which would move the emulation of dame Hecate and the witches in "Macbeth." If bad luck succeeds the treatment, the failure is attributed to the medicine. Sometimes the physic will consist of a grass bracelet, with a shell of fruit filled up with all sorts of rubbish. The hopes and fears of some trusting patients may be associated with the mysterious properties of chips of bone and the gut of some wild beast.

Portions of the insides of some particular animals are assumed to have a curative, or rather preventative, effect against disease and misfortune. But concerning disease, are not all men akin? So long as death knocks at every door, there will be work for quacks in every land.

Every conceivable and inconceivable thing that is foreign to humanity is selected to have an influence over their careers. Pieces of the skin of the lizard and the snake are favourite charms.

The man with the wonderful "head of hair" went on to describe some thrilling adventures, relating particularly to the narrow escapes which the party had had while hunting the second of the elephants whose tusks they had brought. They had followed the elephant for five whole days; but he said he had no fear, because his medicine was of the very best quality, and his aim was unerring. All he wished before going upon another hunt was to have some more medicine from "Señoro." I was told that with a medicine in which they have confidence the people will do most daring feats; but if the medicine is thought unlucky they will return—it is of no use trying to hunt with it.

Da Costa told me that this was his headman, and a very good hunter besides; to be implicitly trusted in every way. With regard to superstition, my friend told me that he was himself a Roman Catholic, but he had long ago given up every effort to make the natives move from the course of their belief or unbelief. He said—and his remarks were worth listening to with attention, for he had spent most of his life among the Zambesi tribes—that it was a hopeless task in any way to attempt to drive away native superstition. They have an ineradicable trust in their own fashions of faith, so that if they begged medicine from him he was in the habit of giving them bracelets of different kinds. This is a favourite plan among hunters. At the same time he told them it was all nonsense, but that declaration they did not believe. They preferred to think that what he gave them was a wonderful medicine, in fact a specific against all danger, and a precursor of luck.

From what I saw and could hear the Angoni were as much imbued with the spirit of witchcraft as were the Zambesi tribes. They had their witch doctors, their rain makers—most important dissemblers—their dice-throwing seers, and their clairvoyant mediums, who, I daresay, would be able to find the "lost chord" we hear so much about if they went in search of it, or follow in fancy the fickle footsteps of a runaway wife. They are the searchers into all things mysterious—the revealers of the secrets of the unseen and the unheard.

As an instance of their grasping at everything that is odd, I should mention that when da Costa had gone into the country, about two months before my arrival, he, in order to "save his bacon," as the saying goes, brought a donkey from the Zambesi country. The people had never before seen such an extraordinary-looking beast. Therefore they were much disturbed and apprehensive lest they should incur its displeasure; to such an extent, in fact, that they brought it corn in abundance, and asked all sorts of questions with regard to the animal's powers.

The belt of the tsetse fly to the north of the Zambesi was passed, and this wonderful donkey then proved the fact that even donkeys will die from the prick of the deadly pest, although some travellers have asserted the immunity of the patient and thick-hided quadruped from its attacks. Donkeys, it is true, are more tenacious in life than horses or oxen when in the fly country, but eventually they pine away and die like other victims.

Night was well advanced when I returned to my retreat, and found that my guardian angel, one of da Costa's boys— a very fat fellow—who kept watch and ward over my quarters, had made the hut his earthly paradise. Enveloped in clouds of choking smoke, he snored in blissful unconsciousness, with his body almost in the fire. I immediately rolled myself in my blanket, and amidst the smoke was soon in a torpid condition, drowsiness being further induced by the soporific resonance of the fat boy's nasal drone.

The climate was healthy and invigorating, but I did not feel particularly frisky, suffering at times a good deal of internal agony, attributable no doubt to the hard fare, that is to say, badly husked rice and corn meal. Constant anxiety also sometimes had the effect of causing restless nights. The night I speak of brought one of the disturbed slumbers to which I was too often accustomed.

A week had elapsed since I had asked the king for boys to take me to the lake, but as yet I had received no word as to what might be his decision, and I was not a little troubled by anxious reflections. The uneasy slumber into which I had fallen was broken by the arrival of my mysterious nightly visitor.

"Mzungo, Mzungo!" said the familiar voice which aroused me.

Sure enough my pombe damsel was there, her face wreathed in smiles, and this time accompanied by two other maidens, with lithe, pretty figures, and eyes so lustrous that they might almost be called captivating.

The pombe was brought in, and the snoring Kaffir was stirred to life, in order to interpret the weighty speechmaking that was about to take place. When the nocturnal conviviality had fairly commenced, I was told that Chikuse was at length satisfied with Mzungo. The satisfaction, I thought, resulted from the present I had given him.

At intervals my merry companion would laugh heartily, afterwards looking at her friends in such a way as though she should say, "Why do you make so much noise?" To me it was evident that whoever boasted of having the young charmer as personal property, were ignorant of her little midnight escapades and wanderings.

The pombe was drunk, and the supply replenished again and again, until the small hours of the morning had passed, and then my fascinating friends took their departure. This was the last visit made by the lady. No sooner had the company departed than my guardian angel was again reclining, and was soon in the land of dreams—would that I could say the silent land! But that would be untrue, for his trumpeting was louder than ever.

Next morning, as I was walking towards da Costa's hut for breakfast—the *cuisine* was now in a much better state—I could see a crowd of men, who I was very glad to find were the Angoni, who had been sent to fetch my few loads from the town lying to the south.

We offered them the payment which had been arranged before they left, but they now refused, expostulating and saying that they must have cloth. We refused to give cloth, and sent word of the difficulty to the king, who decreed in a most unjust manner that we would have to give them cloth, and if they declined to take one fathom we would have to give them two, the scale being conveniently graduated to suit the savage feelings.

Chikuse was evidently suffering from indigestion, which with him always brought fits of capriciousness, not infrequently culminating in the death or dismemberment of some unfortunate individual who happened to heave in the line of his majesty's jaundiced glance. On that particular day he had determined to vent his spleen upon me.

He sent word that I had given him very little, and that he could not give men, to which intimation was coupled the remark that he knew I had plenty of cloth—" I had four loads of baggage, what were they if not the white man's *bank?*"

An extra donation, which I had to get from da Costa, as my supply had run out, produced a better tone, and by next day the wrathful symptoms had passed away—at least from my direction.

There was absolutely nothing to admire about Chikuse. From all I could learn of him he was a dreadful character—an arrant coward in my opinion—although my friend asserted that, compared with others whom he knew, he was by no means so bad as I supposed.

Little surprise can be felt at his general behaviour, when we remember that either in the black or the white absolutely unchecked power always begets tyranny. Cruelties by King Chikuse were said to be very common. For the gratification of freaks of passion, and for minor offences, the most ordinary punishment consists in cutting off the fingers or ears, or destroying an eye. It is marvellous how the poor creatures stand such pruning. Their wounds seem to heal very rapidly, and are not nearly so liable to "go bad" as the cuts of Europeans. One of my followers, a Landin, had one of his ears cut off and an eye taken out. Other indescribable horrors are perpetrated on both men and women to satisfy the whims of his majesty. Such modes of punishment are prevalent throughout all Central Africa.

The Makanga tribe to which I have referred are great enemies of the Angoni or Landin, and among the latter the name of their opponents must never be spoken above a whisper. Hostilities have occurred upon various occasions. Another foe of Chikuse's is Pezéni, who, like himself, is a chief of the Angoni. King Pezéni dwells in the north, and fights a great deal with the people of Chikuse.

The Angoni do not disfigure their faces as do the tribes further south.

Their principal diet is maize meal. The people of Chikuse's town appeared to be very partial to eating rats, considering them a great delicacy. Like most Kaffirs, they are very foul feeders. When an animal is killed every atom that can be swallowed is used. Even the skin, the hair only being singed off, is cooked with pieces of flesh clinging to it.

Food is never more than half-cooked. Some take salt when they can get it; but its possession involves a great deal of labour, as it has to be brought from the valley of Nyassa. They have nothing sweet to use as a substitute for sugar.

They are great beer (pombe) drinkers. As a matter of fact the royal family seemed to be wholly occupied in imbibing this beverage, which is most nutritious, and might account for the fatness of all its members. The natives will live upon pombe for days without touching solid food. I did not find pombe, however, in every town.

It is a very palatable drink, when it is strained, possessing a slight acidity. Great quantities may be taken without inducing intoxication. A bad effect of drinking doubtless is frequently evident, as I noticed particularly during my stay at Chikuse's, where a number of minor troubles arose from a too free carousal over the favourite drink. Were it not for this, domestic quarrels would very rarely occur. Apart from this the native of Africa, under the rule of a powerful chief, is a most exemplary being, manifesting no vices that can injure his fellow-men. I observed that among these people, as among all other tribes with whom I sojourned, the women and men never supped together.

Beans were abundant, and of two varieties. One was the castor oil bean. The oil which it produced was used by the people as a purge. They also rubbed their bodies with it.

One evening as we sat quietly outside the hut a curious incident occurred. A young brave descended angrily upon us, shouting loudly and gesticulating with the utmost energy. His cry was that he would kill da Costa's men. He accused some one of coming too near to his harem; but this appeared to be a hallucination excited in his cranium by the pombe. The man's actions were the maddest I had seen for some time, and he kept up his yelling noise far into the night, running wildly all the time to and fro between his hut and our position.

Had there been any real grievance we would assuredly have heard of it on the following day, but evidently the trouble disappeared with the cause. On several occasions I have seen them in this state, when the slightest indiscretion on our parts would have resulted in very serious trouble.

I observed that the Angoni were not given to dancing and singing to anything like the same extent as other tribes I had fallen among. Nor did they give voice to any of that peculiar melody, distinguishable in the songs I had heard further south. Drums, too, although they had them, were not in constant use as they were in other places.

Some of the young men were seen playing upon a bow-string instrument set upon a calabash, the strung line of gut being beaten with a piece of reed. The Zulus of South Africa have a similar instrument. Singing in a disconnected manner is common.

The women have their heads shaved, but in times of sorrow and trouble the hair is allowed to grow. The dirtier they are, the more complete is their mourning.

Wives of a defunct chief become the property of his successor, who generally keeps those he fancies and distributes the rest amongst favoured friends. Both women and men adorn their bodies with bracelets and anklets of hide ornamented with brass, which shows to advantage against their dark skin. A very small apron of leather, a bunch of feathers, or even a piece of rag, constitutes the only covering of the men.

The women, in some instances, wear aprons of bark. Those of the king's wives, whom I saw, all wore calico round their loins, for Chikuso has a good supply of cloth given him by traders and hunters.

Many young girls might be seen going about entirely nude, while some wore small fringes of beads. They were much delighted on being presented with the smallest piece of cloth, or even a thimbleful of beads.

Not a few of the men carried a small carved wooden pillow, similar to those used by tribes south of the big river. The pillow, which I have before alluded to, raises the head about eight or nine inches from the mat on which they recline. The carving usually is a simple arrangement of circles.

What struck me as a remarkable circumstance was that very little brass-wire or cloth had been generally distributed among the people. In this respect the seeming poverty of all, with the exception of the royal circle, was striking, notwithstanding the flourishing condition of the slave trade.

Some of the men were very good-looking and graceful in their movements; but the general average gave a poor show, for in no respect could this branch of the great Angoni tribes be considered as physically a fine race. There is little doubt that the disturbed life led under the bane of endless warfare, slave kidnapping, and a miserable diet, has had its effect, deteriorating the physique of a people whose progenitors for aught we know might have been the Hercules's and Adonis's of the Bantu group to which Lord Beaconsfield, referring to the parent stock who dwell in the distant south, referred in such glowing terms during the Zulu war:—" These men," he said, " have outwitted our diplomatists, out-manœuvred our generals, and converted our missionaries, and yet you call them savages."

The Angoni are thoroughly a tribe of slave kidnappers, believing implicitly in the idea that the people of other tribes are born for their use. This " fair game " of the valleys and plains has to be hunted. When a propitious period arrives the Angoni horde sweeps like a devastating whirlwind among the neighbouring tribes of Ajawa and Manganja in the Shiré valley.

They lay waste the villages, pillage the gardens, and triumphantly bear away the human spoils, young men, women and children, who soon are offered for sale in the slave markets of the Angoni's rugged home.

The district under the sway of Chikuse is one of the greatest slave-trading centres in Africa.

I have often seen the young warriors playing to show their cunning in stalking and agility in the capture of their human victims. Holding a buffalo-hide shield in the left hand, and grasping a kerry in the right, they would run rapidly forward with a number of wild bounds, displaying numerous excited evolutions of the chase and of warfare. Their contortions were extraordinary. Leaping into the air they would kick their shields while their feet were off the ground, and when they alighted they would wholly disappear amidst the high grass.

During my sojourn in Angoni-land slavery was in full swing, but in Chikuse's town there were very few slaves ready for transportation. Probably this was due to the fact that it was the time of the king's raid into the Shiré valley. Literally on every hand evidences of the slave trade could be seen, but in this instance I refer to the export, or rather the east coast trade, the home traffic being of quite a different character.

The latter branch of the business was exceedingly lively. A caravan of three hundred and fifty, all told, left a town a short distance to the north of Chikuse's, and preparations were being made when I left for the dispatch of another.

Every village shows the familiar sight of the slave in the yoke. After purchase the poor things are taken to the headquarters of the east coast traders—*nazaras*, as the people call the Zanzibar agents—some of whom are constantly in this district. Two I can mention by name, Xuala and Saidé.

At the agents the yoke is made secure, and it is not exaggeration to say that it is often allowed to remain upon a slave for nine months or a year, night and day, without being once taken off. Constant rubbing by the yoke upon the neck chafes the skin, and gradually ugly wounds begin to fester under the burning sunshine.

Slaves, however, are to some extent looked after with a view to prevent serious bodily injury, the appearance of which would certainly depreciate their marketable value.

Until all is ready for a start the miserable slave sits waiting with all the compulsory and hopeless patience of bondage. Day after day he sees the sun rise and set. The

SLAVE KIDNAPPERS. ANGONI-LAND.

dreary days pass by and are numbered into weeks and months, and still the victim is bound by the yoke about his neck.

In his mind, perhaps, he conjures up a picture of the distant and dreaded blood-stained sea; for since his childhood's days, the hideous story has been driven into his ears, telling of the white man's feast on the fattened flesh of the captive slave. Nearly all the natives have the common story that the white man is cannibalistic in his humours.

When first captured or sold, the slave's star of hope has not altogether set. Many escape, to fall perhaps into other traps. But when the dreaded branch encircles their neck, their doom is sealed; the faintest gleam of hope which may have lightened their heavy hearts, is then for ever extinguished. At such a time a crowd of the most fearfully fantastic visions that can be raised by the imaginative mind must fill the brain with heated horror. Happily, however, with him mental misery is short-lived, for fortunately the black slave is a philosopher, and when the first great terror is over, he submits with calm and careless abandonment to the harsh conditions which have overtaken him. Poor creature!

I am not alone in thinking that in this wretched traffic in human lives there are horrors sufficient to cause the most devout to question the existence of mercy. It seems cruel that men should be begotten and should live with hearts as cold as winter's icy wind, and just as pitiless, and whose malignant oppression shows in the saddest form the dismal truth of man's inhumanity to man.

Hard, indeed, it would be to show the slave that his life was anything beyond that of a beast. What else is it? Has he no hope? Yes, he has; with death his hope begins. What a satisfaction it must be for him to think that some day he must be FREE, away for ever from the tormenting tyranny of his fellow-men!

The numbers of slaves in caravans vary very greatly, for, like every other commodity, traffic is regulated by the inalterable laws of supply and demand. Prices also vary a good deal. When there is a good demand, a strong young man is worth from forty to sixty fathoms of Zanzibar cotton.

The time taken to equip a caravan depends upon the quantity of goods or trading articles of exchange which the *nazara* has with him. Sometimes a stay in the country of from four to six months is necessary before they can get all the slaves they require, so that the unfortunates who are first purchased have to sit all the time with the yoke—a young tree—fixed to their necks, the weight of the implement depending upon the disposition of the slave; for should he be fractious, he will be tamed by the employment of the heaviest yoke. Those I saw were very heavy.

This appliance of torture is made from the forked branches of a tree; about five or six feet long—some are much longer—and from three to four inches in diameter at the thickest part. Through each prong of the fork a hole is bored for the reception of an iron pin. This ready, a soft fibrous bark is wrapped round until the whole forms a thick collar of bark, making a sort of pad much rougher than a horse's collar. The forked branches vary in thickness, to suit docile or fractious subjects.

The time occupied during the journey to Zanzibar depends upon circumstances; but, generally speaking, it occupies from one and a half to three months.

Other pens have powerfully described the frightful cruelties which are practised during this miserable journey, so I will not attempt to dwell upon the matter here.

The women usually are chained by the necks or wrists, or

attached to each other by bark ropes from neck to neck. Some of the women carry their infants on their backs, held by a piece of cloth.

The slave-trade existing among the natives themselves—the home supply, so to speak—which may be found in almost every tribe on the African continent, cannot be looked upon from the same rigorous standpoint that we occupy in considering the export trade, which has not a single redeeming feature. The home traffic is different. Slaves born in the country have wives, and in time may themselves become the owners of slaves, and be equal with the free men of the country. To me they seemed to be well-disciplined servants.

Special acts of cruelty by ordinary masters I never saw. These home-bred slaves in manhood become capturers, hunting on behalf of their masters in the human preserves. No doubt the conscience of the Angoni is sufficiently elastic to let him, at a pinch, sell his own kith and kin; but generally speaking this is rarely done.

When a full complement of men and women have been gathered, the export caravan is made ready for the road. The men are coupled by the yokes being lashed so as to form a rigid pole, binding the pair from neck to neck together. With loads on their heads, they then turn their faces to the eastward, and leave their homes for ever.

CHAPTER XIX

DA COSTA, THE ELEPHANT HUNTER.

A visit from Chikuse—The king washes himself—Beads and cloth are products of nature!—No God—Chikuse's wives—Engaging a guide—Music hath charms—The queen mother—A fine old woman—Her love affairs—Bewailing death—Tears and snuff—A scene of murder—Graceful damsels—Looking out for the new moon—Da Costa's kindness—Story of his life—The dreaded Makanga—Cruelty and treachery of the king—Execution of a supposed sorceress—Thrown to the crocodiles—A hunter's life in African wilds.

ONE morning, when Senhor da Costa and myself were having our simple morning meal, his majesty Chikuse came down unexpectedly, and seated himself upon a large mat, his courtiers forming a circle about him, and I at once seized the opportunity of putting forward my case, managing to get a favourable answer, in so far that he promised that men would be forthcoming. Remembering that a savage king only begins to perceive the lapse of time when he thinks that his faculties are failing, I was inclined to ask myself at what time the men would appear.

Da Costa had secured the confidence of Chikuse to a wonderful extent, having even succeeded in influencing him to drink a cup of tea occasionally. This he deigned to do on the present occasion. The performance which followed was comical in the extreme. A brass basin which we were in the habit of using was given to his majesty, along with soap, a towel, and a small looking-glass. With these at hand he went through the operation of making a heavy lather with the soap. This seemed to give great satisfaction, and he took a good look at himself in the mirror, always a source of great delight to the savage mind. A considerable time elapsed before da Costa had been able to persuade Chikuse to wash his hands or drink tea; but ultimately his objections had been overcome, and he became quite accustomed to both these habits of the white man's life.

The admirably easy manner which my friend had in dealing with the people impregnated their shallow minds with confidence; but doubtless his having so large a number of armed men in the country, and the generosity with which he gave innumerable presents to the king, had strengthened his hold upon respect, if not affection.

"You are great fools," Chikuse said. "Why do you not buy people? You are not men. You have been dead for a long time."

As to our statement that the cloth and beads which we had were made by people like ourselves, he would not credit a word of it. No; we found them just as they were, all ready-made by the master hand of nature! The cloth came off the trees.

"People," said the king, "do not make that stuff."

This incredulity puzzled me; for in his own town I had seen a man weaving a coarse cotton blanket in a primitive way. Perhaps the glowing patterns and the fineness of the calico gave it in his mind a spiritual origin.

Instead of revering the white man's curiosities (which they are always glad to get with as little exertion as possible), they continue to view the owner with pity or toleration. Should the black man of these lands see you strike a match, and make instantaneous fire, he does not reason that such a feat is the product of thought and labour.

K 2

Very likely, nay, in truth, after a long acquaintance with white people, this impressionless view changes; but in early simplicity nothing can win genuine admiration from the race. They have, as I before stated, no ideal; and I consider as inaccurate the assertion that the word Murungo, or Mlungo, means God in the same sense that we associate with the omniscience of the Deity. An understanding of this nature has been advanced by some travellers, and the statement that such a word exists I do not dispute; but, speaking for myself, I have never, even upon a single occasion, been able to detect in the very slightest degree the proof that the natives comprehend a divinity. The word they use seems to be applicable to many gods. On being questioned regarding this matter, those who are acquainted with the term will point to one star, then to another, and so on; from which I infer, rightly or wrongly, that the expression is used towards every brilliant orb that gems the firmament. But this is digression.

Chikuse, I should say, was about thirty years of age. He had not lost any opportunity of capturing wives, and then had a very large number—over two hundred; so that he gave good signs of running a dead heat with "the wisest man the world e'er saw," before he reached middle-age. Twelve of the youngest of his very-much-better-halves had run away during his absence from his other town. The report was at that time current that they had been caught, so that in due course a great killing festival might be expected to incite the sanguinary gloating of the staff of murderers. My friend da Costa said he was going to plead for the fugitives; but notwithstanding his interference, there could be little doubt as to their destiny.

Not long after the king had left, a highly decorated man, certainly the best dressed Landin I had seen, came with the information that his majesty had ordered him to see that I got boys to go with me to the lake. Very thankful, indeed, I felt when I heard this piece of good news.

Shona, the man who brought the announcement, was a headman of one of the outlying villages. He said he would not be able to start for some days as he had to carry out a pombe ceremony over his mother's grave. The dissipation was not to begin for three days, and its duration would be three days more, or some uncertain period longer.

Under the circumstances it was arranged that I should get some one else to go, and an older man was brought who seemed to be better acquainted with the southern end of the lake. Over and over again I attempted to explain that it was the white men at this end of the lake whom I wanted to reach, but the effort was unavailing. All manner of arguments sprung up among the bystanders, but not one of them seemed to know anything about the place called Livingstonia; of course that name could not be familiar. The old man said I would have to go far on the water.

Having studied the contour of the country at the southern end of Nyassa, on a small map, I concluded that perhaps I might be able to procure canoes on this side, and thus reach the missionary station at Livingstonia, which was marked on a promontory of land.

The old man proceeded to say that men could be got to go, but they would not go into the white man's town. When we reached the lake I would have to send for my countrymen. There seemed to be some wild stories afloat about the doings of the Englishman.

Stories or not, however, I wanted to get off, and was willing to agree to anything, for I felt if once I was on the shores of the lake, I would surely find my way somehow.

So far no rumours of the Makololo war, of which we

had heard so much on entering Angoni-land, had reached this place. Had they been well-founded they would surely have arrived with all the force of extra colouring and exaggeration, which would have been nothing short of a catastrophe; at all events it would have been a fatal stroke to my endeavours to procure a following. Instant and strong pressure was therefore brought to bear so as to effect a start.

Da Costa and myself passed our afternoons and evenings in various ways. When we approached the hut the crowd would gather and keep up an incessant begging. But cloth in this out-of-the-way place was far too valuable a commodity to throw away for nothing.

The concertina which da Costa played called forth great signs of admiration. Much in the same way as the people had done with regard to his ill-fated donkey, they now began to bring corn on the cob and lay it at the performer's feet. Small wooden vessels full of meal were also brought. These efforts to conciliate the concertina were intensely funny.

On one occasion the assembled mob rapidly dispersed on the appearance of a remarkably stout old woman who was seen approaching our palace of grass, which apparently was thought to contain the magic powers of producing all kinds of goods, a veritable home of an everlasting Santa Claus. The black man looks upon desirable goods in the same way that children look upon toys.

Our new visitor proved to be the queen-mother, the imposing parent of the awe-inspiring Chikuse.

After this important matron had gone through the exceedingly funny performance of squatting on a mat before us, conversation was opened. Great numbers of people had been to see me, as being an extraordinary-looking mortal, but it had taken some time before the dowager had been inspired with sufficient confidence to pay a visit.

Ultimately, however, by the constant assurances of my friend and by the hope of being able to extract a present, timidity had been overcome. When she did perform the arduous journey, she seated herself in a manner as though she for ever abandoned all hope of rising again.

A fine specimen of an old savage was this curious queen; as good as any I had come across. In every way she showed herself to be far superior to her bloodthirsty son, whose cruel deeds she, when alone with da Costa, would deplore earnestly. Even in my presence she expressed her aversion to the readiness of her son to kill people. At such times, perhaps, her mind lingered on the fond memories of her six lovers whom the irate king had given to the hyenas.

Second sight was not required to observe that it had caused the lady the greatest pain to witness the slaughter of her enamoured favourites. This seemed to be *the* subject of her thoughts, and she dwelt long and pathetically upon the theme, how bad it was of her son to kill so many people; he had a hundred wives, and yet, he would not allow his poor old mother the peaceful possession of even a solitary spouse!

She had marvellous powers of sighing, her obesity greatly facilitating the process, and making the effort particularly impressive.

A heavy sigh was followed by the remark:—

"You white men don't kill people; you don't buy people; you are very good people."

When she was before us her slave girls were constantly in attendance with pombe. The latest lover, and candidate for the wrath of Chikuse, accompanied her. He was about twenty years of age and very good-looking, while his ornamentation was of the most lavish and varied description, comprising bangles of iron and brass, armlets of buffalo hide, and anklets studded with brass, which showed well against the deeply-bronzed skin; over all he robed himself in a long blue calico sheet.

Between the ages of the couple there was a difference of about thirty years; but as Mrs. Grundy is unknown in Angoni-land, such facts take no part in making up grievances for the regrets of good-natured friends.

I discovered, however, that the actual reason for his majesty's fury—shown in dire threats at annihilation towards this lover—was due to the circumstance of the favourite being a slave (a homo slave) by birth, the king no doubt thinking that it was sadly *infra dig* that his mother should enter upon such intimate relations with one so far beneath her station. The doom of the young Adonis was evidently sealed, for Chikuse had despatched all the former beaux in succession and without any compunction, requiring only a little excitement over the pombe to put this one out of the way too. The queen, however, at that time threatened that if he killed the man she would leave the country.

I was always an object of great curiosity to the queen. She would look upon me for some time and then make an exclamation "Ugh!" followed by a remark that I was not stout enough, or some other straight criticism on my personal appearance.

It was a treat to witness her getting up to an erect position. First she rolled over on her hands and knees, and then raised the heavier portion of her body on her legs, and last of all shoved herself into the perpendicular by an exertion of the arms. After that operation she got her balance and wobbled homewards.

Soon after she left on the first occasion, there arose the familiar tone of the long wailing cry which told of death. The people were running from all quarters of the town towards a central point. We joined the crowd because I wished to observe their custom at such an occurrence. On the last occasion of a similar kind I had been debarred from being even an onlooker.

The people thronged round the hut where the dead man lay. Holding their hands on their heads they cried aloud, and shed some tears, varying every now and again the pitch of the voice. Some held the open hand to the side of the mouth, like a bo'sun giving the word in a gale of wind, and by that means gave their shout a wonderful vehemence.

The tears that were shed were of the crocodile character. The Kaffir's heart being immeasurable, the only way, on ordinary occasions, to tap his tears is by means of snuff; so that whenever there is any genuine sorrow to be shown the irritant is plentifully employed, with the effect of increasing the water-power immensely.

An observer is very apt to laugh outright when such a scene is before him, no matter how solemn the actual cause may be. The *sang-froid* of the mourners was absolute, and the whole ceremony was little else but a farce. The people hurrying up would jostle their way into the crowd, howl dismally for a short time, and emerge as jolly as possible to go about their ordinary routine of life. Mourning is only a matter of form in more favoured countries, although the artless children of the wilds seem to have no yearning for the goods and chattels of the departed, and give no subject for a hungry picture such as the "reading of the will." One morning, long after the first light of day, da Costa and I were taking our early walk. The sun was high, and both of us enjoyed very much the freshness of the lovely scene, in our rambles chatting so pleasantly and planning movements for the days to come until we found ourselves close to the town, without knowing the distance we had travelled.

Conversation was here interrupted by the appearance of a throng of people, pushing along in hot haste.

"Barbaros," exclaimed da Costa, "they are going to kill another man!"*

Sure enough, on they came, little boys of tender years bounding side by side with the lusty manhood, which formed the greater part of the excited horde, intent upon pushing on the palpitating victim whose hands were pinioned behind his back.

The exultant mob brandish their weapons in the air. The thicket of black fiends sweep swiftly along, all are light-hearted as merrymakers at a fair. A gentle grass-crested eminence is passed. Then in the midst of a wild rush and demoniac shouts, once again the death-dealing assegai is plunged into the side of a writhing unfortunate wretch. So another body goes back to earth, and to another soul the great mystery is revealed.

The excited crowd quickly assemble around the gory scene, boys and men swinging their clubs furiously like the sails of a windmill in a gale. One after another they go up and smash at the lifeless corse. Then follows the sickening act of decapitation and mutilation, after which the remains are left as food for the hyenas. It is only a case of another horror being added to the tyrant's roll of crimes.

On our reaching the town the headman who had been commissioned to procure men, brought the intelligence that the staff was completed, and that we would depart in the morning.

* One man had been killed just before my arrival.

This piece of news, I need not say, gave me unmixed delight, for thus far my stay in Angoni-land had been a dark and dreary experience, and I longed to be once more on march.

In the evening we sauntered out to the wells. Women, young and old, might be seen, both in the morning and the evening, passing to and fro between the town and the wells of Urongwe, to replenish their gourds with its clear waters. The erect and graceful carriage of the women lent a peculiar charm to this scene of savage life. At the wells, just before the sun has gone down, might be seen every stage of human life: the bud, the blossom, and the fading flower. Some there are on whose heads the rudely-fashioned gourd of clay never rests. Their lives are easy, for they are the chosen whose charms have freed them from the toils of work; for Chikuse, unresisted in his selection of wives, could gratify from all the daughters of his tribe the peculiarities of his fickle fancy; all were his, or his to be, should his will be formed. Once the royal lips uttered the words "She must, she shall be mine!" it became a matter of death should another court the charms which awakened the monarch's passion.

Some of the young maids are far from ugly, even to the eyes of a white man, but there is no accounting for taste: the black man's prize may be the white man's horror; the Englishman's delight the Ethiopian's dread.

All who have seen the wild girlhood of secluded Africa must acknowledge that the damsels are picturesque in their movements, surroundings, and personal decorations. In the naturalness of their state the most scrutinising critic of the Grecian model could find a subject for admiration, provided he overlooked the strangeness of cranium, forehead, and features.

Good nature is the distinguishing feature of these black fairies. Even when they have some years to run before they reach the limit of their teens, their forms are true to the perfect lines of nature in comely womanhood. A few brass anklets encircle their lithe limbs, the fetich bangles of the buffalo hide, or the hair of the elephant's tail, clasp their small and shapely wrists; but no ornament, no lines of natural beauty are so pleasant to look upon as are their glowing faces, when brightened by unaffected smiles, breaking into the merry laughter of jest and gossip.

The eyes of these damsels are lustrous and beautiful, usually of deep brown. Should you inquire how many wives a king has, you may be told of many hundreds. But in truth these are the grand total of his women, the majority of whom are workers in the field. Those who belong to the household only work in their own gardens, and some do not work at all.

Although it was quite dark, there was still a faint glow of light in the distant west when my friend and I made ourselves comfortable on the great sheaves of prairie grass, seven or eight feet long, which lay at the door of the hut.

The people are all standing in the street, and are looking towards the west. What are they anticipating? Numbers of the crowd occasionally point in an excited manner as though they see something extraordinary in the sky. Ah! at last they are satisfied. The new crescent moon has just cut through the faint mist, and now shines as a golden band in the starry dome. The people feel that nature is still with them. They can discover something of good import in its first appearance, for they shout and sing in joyous unison.

Omens of good and evil are seen in the elements and changes of the moon, the clouds, the thunderstorm, and so forth. Not the slightest doubt can exist that my visit as an apparition from the world beneath the ground was considered very ominous of something; the wonder is of what?

However, above all things the innate conceit of the ruler of these people was a sufficient safeguard against further apprehension, when he came to the conclusion that I was something other than a man, and when he felt confident that my influence would depart with me, of which they were assured by my friend.

As da Costa and myself lay stretched and drowsily surveying the cloudless sky, we heard the resounding waves of drumming and singing; the pombe feast having reached its height upon the previous evening, while between the intervals and the lessening of the chorus, and borne on the wings of the western wind, came dreadful sounds, which touched the heartstrings and reminded us of the day's tragedy. Harsh and hideous were these sounds—the grim laughter of the hyenas, screaming the mocking notes, as they revelled in the gory feast given them by the dark ruler of the land.

"Well, Amigo," said I to da Costa, "I suppose that tomorrow night I shall have to fall into the old camp life again. I don't object to that, for it does not cost me unnecessary thought. But of all the different tribes I have come across, I have the least inclination towards the Angoni, and certainly the least confidence in them as travelling companions."

"Never mind," was the response; "I will let you have three Maravi of mine. One of them can talk a little Portuguese."

"Well, with them I shall struggle through, I suppose; if they only stick to me."

I here seized the opportunity to thank da Costa for his

kindness to me, dwelling upon the incident of our meeting and of his brotherly treatment of a stranger, remembering that but for him my grave would certainly have been at Urongwe. Chikuse might possibly have killed me; and owing da Costa a deep debt of gratitude, I expressed my feelings freely, as fate, wayward though she be, might never throw us into the same land again.

"I wonder where it will be next!" I said. At the same time I told my friend that I would like to hear some account of his African life.

"Who can say?" da Costa answered. "Probably we shall never meet again. This is a strange life. My path, for instance, is guided by the scarcity or abundance of elephants. As these beasts are driven off, I have to seek them further and in new fields. I have been a long time among these black people, and a great portion of it has been spent in the Makanga country, through which you came."

So trustworthy a man did Eustaquio da Costa seem to be, that I thought the opportunity a good one to hear more of the dreaded Makanga king, Kankune; consequently I asked him to give a brief account of his life with the monarch. I certainly can never forget the days and nights I had passed in his country.

Da Costa then proceeded to tell me something of his career.

He had been in the Portuguese army, and when only twenty-one years of age was sent out to join the black forces in eastern Africa. About a year after his arrival he found himself at Tette, and, although at death's door with the fever, he was under orders to leave for the Makanga country with messages for the king, and to remain there to watch the modes of life.

The fearful scenes enacted in that gloomy and heartless land remained still vividly in his mind. On his arrival the king treated him respectfully, and immediately offered him fourteen maidens as wives, with others of whom he might dispose. None were accepted. He soon learned that the character of the king was deceitful to a degree, although the falseness was well concealed, for he always employed fair words when speaking to da Costa.

He was constantly killing his people. When he intended to slay any one, he did not let da Costa know, because the latter always remonstrated with him. Da Costa, however, invariably heard of the slaughter through a servant he had.

A death, which he personally knew of, was that of the king's uncle. The king one day conversed, eat and drank with his uncle, treating him well and with the greatest respect. In the afternoon the uncle took his leave, with the intention of returning to his town, which was within a short distance of the royal kraal. My friend heard the king say to his relative, "Uncle, you can go now;" at the same time giving him two flagons of brandy and a piece of linen, with the remark:

"Here is cloth to clothe you, and brandy to drink. Come to-morrow and see us again."

After this friendly parting, da Costa saw the king dispatching a number of young men to overtake his uncle on the road. Next morning the young men returned to the king with the intelligence that they had carried out his commands, and, as was customary on such occasions—in positive proof of an execution—they held up portions of the intestines of the victim, with every manifestation of delight in the deed!

Da Costa remained with the king, and witnessed a war with a neighbouring chief, large numbers being killed in battle, and the prisoners, including women and children, were slaughtered in a most fearful manner. Twenty wives of powerful chiefs were among the slain. Fourteen chiefs had been captured, and it was intended that a great execution carnival was to take place at the king's kraal, for the entertainment of all the people.

But the elephant hunter begged hard that the king should refrain from such wholesale butchery, and after the first two victims had been immolated, he had the satisfaction of obtaining the tyrant's reluctant consent that the rest should be in the meantime spared.

The Makanga were deceitful to the last degree, and envious as well, never hesitating to kill their own relatives in a cause of self-interest or jealousy.

In superstition, da Costa said, their nature is just like that of the Angoni. He saw a woman, who was supposed to have bewitched some of the royal wives, executed in the king's presence. Pleading upon that occasion was unavailing.

Her arms were first amputated, and then she was decapitated. The wives, who were supposed to have been influenced by the sorcerer's enchantment, walked in procession afterwards, carrying the head and arms of the victim from eight o'clock in the morning until the sun had set.

Kankune was constantly killing his own wives. Two of these executions were seen by da Costa. Brandy, which the fiend unfortunately procures on the Zambesi, was, alas! and still is, the cause of all this terror. Of the two murders of which my friend was a spectator, the first took place about ten o'clock at night. The unfortunate woman was first felled with a club, and then the contents of a rifle was discharged into her quivering body. In the second case, the king led the victim to the Revuqwe river (close in front of the royal kraal), and with a rope secured her firmly to the bank, there to remain until the crocodiles should come, for this river teems in all its length with these reptiles. About ten minutes afterwards da Costa saw one of the brutes seize the poor woman, who vainly struggled a few moments before the animal carried her off into the river.

With this horror da Costa's narrative finished. I would not have mentioned the circumstances, had it not been that I wish to throw some light upon the horrible life of the black victim to brandy, the leader of a people who naturally follow the king in his example of indulgence, vice, and crime.

In other ways da Costa's brief story is interesting; in particular it shows some of the vicissitudes and dangers of a hunter's life in the wilds of Central Africa, and in a trustworthy way describes real observations of the habits and modes of existence which characterise the native tribes.

CHAPTER XX.

TOWARDS NYASSA.

Departing from Chikuse's—Thoughts of Nyassa—Difficulties—Gifts to slaves—Da Costa's good-bye—Mount Deza—Timidity of women—Mara the Maravi—His fowl-hunts and his wiles—Lying Angoni—Inquisitive blacks—Swarming kraals—Arms of the Assegai—The knobkerry—The Revuqwe—Signs of slave traffic—Slave stampede—"What the devil is the matter?"—Tortures of slavery—Iron smelting furnaces—Arab influence in slavery—Mountain scenery—The land of the rising sun—Nyassa—Salt carriers—"The white man has seen the lake"—How to reach Livingstonia—Crowding natives—The troublesome old men at Pantumbo's—Women at Pantumbo's—Objections to proceed—Look out for the people of Mponda—Distressing march—Fishermen—A disappointing shot—The luckless chronometer—A beautiful scene—"Nyanja senhor!"—Thoughts of the future—Angoni reluctance to go on—Sleep disturbing hippos—Alarm of the Nyassa people—A hostile reception—"These people are enemies"—The party is surrounded—Explanations—On the shores of the lake—Oppressive heat—My first sickness—A wretched night—Canoeing—Livingstonia at last!

Soon after sunrise I was out, and, after the accustomed bodily shake, hastened to da Costa's hut, for it was the morning upon which the escort was to turn up as promised by Shona the headman. The sky was grey and the atmosphere cold. Before we had finished the operation of internal scalding with hot coffee Shona arrived.

Then the people began to gather round, all seeming brighter and happier than usual, so that their change of humour had a cheering effect upon me, and made me long for a start. There could be little doubt that now I would soon be on the road again.

The pombe feast was over; the funeral ceremonies were

at an end. The slave caravan had left for the east coast. The king had gone off to his town which lay close by towards the north. A party of Maravi hunters were to leave for the north-west. All were astir, and I busied myself quickly in making final preparations for the march. Before noon I meant to be *en route* to the lake.

Hurrah for Nyassa! I would see white friends again, and be enabled to equip myself afresh for the journey riverwards to the far Indian Ocean.

At the last moment it appeared as though all the arrangements would have fallen through. The old man whom Shona had substituted for himself duly arrived, and, after receiving payment for the proposed journey, spoke weighty words to the effect that after all it had struck him that the king, having been gracious enough to bestow upon him the most noble Order of the Ring—that is to say, the saucepan affair which encircles the skull—he could not go.

It would be impossible too for his son to proceed, because he had been a mourner at the last funeral, and now that the sun had once more risen upon their kraal, shaving of the head was the order of the day.

Objections of this nature were followed by wild stories of the white men's strange propensities, which made it impossible for the Angoni to go to the town on the lake. While the debate was proceeding another old gentleman appeared, who, like the rest, had his own desires with regard to the supposed inexhaustible store of white man's bank (cloth). His particular line of argument was that he knew all about the road to the lake, and that Shona and the other man were to take me the wrong way.

With the patriarch's patience, da Costa haggled with them all vehemently, but it was not without extraordinarily strenuous efforts that he managed to get ten men together.

I had to be satisfied to accept the old man's substitute in the person of a slave (home born) and other nine Angoni slaves, who all carried shields of buffalo hide, also kerries and spears. My friend had also been true to his word, for the three Maravi he had promised were close at hand. One of them could speak Portuguese pretty fluently.

I made a declaration that I would not go by the southern line which was pointed out, for visions of all manner of dilemmas, even worse than those I had recently escaped from, arose in my mind suggesting the inevitable results of failure. Should I be unable to reach Livingstonia within a reasonable time, we might unwittingly run into the Makololo war, of which so much had been spoken. When at length the direction that was to be taken had been arranged, I made a calculation, and according to the reckoning the line of march would in any case take us far to the north of Livingstonia.

Each of the home slaves who were to accompany me received his contract price in calico. I made it my business to verify the suspicion which disturbed my mind regarding the destiny of articles given to slaves. I was not sure whether a slave on receiving a gift had or had not to deliver it forthwith to his owner. Travellers are often apt to form false opinions upon such matters, and in a case like that of which I speak, the circumstances rather encouraged the chance of inquiries going into the wrong channel. Why did the slaves not make loin cloths for themselves, instead of going about in a nude and bestial state? Because they had higher and better views. The calico did not go to their owners, nor was it used to bedeck themselves. It was immediately handed to their wives, who soon hid the nakedness of nature.

Exactly at mid-day I heard the words:

"Amigo, tudo esta prompto!" (Friend, all is ready.)

All was ready. I had been busily engaged in packing the last sack, putting into it provisions for my personal use, for the men looked after themselves. We had very little provisions, and, comparatively speaking, still less of that which would buy provisions. The vicissitudes of my stay, or rather my entry into Angoni-land, had exhausted my own supply, and already I had drawn heavily upon da Costa's resources.

But as I revelled in the hope that I would soon be in a place where there would be a superabundant supply, I concluded that a few men with featherweight loads and fast travel would fulfil the most desirable purpose, and ensure the rapid accomplishment of this latter part of my journey.

Da Costa, ever generous in hospitality, more than once said:

"If you don't find your friends, be sure to come back. I will make it all right with the king."

"Oh," I answered with all confidence, "never fear; I will find friends on the lake!"

"You can never be sure of anything in this country."

After these few words, and with feelings of grateful emotion, I said farewell to my kind friend, in whom I had found all the bright blossoms of the truest character, enchaining a friendship whose links can never be broken.

The Angoni, carrying the light loads on their heads, with their buffalo shields in their left hands and their weapons in their right, filed slowly out of the reed-built city and on to the rolling prairie, from which I looked back and said farewell to the blood-stained abode of Chikuse.

We struck out in a north-easterly direction, pursuing a course as wavering in its windings as the sinuous track of the snake. But it was with delight that the eye now revelled in the refreshing view of the open country, while the sense of freedom braced body and mind to activity and exhilaration.

We passed to a wide and treeless plain, observing afar the wild peaks of fiery rock, like colossal styles of one of Nature's sun-dials, surmounting the disconnected mountain tops which here and there rose from the far-reaching table-land.

Large numbers of the lovely crested crane gave animated beauty to the sequestered banks of the rivulets. Many huts of the Angoni people were seen scattered at intervals on the plain.

Onward we pressed, ascending and descending ridge after ridge of the rolling land until the day was well spent—too quickly I thought, although we had gone over a fair piece of ground. As we all felt inclined to rest, we halted on a small eminence, from which an extensive view could be obtained. Mount Deza stood close by to the west, its formidable cap wearing a crown of dense black clouds. South-west in the distance, and seemingly far below us—for we had risen some hundreds of feet—was the low mountain of Urongwe, on the bare but grassy slopes of which the deep shadows of Chikuse's town were just visible in the faint light thrown out by the expiring sun.

Vivid memories of many stirring scenes and anxious moments coloured my somewhat sombre reflections. Now the bitter experiences of the past seemed nought but a brief and intensely horrible dream, when I thought of the miserable days and more miserable nights which I had spent in the place—*alone!* The recollection of da Costa's unexpected but timely arrival was like a happy awakening on a smiling morn.

The evening was cold when we rested. A sharp wind

sweeping over the great plain chilled me to the bone. When we were again on the move we made a descent, and soon came to the familiar furrows of the maize gardens, close to a town, or rather a large village, which we entered. Sitting in the middle of the street on the bundles we awaited results.

The entire population turned out *en masse*, being fully alive to the importance of the arrival of the novelty caravan with its white mystery. Not one of the people would approach very near, the women especially being remarkably timid, which was manifested at the first moment they had seen me nearing the fields, when they quickly began to drive in the children, and made haste to reach the dark shelter of their grassy houses.

Huts in this place were lower than any I had seen, the entrances being similar to those which appear in Zulu huts, and necessitate the doubling of a man before he can enter.

The Maravi man—my new high counsellor and groom-in-waiting extraordinary—was of a very different disposition compared with the poor old slave Misiri who had accompanied me during the earlier part of the Zambesi journey, and who always acquiesced to all I said. The new man, whose name was Mara, was of a somewhat contradictory disposition, but possessed of all the good points to be found in the Kaffir character. His contrary nature was at times most entertaining. For instance, he rather ridiculed my Portuguese, thinking himself a finished master of the language.

Poor Mara had one desire above all others, and that was his living. At feeding and beer drinking he excelled, and was a capital hand at foraging for needful articles of food. On arriving at a village he would sit down before me and keep repeating "missanga" (beads), followed by "nkuku" (chicken). Urged by the thoughts of the delicate morsels forming a savoury stew in grease, he would excitedly pursue his winged game until he raised a storm of cackling, and filled the air with feathers.

Chickens and goats are the only domestic animals to be seen. Cattle are not seen in the outlying villages, and pigs, in domesticity, I never saw in Angoni-land.

Mara was a man of rather tricky disposition. Supposing he got a refusal of the price he offered for a chicken, he would turn abruptly away, saying that such was the price that the king declared we were to give, a downright lie, of course; but, for a wonder, in the proper place, for it invariably had the effect of transferring the coveted fowl.

Upon that evening I made some inquiries as to the distance, in day's travel, to the lake; but could not draw out a sensible reply, Mara continually averring that the Angoni lied! His assertion was afterwards found to be well grounded.

The hut in which I slept was half full of old baskets, which had been used for storing corn, and hanging upon the low dark walls were some bows, side by side with a number of barbed arrows. A bark mat, which lay on the hardened mud floor, formed my bed.

Early in the morning—before Mara had extricated himself from the household debris, where he had been snoring and nestling all night—large numbers of young blacks crept up to the door of the hut to see if they could get a stolen glimpse of the sleeping white ogre of the "side show." A nude little urchin, bolder and more inquisitive than the others, pushed his head just inside the door, in order to report to his companions the movements of the monster.

By-and-by the enclosure which encircled the hut was

quite full of men, women, and children, who became panic-striken the instant that I peeped out at the door, all rushing in hot haste to the narrow portal, in order to escape from my baneful eyes. It was a most ludicrous sight. One young woman of rather impressive proportions, with a child on her back, blocked the way, so that those behind had to leap, which they did as if for life, adding greatly to the confusion, which seemed to amuse old Mara vastly. The latter was now busily engaged in preparing food for the caravan, and was doubtless telling the people that his "fancy" was harmless.

The clouds seen on the previous day capping the summit of mount Deza proved to be the precursors of rain. This morning was cold, dismal, and wet.

I had not as yet seen people so miserably deficient in raiment as were the inhabitants of this village. As a rule, they had nothing on their bodies, and their black skins shone with the cold wetting mist and heavy rain, making them look the saddest pictures of absolute misery.

The kraals were swarming with children, and from close observation I was led to believe that the mortality between the ages of childhood and maturity must be very great. Comparatively speaking, youths are not proportionally numerous.

While sojourning in these outlying villages, I also was much impressed with the fact that the Angoni were not in any respect so perfectly or completely armed as some of the tribes further south in South Africa, or on the north side of the Zambesi. Their spears and arrows are certainly well formed, and fairly well finished, but the neatly produced assegai of the Matabeli, with its plaited stripe of raw hide securing the shaft or handle, is far superior to any weapon of the Angoni. The assegais which came from the north end of Lake Nyassa were also very superior weapons in form and finish.

The 'kerry was the universal weapon. It was carried by every male; and was, no doubt, the implement most used in slave raiding, in conjunction with the shield.

This popularity of the 'kerry was disagreeably shown; for when I walked outside the kraal, which was watched in a most vigilant manner by some men who took up their position at the back of my hut, and by turns would remain and scrutinise my every action, little boys would follow me in herds, jumping around and gesticulating wildly with flaunting 'kerrys, as now and then they would make sundry feints, as if about to throw their hard root missiles at my devoted head. To be alone for an instant was an impossibility.

Although the sky was still overcast, the rain ceased. With difficulty the Angoni were gathered together; the task calling for all the strategic tactics that have a place in the traveller's resources. Blacks are prone to vanish to obscure places whenever a town is reached.

On our departure from this village hundreds of people followed us, skurrying out of the adjacent huts, all seeming eager to see the last of the white man. Everybody in the place appeared to have turned out to bid us good-bye.

Women, some of them very stout, with big babies tied on their backs, ran along briskly, evidently reluctant to miss a chance of having a look at the wonder. Swarms of children trooped along hopping and skipping over the numerous ant heaps, and with shrill voices, giving noisy life to the bustling scene.

But we hastened on, and, crossing the Revuqwe river, left the excited crowd on the western bank. At this point we were at the head waters of the Revuqwe, which we crossed for a third and last time. I had seen it where, broad and clean, it emerged into the giant Zambesi, and was lost in the wide blue bosom of the mighty river. We now crossed it in a single stride.

A few hours' steady marching over bare ground, studded with chips of disintegrated granite, winding amidst which I could discern numerous paths well worn, doubtless by the journeys of the slave caravans, and branching in all directions, brought us to the environs of another village, which nestled in a small clump of copsewood. The main trail of the paths I refer to went in a northerly direction, almost parallel with the mountain chain. I am inclined to believe that the larger portion of the slaves taken from Angoni-land go to Jumbés, at Kota-Kota on the lake; thence they are ferried over to the eastern shore, and begin their march to the coast, loaded with ivory.

The men were some distance ahead of me, because I had made a short detour, my curiosity having been aroused by the appearance of a number of slave yokes scattered about on one side of the trail. Examining these, I found that two were broken, but from their appearance I was convinced that no long time had elapsed since they had been employed in their torturing work. On the spur of the moment I thought I would endeavour to take one of the yokes with me as a trophy; and shouldering one instantly I ran on, but soon became tired of the encumbrance, and threw it away, thinking at the time what must be the effect of having such a load about one's neck for months.

I kept up a pretty lively step, for the Angoni were marching quickly, and I had lost sight of them when they had disappeared into a little patch of bushy covert.

Mara, however, had waited and watched for me, and on

my arrival gave the usual reprimand, which invariably was as amusing as it was earnest.

"What are you doing staying alone? The boys are far away, and there is a lot of *gente* [people] in this town."

No sooner did we reach the first hut of the village than a rushing crowd of people was observed, many of whom fell over one another, as though in a stampede through dreadful fear. Some men were coupled by the two-forked yokes, fastened together with bark rope, while others had on the single stick or yoke. A number of women were tied neck to neck.

"What the devil is the matter, Mara?"

No response was made, but on my repeating the question more vehemently and emphatically, the answer came, short and pointed:

"*Gente comprada! Vamos!*" ("People who have been bought! Let us go on!")

But here there was no going on for me. I was determined to see what was being done, hurry or no hurry. The throngs of blacks were jostled and shoved into all sorts of corners, and herded into the cane-wall enclosures of the huts. The meaning of the scene was that I had alighted at a secluded village, where a number of kidnapped slaves had been brought *en route* to some headquarters, for they were not people of the district. The slimy visage of a man robed in white—he himself was of Satanic blackness—suggested to me that the agents of my previous acquaintance, Saiide or Xuala, were bringing in an assortment of the human commodity.

Possibly the reader can guess what my feelings were; I should have liked with a single bound to have been in the midst of the harshly-used creatures, to strip from their suffering bodies the tyrant's thongs and fetters. Under

SURPRISING A SLAVER.

such circumstances these impulses can never be gratified, no matter how acute may be the desire to give relief. The suppression of the traffic cannot in the slightest degree be influenced by the words or actions of solitary passing travellers; any movement on my part would have been madness, even had I a strong caravan of armed followers.

Nothing decidedly advantageous in this way can be accomplished excepting, as in the case of every great good work, by every effort being made by strong organisations, whose work follows the hard and slow course of Time's transforming power.

One indiscreet act on the part of a traveller may cause barriers to progress to spring up, and insurmountably and for generations stop the advance of trade and missions. Every traveller who is influenced by considerations of relative positions must feel how important is the question of his bearing among a people who watch his every action, and when a single imprudent step on his part may cost some unfortunate creature his life.

I think every one is impressed by the very movements of individuals as they turn, twist, and bend under the pangs of pain and fear. In this sad scene of excited action, where anguished fear and doubt were mutely expressed upon many mournful faces, my mind was filled with melancholy emotions, awakened by the forlorn looks and stricken attitudes of the unfortunate crowd: a woeful sight, indeed, a sight that, while memory lives, will ever and anon recall a sorrowful picture, a pitiful story. Some of the slaves might be seen in the agony of despair; in most cases, especially the men in the yokes, wriggling and twisting as they were jostled in the narrow crooked streets, their heads being screwed round so far that I fully expected to see some broken necks. Two very pitiable cases strongly arrested my notice: the subjects were seated on the ground, sheltered by some bushes, and each resting the end of his yoke upon the ground. One was in a frightful condition, with open sores sweltering under the heat of the sun, being chafed to the flesh through the roughness of the bark bindings of the yoke.

Being determined to find out something about the unfortunates, and ignoring Mara's ill-concealed anxiety to proceed, I made the latter inquire of the sufferer what was the cause of his deplorable condition. His reply was that he had run away and had been recaptured.

All the time I was here the black agent looked upon me with an undeniably defiant expression.

Leaving the accursed scene Mara and myself hastened after the Angoni, who had been pressing forward with the intention of reaching the mountains that night. We had been nearing the range for some time, and following the path we passed through another village, in which no captive slaves were seen. At length, after mounting a steep slope, we sighted the advance party.

Further northwards—we ascended gradually, and were then 4,500 feet above the sea—we passed a number of native iron-smelting furnaces, some of which showed signs of having been recently used, as small heaps of slag lay piled beside them. This slag I found to be very vesicular; the metallic iron was in irregular buttons, and had evidently been reduced from brown hematite or hydrated peroxide of iron.

After we joined the Angoni party clouds began to gather, and a disagreeable mist rolled along the plains, bringing a damping influence upon everything, spirits included.

In the evening I had an opportunity of questioning Mara more thoroughly regarding what had occurred at the village where the grim realities of slavery had been seen. The little I could gather from my guide's replies amounted to this: that an endeavour to bribe his captives had been made by the driver, as soon as he had heard of my approach; for he was on the march and evidently knew nothing of my travelling with so small a party. I imagined that this body of slaves had in some manner managed to effect their escape, but had been caught and driven back. The yokes I had seen were probably some that had been thrown aside by the captives, who had found some means of casting them off.

Black agents as well as Arabs are well aware what the efforts of the white men have been in the direction of suppressing their "black ivory" traffic on the east coast, and it is very well known that the Arabs in Central Africa are now more violently opposed to the approach of the white man than ever they were.

As I looked out on the north-western expanse, stretching far away to the poisonous swamps of Lake Bangweolo, my mind was filled with thoughts of the greatest of African explorers, who was struck down on the inhospitable shores of the lake. More than once have I thought, while looking upon some of the horrifying and heart-rending scenes which arose before me, of the words of him who was so deeply impressed with the fact that the devil held the reins of power in the dark continent. "All I can add in my loneliness," wrote Livingstone, "is may Heaven's rich blessing come down on every one, American, English, or Turk, who will help to heal the open sore of the world."

We had a night of piercing cold. The wind swept past in biting blasts, whistling shrilly over the great plateau. I was very glad to hear Mara say the Angoni had told him that in the morning we would cross the mountains. The very thought sent a glow of warmth through me, in spite of the bitter wind. Our shelter was very scant. Large fires had disappeared, like other luxuries of the past, for wood was exceedingly scarce, maize roots and stalks forming the chief kindlings.

When the shivering and shaking night had passed, the unimposing caravan wended its way among the foot-slopes of the mountains, hidden by the dark shadows of towering cliffs. On our left lay immeasurable plains which had just caught the first bright smile of morning, while a bleak and wild landscape opened out far to the westward.

We passed a number of small fields which bore the appearance of having been irrigated to a small extent, for narrow ditches from tiny rivulets led to patches of arable land. Here and there the ground was dotted with short young grasses which, when touched by the glancing sunbeams, gave a refreshing charm to the otherwise barren scene. Pretty flowers, pink and purple, gemmed the smiling greensward, giving a bright welcome to the opening day.

A number of miles were scored during that morning, and in time we reached a deep rent in the mountains. The pathway here turned sharply to the right, and it was with joy unspeakable that I turned my face in the direction of the rising sun.

Walking under the dark shades of the sombre rocks, every step and every turn in the tortuous path showed varied views. Cloud-capped peaks in their rough grandeur contrasted with yawning chasms, which were lost in the profound blackness of lifeless hollows. No sound was heard save the sweet but monotonous murmuring of mountain rivulets, rushing on to mingle their rippling waters with the larger streams which flow singing to the great lake.

At length the region of rocks is passed. Peaks, caverns, chasms, and yawning cañons have vanished from our view. We stand on the eastern slopes of the Manganja range, and feast our eyes upon the vast expanse clothed with interminable forest, lifeless to the view were it not that here and there vultures might be seen soaring high over the dreamy scene.

Yes, 'tis the land of the rising sun! Far away in the east the glistening sunbeams revealed the mirror-like lake flashing in lines of dazzling silver between the woodland banks and the rising mists. A thrill of joy electrified my frame. At last! Hurrah for Nyassa—Nyassa, the great inland sea!

In our rear the frowning mountains defiantly stopped the sunlight; in front the sylvan beauty of the voiceless forest sloped in gentle undulations on to the silver sands of the silent sea, which in the far distant horizon mingled with white downy mists.

We are about to penetrate the stretching forest land. What luck awaits us, what encouragement, what barriers? I became unconscious of my immediate surroundings; my human troubles and disappointments are, for the time being, eclipsed by the extreme grandeur of the prospect before us. My mind wanders away over this wooded wonderland and anticipates naught but joy.

I think I hear the welcome words of friends echoing across the quiet waters, for through the far-off clouds my thoughts speed fleetly to linger on Livingstonia's shore, where stand the white brothers whom I have striven so hard to reach. How near everything seems to be! But yet many occasions have proved that time and distance are not related in circumstances such as mine. Dependance robs me of the pleasures of calculation.

Now I hear some muttering amidst the ranks of my followers. What can it mean? They move onwards, and I see them wending their way slowly down the zigzag path leading into the valley of Lake Nyassa.

Once more we tread the crisp faded leaves which cover the paths of the primeval forest. The hot breath of the confined air makes us long again for the freedom of vision and the cold winds of the high plateau.

A party of Angoni was passed, each carrying a load of salt upon his head. It was packed in neat cigar-shaped bundles, bound with jungle grasses. What stories had they told my company? Not long after they passed a prolonged halt was made, during which a proposal of a return to Chikuse's was brought up. It was evident that the news they had heard had revived the wildest stories, which had terrified every mind for months before we left Urongwe. Assuredly the white wizard of the lake still looked them blankly in the face.

"The white man has seen the lake," said the Angoni. "We said we would show him Nyanja. He has seen it. Now we will return."

At such a juncture nothing could be concerted. Where could a village be found? Go back to Chikuse's— never! I gave the shortest answer I could think of; saying that the white man would not speak until he saw a town, an intimation which was followed by absolute silence.

Thus we walked on through the great forest trees, beneath the drooping boughs of sycamore, fig, and tamarind, whose massive trunks stood like columns supporting their canopies of foliage, until at length peeping above the intertwined undergrowth of jungle thicket we saw the welcome sight of hut tops.

Little time elapsed until we reached the town, where a hut was procured for me, and then seated in thoughtful silence we meditated what would be the next step.

When first I saw the lake I had fondly congratulated myself that, now as it was not very far off, and as the Angoni marched quickly when once moved, troubles and annoyances from porters were at an end. Surely they would never stop when they were so near the lake. I had promised them all that they would be well paid on arrival at Livingstonia.

My confidence had been misplaced, and now it was difficult to determine what was to be done to reach Livingstonia—the centre of all my hopes. I remembered having seen its name printed on some maps as big as though it were a place of the size and importance of Birmingham; and my mind was filled with thoughts of the readiness with which I would dispel the fears of these Angoni followers, when they saw the white men with their abundant stores of pretty cloth. Then I would send them back to their home on the high and rolling prairie with the consciousness that they had found a man outside of their own tribe who would at least keep his word.

All would be well at Livingstonia; but how was I to get there? The cloth at my command would only suffice to pay for canoes which would of necessity have to be found in advance. Under any circumstances I dared not then give goods to the Angoni. My companion—Mara the indispensable—sat in front of me with three hens which he held by the legs while they agitated the dusty ground and sent the down and feathers flying through the air. All the time he kept repeating " Misanga, Misanga—beads, beads."

No business could possibly be transacted before Mara had settled the question of the food supply; but in my anxiety to save time I then felt very indifferent about commissariat arrangements.

If we pushed on rapidly, the village, Mpemba, beside the lake might be reached upon that very evening. But not this time. Mara again seated himself in front, not forgetting his never failing ceremony of shuffling the feet, and stated that pombe was to be had, and perhaps it would be better that we should have some. The demand was not extravagant, so I immediately agreed to it, giving a couple of large gourds to the Angoni.

A big crowd collected around us here. Numbers of old men pushed into the hut and, sitting before me, evidently gave a sharp criticism to my appearance, remarking among themselves upon my glaring defects as one of the *genus homo*. Ere long the hut was packed as close as a fish barrel, and as it was about three o'clock in the afternoon—the time of day when the heat is most oppressive—the close atmosphere about the batch of niggers may be more easily imagined than described.

I betook myself to the outside, but there found no relief; for the people crowded and pressed around until we had an atmosphere of our own that beggars description: it was about as strong as the people were uncouth.

The women seemed to be rather amused and behaved, as they always did, much better than the men, who sat grinning and laughing outright at the novelty of my unfamiliar aspect. This did not in the least way disturb my equanimity; but I would have been satisfied with a little less of their odour. The filth of the surroundings was remarkable. Pigeons, chickens, goats, and black children—a sappy lot—proved their presence to the nasal organs, while dust, feathers, straw, corn cobs, and all kinds of light and unclean rubbish were whirled about the head by sudden gusts of wind.

Mara did not appear until he had demolished everything that he could lay his hands upon if it was soft enough to swallow. On his arrival I sent for the headman of the Angoni, and asked the reason why he had threatened to leave me on the road. The answer was a repetition of what had been said during the descent from the mountains, with the additional information that the white man had lied, (!) for he had not given them the cloth he had promised, and, besides, they had acted strictly according to their agreement: they had shown the white man the lake, and he had consequently reached his destination.

I reminded the headman of Chikuse. Had not that chief ordered them to take me to my white brothers? When there I would give all of them presents. Where were the canoes which were to take me across the waters of Nyanja? The old men of Urongwe had said that I would have to go far by water.

"Where is the village on the shores of Nyanja—Mpemba, Mpemba?" I repeated over and over again.

The old men seated in front, who were the possessors of the concentrated intellect of the whole community, said much among themselves, shaking their heads in an unmistakably decided manner, and waxing loquacious upon the subject, the interpretation of their trouble being the declaration that the village Mpemba, on the lake, could not be entered by the white man: if he attempted to go there he and all his men would be killed.

The Angoni then said they would leave whether I paid them cloth or not! They repeated that I had told them I had white brothers on the lake, and that the old men of Pantumbo (the village we then were in) had affirmed that there were no white men at that end of Nyanja. It was quite impossible to get any information about a place called Livingstonia.

After the palaver was over and the meeting separated, I came to the conclusion that there was nothing for it now but strategy. Before doing anything I said to Mara:

"Are you going with the Angoni to leave me?"

"Nao Senhor-rr! My master said I must never leave you until you see your brothers, and the other two Maravi must do what Senhor da Costa told them!"

This news gave me quite a lift. Had I suddenly got the command of an army I could not have been more elated than I was by the discovery of a single friend who would stick to me in adversity.

With compasses I paced off the distance, roughly, between our position and Cape Maclear or Livingstonia, and found it to be short of fifty miles. I would have to keep to one of the two routes. By that first planned I would have to risk the wrath of Mpemba; the second was a land journey. I determined to abandon the first, and every idea of a short cut in canoes. The land route would be infinitely better, and if Mara would stay with me, we would manage to get on alone, and reach the missionaries, even should my proposals to the Angoni fail.

When alone I cut off a few yards of blue calico, being careful that the Angoni did not see me—if they did all the plan would have been upset, for they would think the supply inexhaustible—and handing it to Mara, told him to present it to Pantumbo the chief, with the announcement that I wanted a guide to take me to the south end of the lake, and that he must be ready for departure in the morning. Far from being my first difficulty, this new trouble was rendered less formidable by the recollection of previous experiences, which suggested what my actions were to be on the following morning. I knew I had a very strong hand.

A stroll among the huts strengthened an impression which had been forced upon me almost on my arrival at Pantumbo's, namely, that the people were in a deplorably poverty-stricken condition. The women generally had old and ugly-looking rags about their loins, and in some instances the bark kilt reaching from the waist almost to the top of the knees—the latter being by no means a repulsive costume for a black woman.

Many of the women were husking millet in hollow tree trunks, while others were reducing the seed to meal in what I have termed the syenitic mill: between two pieces of syenite they grind the corn by hand.

Irregular though the streets were, they were well shaded from the intense heat of the midday sun by the fine foliage of large trees.

There was no river near; consequently the people drew their supply of water from rudely dug wells. The water was very near the surface, for the position was only a few feet above the level of the lake.

By the way, I never saw any of the African tribes burn oil to get light: whenever light was required they kindled fires, throwing on twigs, pieces of corn stalks, and cobs, and the ears of maize.

As the evening advanced Mara began talking about the probabilities of our being soon in a position to gratify our appetites with more substantial food than that afforded by the eternal hen; for that morning we had crossed the spoor of a buffalo herd, so that there were fair prospects of unrestricted feasting. He also minutely related the portentous words of the old men, weighty warnings of the untold dangers that lay in store for us on the shores of the great lake.

Our examination was interrupted by the arrival of a man who came from Chief Pantumbo with the intelligence that he, the messenger, would act as a guide to the south end of Nyassa. He said, however, that there was no white man in that neighbourhood; but this was a piece of news in which I was convinced he was mistaken, for I knew very well where the white missionaries were at work.

The morning air was calm when daylight broke upon us through the sprays of thicket and heavy boughs that shadowed our resting-place; but the familiar haze of faintest crimson once more indicated the intense heat which we would have to encounter during the day.

The Angoni were called to the front. When I had repeated the terms of their agreement with me, I said:

"You now refuse to take me to Mpemba, or to my white brothers. There are two roads, and I will go by either, but remember you can never leave the white man here— never; he will return with you to Urongwe, and again appear before the king! What will Chikuse say? Will he not look for the presents, for the cloth he values so much? You must remember the words of Chikuse, and think again before you dare to disobey the orders of the great king!"

My last trump card was now played, for I calculated upon the unlikelihood of the Angoni daring to face Chikuse empty-handed. After a long parley the headman said that on the south road they were afraid of Mponda, a great chief with whom they were at variance; but I knew that Mponda was on the Shiré river, and promising that I would keep close to the shores of the lake, I induced the malcontents to agree to go, so that by ten o'clock we were heading south-east, making a diagonal line towards the shores of the lake, despite the protestations and farewell harangues of the old men, who continued to shout that there was war on the road, and that all the boys would be killed.

"Look out for the people of Mponda!" was their last injunction.

"Come with me," I said to the men, "and see for yourselves whether it is I or your old men that have lied."

We had pretty stiff work in making progress, for the forest through which we had to pass was very dense with an exuberance of tropical vegetation. We had now to cross tortuous little channels which had been gouged out and torn by the tumbling torrents during the rains. To add to the laboriousness of the march, we came upon belts of high jungle grass, which had to be traversed, although they were pitted with innumerable holes made by the heavy feet of troupes of elephants during their migration in the rainy season. Some of the holes were two or three feet deep, and were now baked as hard as pottery. Almost at every step legs, ankles, or shins came to grief; the whole frame was racked and twisted most distressingly as the feet alighted upon the sharp rimmed edges of the invisible pitfalls, in a way that would be disastrous to weak ankles.

Antelopes were plentiful here, also bush pig and buffalo. We passed through a thin belt of tsetse fly, and of course felt their painfully familiar punctures.

It was hard work; but by noon we found ourselves upon the banks of the M'Vurezi river, a small and rapid stream of clear water.

A very short halt was made, and by way of refreshment cold millet meal porridge, unboiled, was indulged in by the boys.

Only an hour later we reached a small village, occupied by Nyassa people, who were busily employed in fishing, their huts being built upon an inlet of the lake. Their mode of fishing was to dam the narrow waterway, so as to prevent the fish from escaping, after which they would wade in with cane baskets made for the purpose of capture. Some of these baskets were seven feet in length, and the ends were formed in such a way that, once the fish entered, escape was impossible.

A villager here reported elephants in close proximity. I had seen the spoor, but thought it was of the day before. Under this incitement I readily forgot a repast which Mara was preparing, and leaving the party to rest, started on the spoor, the evidence of the presence of game being ample, for in every direction the wide tracks of the huge beasts were to be seen. After going on, however, for about a couple of miles, my guide gave in. Speaking was impossible.

I dared not stay away much longer from my party, for the day was advancing, and I hoped ere sunset to cover at least eight miles further.

On our return journey we cut the spoor of some buffalo, and this time had better luck. A walk of two hundred yards brought us to a thick clump of tangle and dwarf forest, through which we had to crawl on the spoor, our chief anxiety being to keep from making a noise, for even by the breaking of a twig the game is lost. I had to pick the spots where each hand had to be placed, all the while twisting and turning like a snake in order to avoid branches and thorns.

Reaching a favourable point, I looked sharply to the front, and through the yielding thicket sighted clearly the massive form of a buffalo bull, while close before him were a number of others. As these animals irresistibly push their way through the dense network, the jungle closes behind their track, so that it is exceedingly difficult to get a shot. The tangle often turns the bullet.

I had come within fifteen paces of the bull. To go further without being detected was an impossibility, so at once aiming for the well-known tail shot, I banged off the eight-bore. Being in a very contorted position, through trying to avoid the thick branches which stood in the line of sight, the concussion threw me on my side, the recoil of the heavy rifle cutting my face and blacking my eye. For a moment vision was dimmed by the smoke, but hearing a bellowing sound, the thought struck me "he's down!"

But in a second, and before I could get a chance of another shot, the brute had gained its feet and rushed madly past, raising a storm of dust as he cleaved crashing and smashing into the thicket like a well-charged projectile—he was gone!

Buffaloes are the quickest animals in bush that I have ever seen. I had given a good shake to this one, for he had fallen, and had time allowed I would have followed, for there was blood spoor; but as on many similar occasions there was nothing for it but to abandon the wounded game, a thing I was always very reluctant to do. The old plague the carriers were ever being changed from tribe to tribe, and consequently it was never safe to remain long away from the camp. After this disappointment we ran home at a jog-trot, and the heat being excessively strong, we soon looked as though we had been in the water bathing—rags and all. Close to the town I shot a small antelope, with minute horns like those of the duiker, sharp as needles, and much coveted by the Angoni as ornaments.

When we returned to the village we found that a large fire had been started, which roared and crackled in so close a proximity to the huts of straw, that I thought everything would be consumed by the long tongues of flame which swept towards the combustible buildings. Closer examination showed, however, that the creek formed a safe circle of water on the side where the flames looked most threatening.

Mara told me that the guide had decided to take us on a short cut to the lake, as, on account of war, he wished to avoid the villages which lay to the right. I was quite unable to get at the bottom of this story, but conjectured that the slave traffic had something to do with it.

Reluctant, indeed, were the Angoni, as they pursued a weary march that afternoon; a march which was rendered unusually trying through the incessant tumbling into the holes made by elephants' feet, forming, with one exception, the roughest ground I had ever seen or heard of; for nothing could compare with it except the ground covered with the fire-eaten and wind-fallen timber of the Rocky Mountains stacked together after a snow-storm.

Here we again found tsetse fly, but only a few.

As we walked along, a loud thump startled me. I quickly turned round, only to see that my chronometer was down again, and on opening the box a mixture of glass and brass was revealed to the view, the clock being thrown out of its hangings. This was to me, as a like catastrophe had been on a previous occasion, truly a sorrowful sight, but it gave unbounded ecstasy to the Angoni, who looked as though they had never seen anything so pretty in their lives; at first they looked serious, then they grinned gleefully as they saw the thousand glassy crystals that surrounded the changeless face of the defunct time-measurer. Not for a moment did they take in the fact that I was showing them a damaged article, for they evidently thought it was medicine to find the direct road. Oh, that unfortunate instrument! I would think of carrying a baby through the continent sooner than a ship's chronometer.

We struck a belt of thick forest, where walking became a little easier than it was before, and our overheated bodies were sheltered from the fierceness of the sun. Fortunately it was the guide's interest to reach the villages at the southernmost end of the lake as early as possible, so that the march was sustained with a considerably greater degree of energy than was usual, although I heard many mutterings from those who were behind, evidently with respect to the pace, and the desirability of halting for the night.

Once out of the darkened forest, a typical African scene lay before us, and we pressed our way through great meadows of yellow grass, the eyes being relieved by constantly changing colours in the landscape. On the left a low spur ran downward to the lake, while over the high green reeds that skirted the shore we saw the waters of Nyassa, calm and cool in appearance. Coming towards us were seen, nodding above the waving grass, horns and heads of a hidden herd of water-bucks. Within shot on our right was a herd of ten buffaloes, whose black heads dipped once or twice before they were finally lost to view.

Night was approaching. Beneath the gloom of the leaden-hued clouds flashes of aureate light streamed to the distant hills, illumining their dark ridges and crests with resplendent gleams, whose rich light gradually became softened and subdued as its flash disappeared from the drooping foliage of the tall palms which clothed the lower mountain-sides. The softer light lingered upon a scene of surpassing beauty, where the forest mosses clung to stem and bough, their graceful wreaths hanging from branch to branch of the slender mimosa and thorny acacia. Around our camp the earth was smoothly carpeted with young grasses drawn out by the misty showers. Westward, far away, like the rolling swell of the inflowing tide, the long yellow grass expanded, relieved here and there by small deep green bushes, which rose like islets from a grassy sea.

"Nyanja, Senhor!" exclaimed Mara.

"Yes," thought I, "it is Nyassa, and such are the lovely scenes that leave happy impressions on the traveller's mind, the recollection of their beauty blotting out the dismal thoughts of miserable days and incidents!"

That night was especially pleasant to me, owing to the keen feeling of satisfaction which thrilled through my veins, and I thought no one could feel otherwise upon such an occasion.

We had just completed one of the longest and most fatiguing marches of all the journey. Now that I had at last gained the shores of the big lake, how I longed, as I had done a thousand times before, for a companion with whom a few congratulatory words might be exchanged!

Reclining against the trunk of a tree I rested my jaded body, finding grateful comfort in the balmy air of the evening breeze. The soft wind which had sprung up from the lake helped to drive away the numerous mosquitoes which abounded around us.

While pensively observing the leaping flames of the camp fires, as they sprung up and licked the moss which dangled from the overshadowing boughs, thoughts sped rapidly through my mind regarding all that had passed during the long time—they seemed like years—which had elapsed since I said good-bye to the Cape of Good Hope.

Reflections on the past were diverted by pleasant anticipations regarding the future. What lay in store for me during the next few days? Bright thoughts of the morrow dispelled the clouded memories of bygone times; for now it could not be more than a day before we would make the curve round the southern bay, and so reach Livingstonia. My reckoning as to position was, I knew, not far out, and even remembering that we were in Africa—that land of startling misadventure—it was not unreasonable to conclude that upon the succeeding day we would be welcomed with gladdening smiles from white faces lightened by the influence of warm hearts.

Many hundreds of miles had still to be covered before I reached the end of my journey, so that the comforts of a few days' repose, with relief from constantly recurring difficulties and dispiriting doubts, could not fail to be most refreshing. The hardest fact of all was that my pedlar's shop was nearly empty, and the end of barter meant the end of progress. What would follow?

Even such trifles as the day, or date, which was lost, in my journal, would be cleared up, and would not be without a lesson in showing how easy it is to fall, if not into error, certainly into doubt. The most inspiring thought of all was the anticipation of news from the outer world, for as a matter of course there would be a thousand things to talk of. Questions of living interest would have to be asked and answered, and there was undoubtedly some gratification in the knowledge that I was the first letter-carrier to deliver a message from the missionaries of the south to the missionaries of the north: for such was my privilege. Thinking of these things I made some tea with the water of Nyassa, and drank to the fame of the White Wizard and the glory of the Great Lake.

Immediately after this solo ceremony, Mara told me that the Angoni wished it to be understood that upon no account would they go into the villages of the Ajawa; so that, notwithstanding the fact of my knowing nothing as to what the attitude of these Ajawa might be, I had to say a few words of a reassuring nature. The course I adopted was to say that they must obey my orders attentively, and then they would be considered as being *my* people, in which case they would in no way be molested.*

Sleep was very much disturbed by ceaseless snorting and grunting from the hippos, which in considerable numbers were pushing their way through the reeds, sporting and feeding. I might even have been oblivious to their noise, but it was impossible not to be aware of the presence of their tiny winged associates, who never left us for a moment, working diligently through the livelong night, and keeping up an incessant singing in the ears. Altogether, I was not sorry when this period of slumbering, scratching, and swearing was at an end, and the march resumed.

The loads were very light now, for we had no provisions of any description. Excepting their shields and weapons, several of the men were empty-handed.

An overpowering heat fell upon us as we pushed our way through a well-timbered country abounding in large forest trees, with groves of splendid palms near to the edge of the lake, which was fringed with a wide band of high green reeds. A few hours spent in enduring this toilsome march brought us to a number of gardens where women, old and young, and children were seen hoeing and making preparations for the rainy season.

The guide and myself were at some distance ahead of the party, a circumstance which was the cause of a rather unfortunate occurrence. High dark forests sheltered the gardens on the western side from which we appeared.

---

* Further south, that is to say on the Shiré river, the Angoni could not go, on account of their previous conduct in slaving raids.

The Angoni, who had loitered in the rear, now observing that we were about to approach a village, came running on in order to overtake me, and request a halt.

Their haste might have brought on the annihilation of the whole party; for as with shields and clubs they sped excitedly over the open flat stretching from the forest, their unlooked-for appearance struck terror into the minds of the defenceless women, who quickly seized their children and ran madly off, all the time screaming to their husbands in the town. At once I saw that a bad move had been made, and a fight would inevitably be the result.

The Angoni said they would go no further. In the most strident tones at my command I shouted in Portuguese, " Remember what I told you!" By dint of painstaking effort, Mara ultimately succeeded in putting a little confidence in their fickle minds, inducing them to do as I told them.

Then was seen filing from the tree-fenced town * a thick black throng of men. On they came, armed to the teeth. Bows and arrows, flintlocks, spears, and a wonderful assortment of other weapons could be seen. Old men stalked on, holding long knives in their hands, generally with the edges upwards, suggesting the idea that their particular duty as auxiliaries was the mutilation of the dead and quick despatch of the wounded. Now when I look back upon the scene I remember their bearing as being rather funny, which it certainly was *not* at the time, pushing along their stiff old carcases over the furrowed ground, and all the time showing every indication of a wish for direst vengeance.

In the expression of the people's faces when they gathered

* Long poles rising twelve feet above the ground entirely fenced and encircled the town.

around us determination was not unmixed with fear; for perhaps they could read upon the buffalo-shields of my warlike followers the appalling signs of death and captivity written with the fresh blood of their wives and children. As a terrifying emblem of war it is the shield, always carried by the Angoni, or Landin, that strikes horror to the hearts of these usually timid dwellers in the valleys of lake and river.

Unmistakable signs of fear clouded the face of Mara, who was in a perverse mood, and kept repeating the words, "These people are enemies."

There could be no doubt that my Angoni men felt very uncomfortable, and Mara informed me that they had declared they would not stay here, although it was my intention to breakfast at the place, if anything could be bought. Four old men came to the front of the threatening assemblage and, accompanied by Mara, I immediately advanced to meet them. They enquired why I came bringing Angoni to their town. I explained that our mission was to buy food, and that the Angoni belonged to me.

"I am a brother of the white men," I said, pointing in the direction of Livingstonia.

A dubious pause followed this declaration. There were no signs of a tangible response in the shape of materials for the sustenance of life; while it was clear that our indignant and hostile-looking besiegers, who formed a bristling circle around us, had not the remotest intention of quitting.

Very aggravating moments followed owing to the fear of the Angoni, who, determined not to sit, clustered clannishly together, clinging to their shields, and displaying with dismal choruses the consciousness of guilt.

"Mara," I kept on repeating, "tell them to sit down." As to the effect of my words, I might as well have spoken to a stone, and I felt that from our appearance the people had good reason to be dubious. Conciliation was our only chance, and just as this occurred to my mind another happy thought arose. I determined to be lavishly liberal, for suddenly I remembered that in my small bag was stored two forgotten fathoms of a very pretty striped cloth, similar to that which had thawed more than one hard black heart, —and of which John, on leaving me, had had some for his "leetle wife."

Giving way, perhaps, to a little superstition, no doubt owing to constant contact with witchcraft, I inwardly thought that this was lucky cloth. Without losing a moment I ripped open the old sack, which was smothered in bark lashings that would have almost defied a dexterous tar to disentangle.

A moment later and the heart-healing cloth was the property of our fearful besiegers. Then their suspicions were lulled, and their hostility softened. The hoary-headed old fossils said we were free to pass, and we had besides a good excuse for an abrupt leaving. The men, I said, were hungry, and we would have to go on quickly in the direction of plenty.

No opposition was offered to our departure, so that we moved deliberately away into the welcome shelter of the jungle.

In the course of our advance we passed a number of men busily engaged in making canoes from the trunks of some very large trees which had been felled.

Frequently we lost our way amidst the masses of netted vegetation; particularly in the palm-forest, where the illusory windings of numerous little trails leading to detached villages decoyed us more than once into belts of almost impenetrable jungle, to emerge upon expanses of high green reeds. Trails of this kind seemed to go in every direction excepting the right one. Not one of the party knew the route, for at the last village we had passed the limit of our guide's geographical knowledge of this region.

We soon found ourselves, however, in the southern bight of the lake, a lovely spot where the bank sloped gently to the shingled shore, and the glancing waters gave invitation to an invigorating bath. It was a place upon which nature had bestowed her richest attractions, seemingly on behalf of wayworn travellers, who under the drooping luxuriant trees could find shelter from the garish sun. Butterflies, the most beautiful it has ever been my lot to see, were here fluttering brilliantly in the air.

The plagues, toils, and woes of the previous few days had affected me more ruefully than the worst experiences of any former stage in my travels. The heat had been more oppressive, and had a more exhausting effect than I had as yet suffered from.

Food, of any kind, was extremely bad. We had not been able to procure anything eatable since the previous day, when the rations had been lamentably limited as well as insipid; my share consisting of copious draughts of green tea.

In this torrid zone the Angoni felt the change of temperature sadly, for it made a bad comparison with the high and, so far, healthy lands of the plateaus. Streaming with perspiration they no sooner saw the gleam of the clear water than they instantaneously cast aside their light loads and plunged headlong into its inviting embrace, where they merrily romped like black Tritons glorying in the coolness of the caressing waters.

The arrival at this southern bay had occupied more time than I had calculated upon, so I could not allow much time for sport, and therefore no sooner was the bathing over than we again dived into the jungle thicket. It seemed to me as if we were describing a circle, sometimes falling into indentations like ditches in the broken ground, and filled with high sappy reeds, until after an hour of aimless rambling and scrambling a village was sighted. Here I took the lead, and marching at the head of the line soon reached the centre of the town. Our arrival evidently astonished the people, but they were quite friendly on seeing the white man.

Possibly it was cruel not to have stayed at this village to rest and buy meal for all; but in spite of our starving condition such a delay was undesirable, for the actions of the Angoni could not be depended upon. A few gourds of pombe were bought, after which liquid encouragement we proceeded on our way, and soon turned our backs upon the southern extremity of the lake, so that when the shades of evening were falling we found ourselves entering the village of Mpanga, only five miles south of Livingstonia.

For the first time in the long and toilsome journey my head ached; I felt tired, sick, dead beat in fact. But anxiety had left me, and in its place came the confidence that there were barely two leagues between our party and relief, plenty, and a hearty welcome.

Orders were at once given to Mara to buy all that was wanted, and to give everybody plenty to eat, for I could now afford to dole out the humble remainder of my dry goods wealth.

I then devoted my somewhat jaded energies to securing a little comfort for myself; but found it an unusually difficult task to make much of my bed, an operation which meant the rolling out of my blanket on the hard mud floor under the verandah of a small oblong hut. I do not mention the hard bed as a suffering, for I had slept upon the ground so long that this particular was a matter of indifference. My pillow consisted of jacket and hat rolled together.

Since we had left the last village the sun had seemed to strike home to my brain, and mile after mile I had trudged on with my teeth firmly set, not venturing to sit down, for that would have ended the march, and necessarily I had to get food for the Angoni. I could not conceive what trouble had overtaken me. At first I thought it was the beginning of fever, for there were indications that some poison in my system was now asserting its presence. But I soon came to the conclusion that it could not be fever, for perspiration flowed from every pore, while the most acute pains shot through every fibre of my body.

I had no liquid spirits; but I recollected that in the medicine chest, about as big as an octavo volume, there was a small phial of *sal volatile*. I was at a stage when *eau de Cologne* would have been quaffed with avidity.

When I looked around nobody was awake. The boys had gorged themselves and were lying in heaps, with their senses wandering in dreamland. I was ill, irritable, and cross, and felt as though I must break something; but strength was only in the thought. Mara's head was the nearest object, but any effort upon such a cranium would have proved a failure.

I managed to creep over to where the bundles lay, and ripping up the innumerable bark strappings that wound round the sack, succeeded in bringing to the light of the fire the bottle of *sal volatile*. By the uncertain flicker of the expiring flame I could see the large label marked S.V., but in the bottle there was nothing to back up the printed lie: the stuff had leaked out—every drop of it. Enough! I can say no more of that miserable night.

ARRIVAL AT LIVINGSTONIA.

Although weak and racked with nocturnal tortures, my agonies had vanished in the morning. Overpowering heat, over-fatigue, and bad food had no doubt been the principal cause of the troubles. Starvation and draughts of hot water helped to cure, but made me feel like a "left-off" man.

The walk over the rocky hill that lay between us and the mission-station had no charms for me in such a condition, for the frame revolted at the slightest effort. Seeing a few canoes lying on the beach, I made up my mind to paddle round the point. The bargain was made, and the water bailed out of the diminutive craft—a scooped-out tree in a very leaky condition. The Angoni ranged up the rocky breast of the mountain, while Mara and myself in the primitive "dug-out" with the guns, from which I had never parted, shoved off, and found ourselves floating upon the smooth waters of Nyassa.

As we drew near to the mission-station of Livingstonia, crowds of people—in the midst was a man with a red umbrella—were seen coming down to the beach. The bows of the small canoe glided upon the sands of the long-looked-for shore, and I stepped out with the carefully cherished letter of greeting in my hand.

CHAPTER XXI.

LIVINGSTONIA.

An ill wind again—Desolation—The man with the red umbrella—"All dead; all gone!"—Searching the deserted town—"It was the white man who lied!"—Shattered hopes—A letter to da Costa—Flight of the Angoni—Days of solitude—Mara's pessimism—The races of Nyassa—Fashions—Huts—No tsetse fly—Supplies exhausted—Mara has a full stomach—Teeth filing and tattoo marks—An odd cup of milk—The "look-out" on the lake—Fishes—A sick chief; medicine wanted—Doctoring the invalid—My patient a faithful follower of Livingstone—"All men are liars"—Mara's boon companions—Hard fare—Dysentery—Plucky natives—Stalking a dove—The stomach very near the heart—A sail!—Animal companions—Missionary sacrifice—The spirit of philanthropy—The spirit of the Church—Saddened thoughts—"Mzungo, Mzungo!"—"Steamer ahoy!"—The grasp of a white man's hand.

IT was night, and, in a deep reverie, I sat on a long bench watching an inch of candle burning slowly way. The surroundings were four whitewashed walls heavily draped with cobwebs, for I was in the deserted home of a missionary.

The silent scene formed a striking contrast to my exciting experiences among the savages of Urongwe. But disappointment again.! I seemed to have been smitten by the bitterest blast that could give the lie to the venerable adage "It's an ill wind that blows nobody good."

Again and again I thought of the day's proceedings, and every incident that had occurred was re-enacted in meditation. Above all I remembered the feeling of surprise when walking up the beach followed by a motley crowd of blacks.

I only viewed the cheerless sight of abandoned houses which lined the streets. In a moment all my long-cherished hopes—the hopes that had chiefly cheered me in protracted adversity—that I would be welcomed with the smile of a British face and the warm grasp of a British hand, were dashed to the ground! Every bright anticipation was cruelly obliterated. I had walked along the lonely street looking in vain for the WHITE MAN! Deserted houses appeared on every hand. A few sad-looking tombstones half buried by rank vegetation added to the gloom of the view, the long creepers coiling and drooping to emphasise the sorrow. Nature, mankind's only true friend, never forgets. The vicissitudes I had passed through of late had certainly been many and varied; but this last unlooked-for experience put every former affliction entirely in the shade.

Even the most sombre scenes and the saddest experiences have comical sides, and in this instance I remembered the appearance of the odd creature with the red umbrella. Disappointment had not been wanting in its share of comedy. When I stepped ashore I proceeded with the greatest confidence towards the brilliant umbrella, being fully convinced that it was the grateful shelter of some Christian divine, but on nearing the emblem of civilisation I found a very black and sorrowful-looking individual under the tattered and torn gingham.

This melancholy mortal could speak a few words of broken English, so that when I inquired where the white men were, he had said:

"Veree seek contry. All dead, all gone!"

When I with a slight difficulty explained that I wanted to see one white man, he began to count on his fingers—

"Mees—dead. Mees—dead!" until he had counted seven;

and then he ended up: "All dead. Verce seek contry. No good white man—all die. All gone Bandawe." With this information he pointed across the lake.

The story was sorrowful enough, but still the manner in which it was told was irresistibly droll.

Not for a moment since I put my foot upon the shore had I been idle. I had walked through the station and ransacked every house. Through the kind help of the man with the red umbrella I had burglariously effected an entrance into the well-secured house, which had evidently been used for keeping stores, and on entering had discovered various articles such as anchors, kedges, and chains. Had I been superstitious the emblem of security might have been encouraging. Dust lay thick upon the empty shelves, and substantial cobwebs festooned the dingy ceilings. Boxes piled in the corner told only of the good things they had at some time contained.

Two rewards of my diligent and painstaking search were a small tin of biscuits and about eight yards of strong pink calico.

I had almost forgotten that in the room adjoining that which I occupied, and underneath a rudely-made bier, beside which no doubt many a sorrowful burial-service had been said, I found the small piece of candle which was now flickering its last light as I meditated upon the rough experiences of the day.

When the dim light was totally extinguished my discomfort reached a climax. I felt as though I was sitting in a sepulchre. A yellow flag of sickness or the black flag of death would have represented the situation, which was one of sickness, desertion, desolation, and death.

The Angoni, when they saw that no whites were to be found, said:

"The old men at Pautumbo spoke truth: it was the white man who lied."

Surrounded as they were by their natural enemies it would have been absurd to expect them to stop in this country. They would be sure to desert me. Where was the cloth I had promised them on arrival?

My only hope now was to make for the Shiré river. Difficulties as usual were numerous. How was I to get there? How was I to pay off the Angoni? How was I to pay boys to take me there? How was I to buy food even now?

These were serious questions for me to decide. Above all I thought of my kind friend da Costa, who in all likelihood would have to bear the brunt of the awkward misadventure; for assuredly Chikuse would be told the wildest lies by his disappointed people, whose troubles would magnify during their journey across the great mountains and the wide plains.

It was impossible not to think that my friend would be deeply mortified by the inevitable imposition, for he would be compelled to pay a monstrous indemnity by that sly scoundrel Chikuse. Remembering da Costa's position I determined to pay the Angoni as much as I possibly could, even if I was deprived of the last rag. I had promised to pay them on arrival, so I made up my mind to do so that very night and take the chances of their bolting.

This resolution was soon put into action. Having made a small fire in the centre of the floor, I wrote a few lines upon a sheet of my journal paper telling da Costa of the predicament in which I had been landed; of my having found the nest, while the birds had flown; but I hoped to be able somehow to work my way to the Shiré river; and with that view would try to keep the three Maravi with me. Coins to the natives were worth about as much as porcelain beads, so I wrapped a few sovereigns in my letter to da Costa, begging him to be so good as to pay the Angoni the remainder of the cloth which was justly due to them.

From that eventful night until now I have not heard anything of the result.

A cheerful thought came to my mind. The Angoni might follow me to the eastern shores of the headland to one of the Nyanja villages; now then I might be able to get canoes to proceed down the Shiré! I would try them. It was my only chance.

At the back of the house the scene wore a more lively aspect, for great camp fires were blazing merrily. The Angoni, being very clannish, were crouched over the friendly flames, evidently indulging in a big talk. The Maravi were seated beside them.

Much now depended upon the straightforwardness of Mara, and I called him into the house, where by this time I had the cloth ready torn off in pieces of the required length.

"Os Angoni fugirão!" (the Angoni will run) were his first words.

Explaining the position occupied some time. My guide, philosopher, and friend was in one of his thwarting, antagonistic moods. It would have been beyond the powers of persuasion to induce any of the Angoni to carry a letter; for such a burden would unquestionably be thought a bewitching element of extraordinary power in a mischievous direction. Sufficient indeed to cause the sun to hide its face would be this white leaf from the white-skinned mystery.

The letter was therefore wrapped around the gold, and along with two or three handfuls of rubbish tied up tightly in a piece of blue calico. When this had been done the headman of the Angoni was summoned.

"You see that the white men lived here," I said. "Do the black men live in houses such as these? Stay with me. To-morrow we will go one day to the east, to the villages of the Nyanja people. Then you may leave me."

The cloth, part of what I owed them, was then given. An awkward circumstance was that they would not take the pink calico I found, saying that Chikuse or his son were the only people who could adopt that colour, so I had to sacrifice the remaining yards of blue calico, which was accepted with avidity. Then I repeated that they should wait to take me to the Nyanja villages. The small blue bundle was given to the headman (for I dare not risk their going back without a note to da Costa), with the request that he would deliver it to my brother at Urongwe, when he and his men would be paid the remainder of the cloth that was due to them.

"The white man will have gone," was the quick response.

"No," said I, "he will be there yet for one moon."

So as to avoid the chances of an out-and-out stampede taking place during the night, I decided to have the three Maravi—Mara and his two companions—under my personal charge; so after the conclusion of the various palavers, I shut them into the sombre-looking dwelling along with myself. I dared not sleep before my prisoners had dropped off, so I sat nodding over the fire, and cursing the vexations of the day. The shake of the previous night had left me in rather a weak condition; but my anxiety in case the Maravi effected their escape kept me pretty wakeful. Hours thus passed, during which I continued to sit watching and wondering over the smouldering embers, every dying spark seeming to start a new train of thought in my perplexed mind, until my endurance failed, and I fell into a profound slumber.

> "Night's candles are burnt out, and jocund day
> Stands tiptoe on the misty mountain-tops.
> I must be gone and live, or stay and die."

These lines speak of my feelings when, shortly after the grey dawn, I went out to reconnoitre, and to learn, if possible, whether my plans of pushing on another day's march eastward could be realised.

Where were the Angoni? There were the ashes of the fires of the previous night lying at the back of the house. I looked into the deserted kitchen, which smelt strongly of soot, and looked quite as black. Not a soul was to be seen. My presentiment had not been groundless. The Angoni had fled!

What a lovely dawn smiled upon the earth! I walked down to the water's edge. White-necked fish eagles piping their shrill and wailing notes soared high in the fresh morning air, and perched on the branches of the large baobab, which reared its lofty form close to the deserted house. Male and female cried alternately to each other. Fish-hawks in large numbers were busily at work searching for their morning meal, while clearly and grandly the sun silvered every ripple of the great lake. Around the shore Nature seemed to rejoice with the waking day, giving a glorious welcome to the dazzling orb which brought light and life to the grateful earth.

No matter how bleak, how black, how weary the night may have been, uprising day, graced with a bright unclouded sky, rarely fails to bring to the traveller a little liveliness of hope, along with fresh ideas and new aspirations. Mentally his plans under such conditions are gilded with triumph at their very birth, and he feels inspired with boundless energy of purpose and self-confidence to face emergencies, and overcome every obstacle by which he may be confronted.

To detail how the days following the desertion of the Angoni men were passed would be a tiresome and unprofitable task, for monotony is their chief characteristic in the tables of my memory.

Every morning I walked about with my rifle, wandering alone among the hills and along the shores of the lake, visiting some villages of the Nyanja. From these expeditions I seldom returned until night. One morning, during a ramble of this description, I found a pile of wood stacked close to the water's edge. Two men were close by basking in the burning sunshine, and I persuaded them to come back with me.

Mara then interpreted the intelligence that the wood was sold at intervals to the mission steamer. I had often read of this steamer which was employed to supply the stores of the missionaries, but at that time I could not imagine what she could do in that locality, which was certainly out of her course, while there was no one to supply. The men counted with their fingers, and, as usual, got very much mixed, one holding up the little finger, the other the index finger, while both squabbled violently about some numerical discrepancy that bothered them. All this trouble was in the endeavour to show me how long it had been since the steamer had been at the spot.

"Mentem," said Mara, which meant that they lied, for my man put no faith in the news. He had an awkward habit, too, of instantly and malevolently extinguishing all my fond predictions of good luck. I was getting sick, and Mara was getting fat. We could not agree, and I sometimes even wished that our mental conditions could have a better balance—he receiving some of my hope, and I a little of his doubt.

The races dwelling in the villages on the southern shores of the lake seem to be very confused, for little or no regularity could be noticed in the arrangement of their markings. Some had their bodies striped with scars in long continuous lines in sweeping curves from neck to waist. The faces were covered with cicatrices. Others were seen who had not a square inch left upon their bodies upon which they could show a little extra ingenuity of design, for from head to foot they were covered with a perfect maze of lines and scrolls. Not a few wore ornaments in holes pierced in different parts of the face. The favoured places seemed to be the upper lip and the ears; but sometimes the nose was drilled in one nostril, and a rivet-like ornament placed in it, similar to that worn by coolie women of the East Indies. Upper and lower lips were also pierced.

The women wore a great profusion of beads—blue, pink, and red—linked together until the roll assumed the appearance of a porcelain cable, brilliant with colour. The universal anklets and bracelets of brass, neatly made of wire one-eighth of an inch in thickness, were seen everywhere. Forearms in some cases appeared to be a mass of beads. Some of the people wear square combs of cane and bone studded with black and white beads, and stuck carelessly in their woolly hair.

Fashions in this neighbourhood, I found, were different from those of Angoni-land. In the latter place they had a marked partiality for blue and white calico, also yellow, blue, and green beads; no reds at all. On the contrary, in Nyanja red beads were the treasured gems of the black Venus' jewellery, while calico of every colour was acceptable.

Yellow beads were of little value, and it was of these that I had the best supply.

Huts here are of the wonted circular form. Those seen in Mpanga and close to the mission are an exception, being oblong. The houses of the missionaries had been well built, considering the class of materials that was at hand. Being high and airy, they were doubtless comfortable when inhabited. Their frameworks were of poles and thatch, plastered with red clay. Insides and outsides were white-washed. Roofs were of grass thatch, and mats made from split reeds were tacked up so as to form a clean and tidy ceiling.

No tsetse fly was seen here, but it is more than probable that the deadly insect is as migratory in its habits as the game on whose dung it breeds.

A week had passed since our arrival, and every day I had occupied in fostering plans to effect an escape from the sink of sickness. Numbers of women had visited me so long as I was a novelty. They brought meal and hens, and sat from early morn till dewy eve, in the hope that the mean Mzungo would buy from them or give them something; but the pertinacious beggars, on finding that nothing was to be had, left me undisturbed.

By this time we had reached a close corner in the way of dilemma, for the pedlar's shop was completely run out, excepting about three-quarters of a pound of yellow and blue beads; the former the Ajawa would not look at for a moment.

I thought that possibly there might be another mission station in near proximity, but if there was the natives did not know of it, the only information I could get being that there was one ten days' march down the river. As a matter of course, I knew that they referred to Blantyre in the Shiré river highlands.

The Ajawa, or Nyanja, would not risk their canoes on the Shiré river, owing to a fear of the hippopotamus; and not a man could be enlisted as a carrier or guide without payment in advance.

Amidst all these annoyances a trouble that could not have been unlooked for, but was a crushing addition to my misfortunes, fell upon me. Through the wretched living, I was stricken with dysentery. Owing to this I could no longer support the Maravi. I could not walk as I had been doing, therefore game could not be had, for there was none to be found within easy distance.

With an impressively solemn face Mara would come before me shuffling his feet as he said:—"As fazendas estão acabados! Oh! que faremos agora?" (The goods are done. Oh! what will you do now?) "What will you do?" I would reply, answering his question by asking another.

"Tenho a barriga cheia!" (you see I have a full stomach) he would say, looking down with the liveliest satisfaction upon his distended abdomen; for poor Mara had but one ambition, and that was to increase as far as possible this telltale curve of plenty.

The other two Maravi had by this time taken French leave.

After a conversation of the kind I speak of, Mara would leave me; for evidently he had found snug and hospitable quarters in some of the near villages. In the evening he would return, bringing with him a small calabash of pombe, which he would place before me with a knowing nod, as much as to say drink that and be strong. I can never forget the old fellow's ridiculous stories of how people were fattened. He informed me that once he had a good master on the Zambesi. He had first gone to him very thin and very tired, being exhausted by many days' journey in the heat, with no sustenance; as a matter of fact he had arrived a thorough skeleton. But in only a few days, through the bountiful supply that was given him, he became quite fat, a circumstance which he endeavoured to illustrate by movements of his hands, intended to show the extraordinary proportions he had attained under liberal treatment. All this performance was gone through in the hope that it would act as a tonic for my unfortunate self. What he could have looked like in the days of plenty which he described with so much affection I cannot pretend to imagine; but his picture, as he sat beside me there, might be portrayed most exactly by the use of a pair of compasses, for he was all radiating semi-circles. Mara told me also that he had wives and fields on the Zambesi, and belonged to a good master.

One morning an old Nyanja chief, one of the tallest black men I had seen, visited me. His loins were scantily draped with skins, and he had very few tatoo marks upon his body, although a conspicuous peculiarity was that his upper teeth were neatly filed each in crescent form with the horns downwards. No distinct tribe which I have come across seemed to have a regular mode with regard to teeth-filing except the Mashona. The different tribes necessarily have their distinguishing tribal tatoo marks; but there is no recognised rule in connection with the piercing of holes for studs, ear-rings, lip-rings (ja-ja), &c., or for the filing of the teeth.*

The Banyai tribe, which I encountered on the Zambesi, I have already referred to as having a practice of knocking

---

* All the women I have seen belonging to Msenga on the Zambesi wore the upper lip ring ornament.

out the upper front teeth. That case seems to indicate a tribal mark, not a voluntary act of mature years, but the work of the painstaking parent. Tribes cannot distinguish aliens by the teeth, but by the tatoo marks.

The old Nyanja chief when he visited me was accompanied by a slave-girl, carrying a cup of what was the dirtiest-looking compound that I had ever looked upon. Mara informed me it was milk, and it was accepted, notwithstanding that it looked as if the whole tribe had rinsed their hands in the offensive liquid. Kaffir presents mean nothing but exchange, so in return I handed over some of the yellow beads of which my visitor did not at all approve, and it was useless to tell him that no others could be had.

When I asked him for boys to go to Blantyre, his reply was that for seven fathoms of calico he would show me the way! We could not come to terms, for he was not to be prevailed upon to agree to take payment when the mission was reached.

Ever clinging to the hope that some day my ship would come in, as the saying goes, I had found a convenient open spot high up among the bushes and rocky slabs and boulders that lay close to the back of the village, and that position became my "look-out."

Daily, at all hours, my looks were cast in every direction. I lay under the shade of the trees. Between the hills of loose lying rock and scrub lay stretched the corn patches of the Ajawa, primitive tillers of soil, whom I watched going through their operations of piling and burning heaps of rubbish, wherewith to fertilise the land, and likewise clear it, for seed time was close at hand. Some of the young wives, although weighted with ornaments, were devoid of disfiguring stripes, and even picturesque when negligently adorned with their encumbering decorations; for their heads were like mops of beads, and their brass-clad arms and legs shone brilliantly in the sun. Upon their backs their tiny offspring were spread like toads and tied tightly with a wrap of cloth. The small head was allowed perfect freedom as the mother turned over the earth with her heart-shaped iron hoe, and nod, nod, nod, it went at every stroke, the mouth—wide open like the beak of an expectant young bird—inhaling the fire of a tropical air.

The old women in such circumstances always appear in strong force, and seem to accept the situation as life-long drudges with the utmost equanimity, chattering during their work with all the vigour of the sex.

Occasionally canoes might be seen putting off from the shore to seek the produce of the lake, the fish resembling a perch in shape. From whatever cause, the people appeared to be very lazy fishermen, and were very reluctant to part with the fish they did catch. One day I managed to persuade a little speechless boy that yellow beads were much nicer than fish, and in this way had an opportunity of cooking some by passing a stick through them and holding them over the fire. They are tolerably good but very bony; I may even say delicious but dangerous.

So long as daylight lasted I managed to keep both mind and body active; but the evenings and nights were long, and always brought lowering thoughts of troubles and cares. Often I attempted to write by the light of the moon, but on a particular occasion which is now in my memory, writing was impossible; for the wind blew with great violence from a north-easterly direction, rolling large waves shoreward to break wildly upon the beach, while through the dark gorges of the rock-formed hills it swept along howling and whistling with the anger of a tempest. I lay under the trunk of the big baobab tree, whose creaking boughs intensified the shrill chorus of the storm.

From an excessive heat and brassy skies this change was delightful, and I fairly revelled in its wild enjoyment.

These moments of content were interrupted by the arrival of some young men, who beckoned to me to come to the house. An interpreter was indispensable, and consequently Mara had to be ferreted from his earthly paradise. I fully expected that some important news had come from some unseen and unknown quarter. Such luck, however, was not for me. The messengers were the sons of a chief, who said that their father was dying, and he had sent them to ask the white man for some medicine.

This was a strange mark of confidence; a black man asking a white man for medicine! No thoroughly wild man would ever do such a thing, and so I came to the conclusion that this applicant must at some time have been treated by missionaries.

Judging from the description which his sons gave, I inferred that the old man was suffering from the same complaint as myself. Therefore I went forth equipped with a bottle of chlorodyne, and was guided to the village, which, much to my delight, was close at hand.

I was ushered into a good-sized rectangular hut. At one end a small apartment was partitioned off. Not even the usual fire was burning, and I felt my way as far as the door of the exceedingly dark room, or, to speak more accurately, corner. Fearing that I might plant my foot into the mouth of the suffering chief, I did not proceed any farther. I could not see, but out of the pitchy darkness the dismal groans of the sick one fell upon the ear. How like the Kaffir! Courageous in many things, yet pluck soon deserts him in sickness; it is the only enemy he will not fight.

I took a few handfuls of grass from the roof and put a light to it. Then I administered sixty drops of chlorodyne, and left in order to take the same dose myself.

While walking back I thought—human like—that this doctoring might prove a stroke of good fortune; for if I succeeded in curing the man, the least he could do was to get me boys to take me on.

Little did I imagine at the time that I was doing a service to a man with a history; to one who had faithfully followed the intrepid Livingstone, and had been among his "faithfuls," when his wondering eyes first viewed the new found waters of Nyanja, stretching a hundred leagues away to the north.*

Yes! my patient was no other than Chimlolo, the Makololo chief, who, among other Makololo, was brought to this region by Livingstone in the early days, and placed as chief over the Ajawa and Manganja on the Shiré river. This is the reason that on some maps we find Makololo marked as the names of tribes on the Shiré river.

My remedies worked wonders on the old chief. In a few days he appeared tottering, and in a very weak condition, at the door of my abode, and expressed himself as being very thankful to me for my promptness in supplying him with medicine. He said he had been at the point of death, but I had saved him, and continued to repeat, "You must stay with us."

But I had an eye to business, and lost no time in putting the question of transportation before him, and succeeded in making him promise to find me boys, I only wanted eight, and the payments were to be made on arriving at the station of Blantyre.

* Lake Nyassa is 1,525 feet above the sea-level; is 310 miles in length, and 60 miles in width. At the deepest part a deep-sea lead-line does not touch bottom.

"But you cannot travel until you get better," said the old chief. "The journey from here to the Shiré is far; the sun is hot, and, next moon, it is very bad for the white man. If you go away you must come back and live with us."

Just then Mara came to me with the information that he was afraid his master would be leaving Urongwe, and that he would like to get back to him. Further, he said that the Mzungo (white men) would never come. "All men are liars," was the grand result of Mara's meditations. I told him he might do as he liked, but now I had been promised boys, and I was confident the old chief did not lie.

"Anyhow, Mara," I concluded, "wait and see me start. You will then be able to tell your master that you did not leave me, but that I left you."

The good fortune of falling in so opportunely with Chimlolo might, I anticipated, prove the turning-point of all my troubles; but at the same time it would be madness to forget that a start, with no food beyond the wretched gritty stuff that could be had here, and absolutely nothing to buy provisions on what must of necessity be forced marches, would be to court destruction, considering my weakened condition, and the intensity of the heat. By staying where I was I thought the final collapse would be inevitable. Of the two evils I preferred that which offered a change of life and scene.

I seldom saw Mara and his boon companions now, for they had to look after their own appetites, and the constant carousal of beer-drinking kept them fully up to their ambition with respect to fatness. This beer was so full of husk that I could not, in my condition, drink even a small quantity without feeling excruciating pain. Even when strained through a handkerchief the beverage was far from being beneficial.

DYSENTERY.

In view of a protracted stay, I economised my slender supply of beads, only a few ounces now remaining. No purchases could be made, and I lived on the large fish-eagles, doves, and occasionally a fowl boiled down to rag-soup. One bowl of this per diem was the whole extent of my diet. Short rations, however, were a part of the treatment in my battle against the dysentery.

In the small bag, which contained a stock varying from a lancet to a family of cockroaches which lodged in the crevices and lining, I discovered the remainder of a couple of pounds of sago, which I jealously saved. I had received it from the missionaries at the Tati gold-fields, and they had cautioned me thus: "Never use this until you are sick; you will want it some day."

I hope that if ever any of my benefactors on that occasion should read these lines, they will understand that sometimes the feeling of gratitude may exist in the breast of an exploring white man.

Sixteen days and nights passed away, and no change appeared in the melancholy surroundings, while the combat with wasting sickness still continued, although for the last few days I felt conscious that the enemy was getting the best of the fight.

It had almost overcome the power of will, and the very next day I was to have the boys promised by Chimlolo. In defiance of the ailment I was determined to make a start, knowing full well that change is often the hidden agent that brings back to the enfeebled body the boon of health. I never failed to take my daily exercise; even though it was a struggle, it was a necessary adjunct to any medical treatment, besides being the only way I could get something to make soup.

Seeing me shoot my fishy food was a source of great

amusement to the natives, for to witness anything brought down while on the wing afforded them the greatest gratification, while it also gave them grand opportunities of showing to advantage their aquatic daring and powers of swimming.

Heedless of the constant proximity of enormous crocodiles, frequently floating on the surface of the water, they would swim out a long distance to fetch a wounded bird that I had shot. One of the young lakists could do the hand-over-hand stroke with extraordinary dexterity, making wonderfully rapid progress through the water, worthy of a Johnstone or a Webb.

But now, from a sportsman's point of view, I had come to a very demoralised stage. Having only five cartridges left, necessity compelled that every bullet should have its billet, and bring to the ground a substantial meal. Fearful lest I should miss, I would crawl slowly along the ground, holding my breath, while I anxiously took deliberate aim at a dove sitting. The gap which separates the savage from the civil quickly disappears when an appeal is made by a starving stomach; that sensitive governor of the world:—

"For, says the anatomic art,
The stomach's very near the heart."

How naturally I would be impelled to lapse into the state of the barbarians with long hair, and kill all prey with tooth and nail. One touch of panic—shall I say nature?—and savagery dominates every human breast.

Bang! Down comes the unfortunate feathered emblem of love, which when plucked is no bigger than a duck's egg. With the food the finer feelings come back. All depends on the manner in which necessity is supplied. Surroundings only make a man what he is. From accident comes every good.

By this time it was about as much as I could do to reach the "look-out" high amidst the rocks, from whence could be seen the tops of the houses that formed the village streets peeping up above a maze of faded and sun-parched leaves, and looking like the tops of hayricks.

On every visit to the "look-out" I earnestly scanned with the telescope the north-eastern horizon for the long hoped for sign of smoke. Upon a day that shall not easily be forgotten, I gazed longingly at the far-off stretch of the silent inland sea lying undisturbed by wind-tossed waves. All at once a distant speck attracted my wakeful attention. It was long ere I could distinguish the form of the object, but in time something white struck out from the distant blue. It was a sail! I watched its appearance eagerly as it grew larger and larger, making my heart thump with the thoughts of rescue. For a long time the vessel remained in view, drawing close down upon Elephant Island. Was she making for the bay? No, the breeze soon strikes the white expanded wings: they fill, and she scudded along, borne by the western winds, until she faded into the distant veiling mists and utterly disappeared.

Ah! afar off, on Nyassa's waters, I had seen such sights before, awakening all the bitter grief of falsest hopes; for the vessel proved to be a slave dhow, of which not a few sometimes hove into sight and disappeared.

Monkeys, a numerous family, were my only companions during these long watches in the "look-out." Nimbly they climbed the trees, chattering ceaselessly amongst the leafy branches, and sometimes peeping inquisitively over the tilted slabs of rock to have a glance at the pale intruder. Great fish-eagles, appearing first like minute specks in the distance, would draw nearer and nearer, piping the wild sounds of their strangely weird cries, which found a sad echo amidst the lifeless rocks. With a swoop they would swiftly fly past the "look-out," until their still and outstretched wings could be seen floating daintily downward towards the lake buoyant on the soft langour of the evening breeze.

Often from this favourite retreat I watched the signs of opening and departing day, bathing with varied glories scenes that were lovely beyond description. Now, however, wearied as I was, and too conscious of failing strength, I followed with vacant eyes the decline of the orb of day slowly disappearing over the soundless waters of Nyassa.

> "The whole wide lake in deep repose
> Is hushed, and like a burnished mirror glows."

Returning to the beach at night-time, I threw my miserable body upon a pile of logs, so as to get a last look at the shining lake and the departing sun.

Poets for ages past have sung of thy glories, thou mighty orb! for thou art the life as well as the light of man: but still thou art only a glow-worm in the eternal universe—a thing that wakes and dies!

Slight encouragement could be found in looking at the deserted streets of Livingstonia, which only aroused thoughts of desertion, and of the fruitless labours of the missionary who has sown in barren fields, and even sacrificed his life for his controlling belief. The throbbing noise I could hear was the beating of the batuka, mingled with the shouts of the beer-drinking feast-makers, the sound taking the place of the inviting cadence of the bells of church and school. To me the mission seemed to be a thing of the past.

How strange is the Spirit of Philanthropy! Its failings belong to an oft told story. We continually hear of the sons of the Holy Churches seeking in distant lands the inspiring thoughts which stir their anxious hearts. Setting lucre aside as a mean instrument, how are human lives to be considered—I mean such lives as are laid fearlessly down to give the Bible to the black man?

In thousands of streets and thousands of lanes and alleys in the big cities of England, the desolate, the degraded, the starving, are to be rescued by the million. Do not let me hear people say, "Oh, that is an old story!" It is emphatically a sign of the times. We have half-tilled soil at our own doors, and neglect to cultivate it. Religious labourers of our day are becoming lazy: they do not keep themselves abreast of the age, either in action, in thought, or in sympathy. There is too much shouting about easy charity, and too little heard of the doctrine of self-reliance.

The sadness of the scene at Livingstonia must have a cause. Where was it to be found? Could it be attributed to the empty houses, the desertion or the absence of whites? No! again we must go to the threshold of the unknown, to the great inpenetrable mystery, Death!

> "Life is vainly short,
> A very dream of being; and when death
> Has quenched this finer flame that moves the heart
> Beyond is all oblivion, as waste night
> That knows no following dawn, where we shall be
> As we had never been: the present then is only ours."

Livingstonia had its skeleton in every house. Men had lived there in love, and died in faith. Often, indeed, must the piteous cry have ascended heavenwards: "My God, my God, why hast thou forsaken me?"

Awaking to the realities of my harshly solitary position, I heard the hawk's high call and the strange long notes of the fish-eagle dying upon the wind as they left their watery fields of food, and sought their roosts high in the trees amidst the rocks. The native fishing canoes had been beached. The sound of the drums which had echoed over the still waters gradually lessened and ceased.

A few people passed to and fro over the gravelled paths, the soft tread of their naked feet being scarcely perceptible as they hurried rapidly along; the Ajawa being far from home when he is outside his hut at night. They think that the evil spirits of the departed are out and about seeking for whom they may devour.*

Through the dark veil of night bright Cynthia smiled, and under other circumstances my perceptions of a beautiful scene might have been quickened, even the solitude giving a deeper sympathy with nature.

But how long, how dismal those moments of loneliness seemed! The feelings they aroused are utterly beyond description, even were description of any use; for no one can appreciate the despondency of a man being thrown entirely upon himself, except those who have been similarly placed.

The wind that nightly whistled through the stunted boughs of the baobab died with the sinking sun, and anon the atmosphere became gloomy with gathering mists which masked the stars, leaving the still scene in a darkness as black as the pall of death. Nothing could be heard but the murmuring wash of the restless waves beating and playing upon the shore.

Retiring from the scene I was soon wrapped in the folds of the familiar plaid, and being exhausted in mind and body, unconsciousness was soon upon me.

Rattle, rattle! went the clattering window-frames. "Good heavens, how it blows! No rest for the weary in this

* The Ajawa believe in the existence of all manner of hidden influences wishing to eat their dead.

unfortunate place!" The disturbance occurred in the middle of the night, and half awakened me. I tried to sleep, but the noise was repeated louder than before, and I was now startled by an accompaniment of excited human voices.

"Mzungo! Mzungo!" was shouted vigorously, and the sound was not noise, but music to my ears.

"White men!" I shouted, as I sprung from the blanket as quickly as could be done at a fire alarm, and actually leaped through the window; failing energies being braced to a wonderful extent by the suddenness of the incredible news.

Getting to the outside, I heard the story. It appeared that Mara and two others were coming back late from a pombe feast, and were now before me declaring that they saw a light far out on the lake. They said "it was the white men's light."

As fast as I could I ran along the beach, and sure enough in the pitchy gloom soon distinguished a dot of faint light twinkling in the distance over the waters. It did not take long to set fire to heaps of the dry grass which lay along the verge of the beach, and soon a blazing bonfire was sending its ruddy rays far across the darkness of the slumbering lake. My sensations as I watched the shifting light are now an indescribable memory.

Joyful indeed it was to see the bows of a small steamer emerging slowly and cautiously from the gloom. Even at this moment of happy expectation doubts arose. Perhaps she had only come for anchorage, and might leave ere daylight; so, with all the energy I could muster for a last effort, I shouted "Steamer ahoy!"

The vessel crept slowly up until she was within gunshot of the shore, and by the gleam of the fires which the boys were keeping up upon the sands I could see plainly a good-sized steam launch riding upon the waves.

Two men put off in a small boat. How strange a meeting! In black midnight, with its darkness made more apparent through our rude grass fire, I as in a happy dream suddenly clasped the hands of white brothers as they stepped upon the shores of Livingstonia Bay! Both were thunderstruck at finding me, and many were the questions they asked as to where I had come from, where was my party (!), and what I was trying to do.

MIDNIGHT RESCUE ON THE LAKE.

CHAPTER XXII.

ON LAKE AND RIVER.

Farewell to Livingstonia—On board the *Ilala*—Lieutenant Giraud and the rescuing party—Mara's good-bye—An enticing supper—A hunter shot dead—Eaten by a crocodile—Slave dhows—Routes of slave caravans—Danger of releasing slaves—The road to Tanganyika—Origin of the Makololo war—A tragedy of the Shiré river—The banks of the Upper Shiré—Bird life—Crocodiles and hippos—Matope—Abundance of game—An animated scene—Canoe upset by a hippo—Carriers from Blantyre—Revived strength and hope—Cure for dysentery—Blantyre—The trading station—Comfort at last—Routes to Quillimane—Scarcity of food—Leopard attacks on goats—Death of Captain Foote—The employment of a consul at Blantyre—A bootless expedition—Makoka—Katungas—The significance of *Ilala* and *Blantyre*—Livingstone's tomb in Westminster Abbey—A request for black overalls—A troublesome chief—The incorrigible Fred—Bargaining for a lion's skull!—Superstition at Katungas—Ula and Muave—Muave drinking—Ordeals of guilt—Hunting superstitions—Marriage and other domestic customs.

THE morning of our departure from the tranquil bay of Livingstonia was beautiful; but I had no feeling of regret as I looked back upon the vanishing scene, although it was kept in view until the deserted mission station was lost in the distance. Gradually the horizon widened as we steamed into the open of the lake, the smoke of the steamer rolling in black volumes from the funnel, and contrasting strangely with the streaks of fleecy clouds sailing slowly across the high heavens. The pulse of the tiny engines throbbed a hundred and one to the minute as the little *Ilala* boldly breasted the billows on the broad bosom of Nyassa.*

* The *Ilala* is a small steamer belonging to the African Lakes Company. She supplied the missionaries at Bandawe, on the lake.

A buoyancy of exhilaration was felt during this progress, which put into the shade the happinesses of years. The refreshing kiss of the soft breezes which swept over the big water was not only soothing, but strangely delightful.

I had every reason to be contented with my new surroundings, and especially with my rescuers and companions, who one and all did everything they could to make me comfortable. Ceremony was absent here, for in such wild surroundings men soon fall back into the natural state and learn each other's ways.

The rescuing party included Lieutenant Giraud, the intrepid French traveller who had been in command of an expedition sent out by his Government with a view to explore the little known regions surrounding Lake Bangweolo. Lieutenant Giraud's expedition was successfully accomplished; but through intimidation by Arabs his Wangwana followers, from Zanzibar, had, with the exception of six who remained faithful, deserted him on the shores of Lake Tanganyika, carrying off his guns and stores. Procuring assistance at the Belgian station, under M. Storms (whom I have seen mentioned in English newspapers as the Emperor of Tanganyika!) Lieutenant Giraud made his way to Karonga, at the north end of Nyassa, where he had embarked on board of the *Ilala*.

The other members of the party were the captain, who was a German named Fredericks (since dead through climatic effects), and the engineer, Mr. W. Harkess, a Scot, to whom I am indebted for many favours and not a little information.

They had put into Livingstonia Bay owing to their running short of wood, hence my never-to-be-forgotten stroke of good fortune.

I must not omit to say a word about Mara, who had

bidden me "Adeus!" with much fuss, shuffling of feet and clapping of hands, his face all the while being as round and radiant as the full moon. Sincere satisfaction fills my breast when I look back upon the turn of fortune which enabled me to send him and his comrades with lighter hearts and heavier loads back towards Urongwe, bearing also the news to da Costa that I had at last been

LIEUTENANT V. GIRAUD.

taken away by the white men of the lake. Mara would be in a position to tell the true story of my experiences; of the misadventure with the Angoni and the long delay.

Just as we were embarking in the small boat, an odd occurrence had taken place, several boys running down to the beach to tell us that a number of Angoni had been seen in the village without their shields, pretending that their mission was to sell some chickens; but it is beyond doubt that they were spies sent by Chikuse, to see what I was about. The suspicious mind of the king would be soothed when he heard positively of the final departure of the white mystery.

All's well that ends well! Now it seemed that progress would be all downhill or down-stream.

The steamer could not take us very far on account of the cataracts separating the Upper from the Lower Shiré. As we proceeded the wind freshened until it was blowing half a gale, compelling us to run for shelter in the lee of the land, where, just before night time, the little vessel was anchored in a snug bay close to a mountain that had a history.

Riding at anchor that night the small craft tugged and jerked as though she would part her cable. The cabin, a sort of deck shed at the stern, was a tight fit for four; the berths on each side being occupied by Fredericks and Harkess, while M. Giraud and myself made our beds as comfortable as possible on the benches beside the small table. Right in front of the cabin door was the engine and boiler, the fore part of the launch being used for cargo, such as ivory, of which there was a fair quantity. Lying like logs upon the deck were Giraud's six Wangwana, or Zanzibar men, and three black sailors.

There was an unwonted attractiveness inside the cabin, for supper was ready, and the warm light of the oil-lamp swinging from the ceiling gave the little snuggery an air of comfort, and even luxuriousness. Tin cups, brimming with hot tea, steamed up, perfuming the atmosphere with a welcome aroma that told of plenty, while the pile of bread and the pot of Moir's jam gave the rude table quite a homelike appearance; to my long unaccustomed eyes the turn-out seemed a veritable feast. Bodily ailments, however, precluded me from sharing in the good things; so I looked on and listened to the story of the mountain which reared its form above the bay where we had found shelter from the violence of the storm.

Like most African tales in which Englishmen are concerned, it was not without its load of disaster and its dead man. On the cone-shaped mountain, covered with loose broken slabs of rock and wild scrub bushes, an Englishman while hunting baboons wounded one, and coming to close quarters struck out at it with the butt of his gun, experiencing the inevitable result, of course: the gun went off, and he fell dead upon the spot.

One story led to another, and so on, in the usual way; but while listening, I suddenly remembered that on leaving the Diamond Fields in South Africa, a young man ran up to the stage, and said to me—

"Should you ever meet any one named B—— in your travels, remember me in speaking to him. He is a great friend."

I asked Harkess if he had heard of such a man.

"Oh!" was the answer, "poor B—— was eaten by a crocodile not long ago, while bathing in a river near the north end of the lake. He was with Captain P——, the elephant hunter; but before assistance could be given, the monster had carried him to the middle of the water, all the time holding him up to the view of his horrified friends. Then the brute dived under the water with his prey, and nothing more was seen."

Inquiring about the white sails which now and again at Livingstonia gave me so many false hopes when they hove into view in the horizon, I was told that in all probability they belonged to large dhows sailing between Makinjira's and Mpemba's for war purposes. On getting this piece of news I had little difficulty in coming to a conclusion as to why the Angoni would not take me to Mpemba's village, which in my ignorance I was endeavouring to get at, with a view to canoeing to Livingstonia.*

The greatest slave ferryman, I was told, was Jumbe, at Kota-Kota, who builds large dhows for this special traffic, the sails being made of American sheeting, which is a strong kind of calico sold by Arab slavers. Jumbe's vessels take their human cargoes to Lozewa on the eastern shores of the lake; whence they go directly eastward to the coast. Most of the slaves from Mpemba's, however, passed round the southern end of the lake to Mponda's on the Shiré, which they cross, and go straight to Matakas, a notorious slaving centre, about a day's march to the north-east. The Universities Mission once had a station here; but through the ill-timed zeal of an Englishman, who released a caravan of Mataka's slaves near the sea coast, that chief retaliated by robbing the station while the missionary fled to Zanzibar.

"This," continued my informant, " is one of the dangers of thoughtlessly releasing slaves. By so doing, we are apt to harm others of our own race, for the natives look upon all white men as belonging to one tribe."

Further, I learned that the work on the carrier's road which was being cut between Lake Nyassa and Lake Tanganyika had been delayed on account of the death of Mr. Stewart, the engineer. Mr. McEwan,† a young and ener-

---

* Recently I have learned that the forces of Makinjira and Mpemba actually met in deadly conflict, Mpemba being killed. Makinjira dying soon afterwards, the oracles and witches of Mpemba say that his death occurred because he had killed their chief.

† Since dead.

getic man, had just gone up to continue the work; but it seems that the part of the road which is cleared one year, is overgrown during the next through the strength of vegetable life, while it is notorious that if the work is continued with the same disastrous results as heretofore the whole route may become a cemetery, rivalling the railroad across the Isthmus of Panama, in which every sleeper represents a sacrificed life.

Part of the gossip of the lake was that a mechanical engineer* was then busily engaged in putting together a steamer intended to run in connection with the missions at Tanganyika.

The much spoken of Makololo war was also a subject of conversation, and the reader will remember how the rumour echoed in our ears all the way through Angoni-land to the lake. It appeared that an English ivory hunter named Fenwick had fallen out with a chief called Chiputula on the Lower Shiré. During the heat of the quarrel the chief was killed, and then the people rose *en masse* and killed the white man.

The steamer which ran between the missions on the lower portion of the Shiré (between the Zambesi and a village called Katunga, near Blantyre) was sunk by the enraged subjects of Chiputula, the cargo being stolen. The last news was that the steamer had been raised, and was then supposed to be undergoing repairs. No further intelligence could be expected until we reached the mission station in the hills. These mishaps on the Lower Shiré had caused very hard times, especially by making provisions scarce on the lake.

My long lost twenty-four hours were now put right. A careful perusal of the journal showed that the unrecorded

* Since dead.

day was that on which we had made the start with the Unyamwenda from the borders of Mashona-land in June, 1884.

Before dawn the wind had fallen, and the little craft was soon under weigh, pitching full speed ahead as she was steered straight towards the narrow gates of the lake. On each side the land converged as we neared the southern outlet; gradually a current was perceptible, becoming swifter and stronger, until, with a rush, we darted through the high reed-walled portals of Nyassa, and the great lake was left to the north. Two hours later Lake Pamalombe, girt with tall and trembling reeds of a deep green hue, is passed, and we enter upon the waters of the Upper Shiré.

As we glide quickly and swiftly past the river's banks, the grass tops of numerous village huts are seen; and twice the white-robed robbers of liberty could be distinguished standing in groups with their numerous followers, their garb of purity glaring in the sunlight. Speedily, however, the scene of slavery was left behind, passing away like a moving panorama, as we went on to the land of unenslaved and wildest freedom.

Wonderful were the new scenes which surrounded us as we entered these regions of teeming life, in which both air and water were animated. As the steamer ran rapidly along, panting and coughing forth volumes of spark-charged smoke, out from the silent and seemingly lifeless trees came immense flocks of waterfowl—divers and ducks, spoonbills, kingfishers, fish-hawks, and open-bills; black ibis, too, filled the air, uttering their vociferous screams of protest as they flew away in every direction, dazzling the eyes with their rich purple-green plumage, flashing in the mellow light of the evening.

Less pleasant to look upon were the amphibious and

creeping things, which were sadly disturbed by our progress. Numbers of crocodiles could be seen on every hand, with waddling steps hurrying their loathsome bodies from jungle and from mud-bank, to slide into the darksome deep.

The ponderous hippo with his great yawning cavern-like mouth was seen in herds, all in sportive mood, gambolling, gaping, and grunting among the waters. Some of these monsters would wait until the bow of the launch was within a few feet of their broad-beamed heads, and then, with an angry snort, would plunge away from their too formidable rival, to writhe and roll with leviathan lunge, and double on the stream.

All day long we had lived in the hope that by sunset we would reach Matope; but at various portions of the way the water had been so shallow—owing to the gradual silting up of the river—that we had frequently been bumping bottom, and so ran the danger of unshipping the rudder, or, worse still, driving a hole in the hull. These contingencies had necessitated a reduction of speed, so that ere long the stars were seen shining brightly above the line of trees which studded the river's edge. The lively *Ilala*, however, was well handled by Fredericks and Harkess, and cautiously groped her way along in the dark. Another four miles was over, and then the launch was safely moored close to the bank at Matope.

No time was lost in despatching native carriers with letters to Blantyre, about thirty-six miles distant. M. Giraud and myself in the meantime amused ourselves by hunting during the early hours of the morning; usually starting about daybreak and returning before noon, when the heat became excessive, and the task of writing up journals was thought more conducive to comfort than wading in long prickly grass and jungle. Abundance of game could be found on both sides of the river, but more particularly on the west side, where it swarmed in great variety. Never, on even a single occasion, did we return home without bagging.

Early one morning as I walked up the right bank of the river, I saw a most marvellous sight upon an open flat which verged the banks, and was studded here and there by a few stray bushes and dwarfed trees. The situation commanded a full view of a big bend in a broad part of the stream.

Animal life seemed to fill the water, the land, and the air. Feathered flocks were indescribably numerous. Crocodiles and storks mingled together in blissful enjoyment like the members of one family, in fearless intercourse. Hippos were out in full force, some being partially immersed, whilst others showed only a part of their ugly heads above the water. On the brink of the bank was a herd of bush pig; further inland towards the centre of the flat were reed-buck and impala, while close to the borders of the forest was a large herd of buffaloes and nearly a score of zebras.

Buffaloes were rather hard to stalk, the young forest of thin-stemmed trees affording very poor shelter. However, on that day a zebra and a boar fell to my rifle. When walking home I came to within fifty yards of a small herd of water buck, but they behaved so well that there would have been no more pleasure in shooting them than in shooting tame cattle in an English park.

At the side of the river an ancient hippo came within easy range, and as these animals are always fair game I sent a three-ounce ball crashing through his tough old head. *Apropos* of these most formidable creatures (formidable when in the water only) some gentlemen from the mission were once crossing this part of the river when a sportive hippo elevated the boat, party and all, into the air, consigning the occupants to the tender mercies of the water; the ducking being nothing compared with the horrible thought of falling a prey to the devouring crocodile. All had a most miraculous escape as they succeeded in scrambling to the shore. The valuables as a matter of course were utterly lost.

The hippos have been very destructive to the mosquito fleet of the missionaries, some of the best boats being sent to the bottom.

Coming back from the morning hunt I found that Giraud had reached the launch before me, having killed two reed-bucks and one impala antelope. Upon that and succeeding days there was great feasting for the villagers of Matope.

On approaching the village I perceived a large number of blacks assembled on the banks, each with a cloth around the waist; quite a civilised lot of men, I thought, as I remembered how long it was since I had been in such decorous company. They were the carriers from Blantyre.

Mr. Harkess handed me a small bundle of letters which had been sent on by some ever mindful friends to the care of the missionaries at Blantyre, who doubtless wondered from what direction the mysterious man was to appear. Friendship's missives are always welcome wherever we may be, but how thoroughly they are appreciated when they happen to be the first we have received after a long and enforced silence!

In this instance the only letter that could be of any interest to the reader was that of Mr. Moir, Manager of the African Lakes Company, which briefly stated that we would be welcomed at Mandala (Blantyre), and that a number of carriers had been sent to fetch our luggage. Mr. Moir added that our mode of reaching the coast would be a subject for our own decision; because the steamer *Lady Nyassa*, of the lower river, was high and dry undergoing repairs. The latest accounts told of war upon the river; but Mr. Moir said we might be assured he would give us every assistance in his power.

At Matope a number of new cases lay on the river bank. They contained the outfit of Mr. Harris* of the London Missionary Society, a young clergyman who was bound for Lake Tanganyika.

By this time it was evident that under present circumstances there would be some trouble in reaching the coast. M. Giraud and myself had common interests; both of us had been deserted, and both were anxious to reach the coast. In my new found friend I could see many manly traits of character, and his whole demeanour was such as to encourage the forging of a link of good fellowship. We agreed to remain shoulder to shoulder and together find our way to the sea, a compact which I never had any cause to regret. Future progress I then thought would be child's play compared with the weary past.

With the change from solitude to companionship, from despair to hope, and from starvation to plenty, all doubt and all anxiety fled from my mind. This sudden revolution had been productive of good results: the dysentery had disappeared and the appetite had returned, so that I again felt quite fit for the road.

For the benefit of those whom it may interest I may as well state the cure, which was given me by M. Giraud, who had himself suffered during the early stages of his long journey. The remedy consisted of one ounce of sulphate of soda taken in doses of one ounce to begin with, and

* Since dead.

diminishing daily, the accompanying diet being rice-water only—the rice boiled out, strained, and allowed to cool. The treatment was a speedy remedy in my case.

The time soon came when we had to say good-bye to Harkess, Fredericks, and the crew of the lively little *Ilala*. For my part, memory of the first sight of the welcome craft coming through the gloom of the dark night on Lake Nyassa, and of the first meeting of those we were now about to leave, impressed me deeply, indescribably I may even say, as I remembered especially the kindness of their relief and care.

Two days after the departure of Harkess and Fredericks, my friend and myself, severely tattered in apparel and tarnished in general appearance, through constant exposure, but nevertheless in capital health and spirits, marched with cheerful steps at the head of a long black caravan. The men were laden with ivory and horns; also spears and baskets of native make. The white sweeping curves of the tusks which crowned the heads of the Yao porters, whose loins were decked with folds of white calico, gave a curiously picturesque appearance to the chainlike column, as it entered the long gravelled street of Mandala, where the slight stream of sparkling water played, and an avenue of the eucalyptus waved gently in the morning wind. The leaves danced beneath our feet, and borne by the breeze floated upward as we stopped to salute the British flag flying proudly over the mission station in the highlands of Blantyre.

Passing down the street we saw that the ground was enriched by fragrant flowers, in lovely bloom, which wreathed the heart-shaped borders of the nursery beds, whose smiling verdure and radiant tints contrasted pleasantly with the bright red brick houses that lined the street.

Still further we descended, sheltered by the cool foliage of red and blue gums. On our right a field of young coffee trees, ranged in lines, was budding and bursting into blossom, shaking from their pearl-like petals the silver dew-drops of early day.

We crossed the Mudi mountain torrent, hidden beneath dark evergreen leaves of giant fig-trees (*Mkuyu*), and thus passed from Christianity to Commerce, the creek dividing the mission station from the quarters of the African Lakes Company consisting of the store and the manager's house.

Ascending the steep hill leading to the trading station we passed the gateway in the loopholed stockade of Mlomba trees, covered with creepers of impenetrable thorn, and arrived at the porch of the spacious dwelling of the white chief Mandala, the name given by the natives to Mr. John Moir, the company's manager.

Descriptions of Blantyre and its surroundings have been printed so often that it is quite unnecessary for me to add to those which have already appeared. I must confine my words to a narration of our travels onward to the sea.

Mr. and Mrs. Moir gave us a very hearty welcome, and we soon found enchantment in the civilised surroundings of our comfortable quarters. The sight of jugs and basins, iron bedsteads with neat brass knobs, sheets, towels, and looking-glass, with a Bible lying upon a prettily covered table, awoke both in Giraud and myself long dormant thoughts. Perhaps they were something like those of Devilshoof, in the Opera of *The Bohemian Girl*, who lights his pipe with leaves of books and starts aghast when he looks in the truthful mirror which reflects "himself as others see him," an uncouth weather-stained individual with dishevelled hair, who tries the springs of cushioned mattresses for their virtue as springs, and not as downy protectors of sparsely fleshed bones.

That we enjoyed the change goes without saying. We endeavoured to occupy as much of the commodious beds as we possibly could, stretching a toe to each foot-post while with our hands we clasped the cold iron, right and left. Had our hair been cut, the touch of civilisation might have been complete.

Mr. Moir explained the facts about the two possible routes to the sea which were open to us. First, the river was in a very disturbed condition, on account of a war which was being waged between the Mazinjiri and the Portuguese army from the Zambesi. As far as they—the people of Blantyre—were concerned, the difficulty that had existed between them and the so-called Makololo on account of the chief Chiputulu having been killed by Fenwick (an incident already referred to), which was followed by the sinking of the small steamer belonging to the mission, all the trouble had been hushed. The steamer had been raised and was then undergoing repairs, but it would be some time before she would be in a fit condition to depart for the Zambesi.

The other route was an almost direct line from Blantyre overland to Quillimane, a good march of fifteen days.

Mr. Moir could not advise us to go by the Shiré river, a journey which at that time promised nothing but uncertainty, that is to say, insecurity of life and property.

M. Giraud and myself took a very short time to consider the matter, the result being the conclusion that we had had enough of tramping, and therefore preferred life in a "dugout," with the chances of safely running the gauntlet of any hostilities on the river. At any rate, it could not be much worse than weary walking to the coast through excessive heat and rain, although the land route certainly gave better prospects of security.

The burning questions of the hour were: Could canoes be got from the chief Katunga? Would it be possible to procure men to go with us in defiance of the wild reports which were daily arriving from the lower regions of the river?

Even had we chosen the landward route, some time would elapse before we could bring together a sufficient number of carriers for the purpose of transit.

With all its mysteries the river seemed to suit us best; our hearts were bent towards having flowing water all the way to the sea, and no more long, dreary, and nagging marches.

Our kind host Mr. Moir very considerately gave us the benefit of his knowledge and experience of the natives. He departed for Katunga's with a view to negotiate for men to accompany us.

The few days which we had here were occupied in making cartridges, in writing up journals, and in reading back numbers of newspapers. M. Giraud's Wangwana boys were occupied in polishing everything that could be polished by sand and water, even to the extent of scrubbing the browning off the rifles, until they shone like rods of burnished steel. Fortunately they had not unearthed mine.

While in Angoni-land I had often wondered where the detachments of slaves had come from, which were seen passing in and out of the villages. Little by little I began to understand that during my sojourn, or rather journeying in Chikuse's country, his men—the Angoni—were away gathering their human harvest on the Shiré river. The Ajawa and Manganja people, who knew of the white chief Mandala, had fled from their much dreaded foes, crowding towards the Blantyre highlands. All who could sought security within the thorny bulwarks which surrounded Mandala's home.

Provisions were scarce, for in their hurried flight from the sweeping onslaught of the Angoni few had been able to collect sufficient sustenance to tide over the slaving storm; consequently the influx of so large a community had drawn heavily upon the resources of Blantyre; so much so that when we were there a chicken was very difficult to obtain, and what with calls for flour and rice from the missionaries on the lake, and the war on the lower river cutting off regular communication, the inhabitants of Blantyre had good cause to complain. Food and other necessary supplies were obviously scarce, and were diminishing every day.

Another cause of want was the wholesale slaughter committed in the vicinity by leopards, who reduced to a serious extent the slight herd of goats. A few nights before our arrival twelve had been killed; and as we walked out one morning we saw a number of goats lying in Mr. Moir's yard, close to the house, all dead; being killed so deftly by the long fangs piercing each side of the throat, that not a drop of blood could be seen, or the slightest sign of mangling. Most extraordinary of all was that in these midnight ravages by the leopards, goats and sheep that were killed lay close together, showing that no attempt at a stampede had been made.

We heard of the sad death of Captain Foote, who had recently come out to act as consul, but succumbed shortly after his arrival. Mrs. Foote and her children were still there. The vice-consul, named Goodrich, also Dr. and Mrs. Scott, and other members of the Free Church of Scotland Mission, extended to us every office of hospitality and kindness.

To find out why a consul is planted at Blantyre would be as big a puzzle as any I know of. Without the pleasure of hard labour being attached, the man is much to be pitied who receives this appointment as plenipotential exile. The appearance of a British representative where he is almost powerless to act is rather farcical. He is reduced to the position of a Kaffir policeman, without having even the pleasure of using his club. Unquestionably he is invested with sufficient powers to advise corporal punishment on a few thieving natives, but the active exercise of administration is even denied him, and given to a subordinate, so as to avoid a breach of consular etiquette. The ways of the Government are wise, and who shall know them? Posts of this kind are not absolutely useless, but do not let us send good men to them; they would be excellent sinecures for political nuisances, demagogic windbags, and others.

No matter how agreeable may be the luxuries of a home, I invariably feel, after protracted experience of open-air life, a feeling of suffocation on my return to domesticity. Two nights of civilisation sufficed to make me restless, so promising M. Giraud that I would return in three days, I set out with four boys, bound for the Upper Shiré and the game country.

The distance to be covered before we could reach the hunting-ground was too great for the time at our disposal. We covered about seventy miles of ground, and only had the satisfaction of smelling the menagerie. I saw lots of buffalo spoor, but never discharged my rifle—not once. I simply got rid of a lot of bottled energy that it would have been much better to have reserved for more exacting days to come, as we went on in our descent towards the sea. My excuse for introducing this is to show how difficult a matter it is to suddenly become quite tame after a long spell of acting the wild man.

Simultaneously with my return from this bootless expedition, Mr. Moir arrived with the report that he had been successful in procuring a very fine canoe from a chief Malalima, above Katunga's. He also had the promise of men, who were to be ready to start within two days; but on account of warlike rumours it was very difficult to get them to agree to go down water.

Disturbance seemed to be rife on all hands. Intelligence was brought in by some men who had come from a village beside the Shiré rapids, that a Portuguese trader had been robbed of a hundred guns and a quantity of ivory.

In the afternoon a number of the wives and daughters used to congregate about the corners of the house, listening as Mr. Moir impressively read a chapter from the Bible in their own tongue. After the reading was finished, the happy and heedless creatures would break up and scamper away, laughing and rollicking, being apparently highly delighted with what they had heard. One Ajawa with whom I spoke told me that they all liked to hear Mandala's stories.

Early rains had set in, and some heavy showers had fallen over the mountain regions.

At length the time of departure came, and the morning was grey and dull; the mists that at first hung in white columns through the forest soon changing to rain, under which we continued to press on our slippery way, passing a few Yao villages nestling in the heart of the forest, some of them resembling small hayricks tilted sideways by the strength of the storm. Between them shallow courses of water rushed along, heaping small piles of corn-stalks and rubbish at every rock and stump. A few solitary goats, standing with their tails turned to the storm, and keeping closely under the lee of huts, completed the dripping rural picture.

Having heard that one of his employés at Katunga's had fallen sick, Mr. Moir had started on the previous night. On reaching Makoka, about twenty-five miles from Blantyre, we thought we had had enough of it for one day; so we made an attempt to be comfortable, the time being 11 P.M.

Mr. Moir arrived with his "sick man," and after a short stay proceeded homeward, the weather having cleared.

Ten o'clock on the following day saw us at Katunga's, on the Lower Shiré, where we intended to embark on our southward voyage.

The view from the brow of the hill before the descent was commenced was very extensive. The azure outlines of the distant mountains which form the natural walls of the great Shiré valley were seen dim in the distance, resembling the clouds of a lowering sky. Forests stretched afar upon the broad flats which flanked the river, giving them a mantle of the deepest green. In the centre, deviating in unequal curves, like a retreating serpent of silver and blue, the widespread forest scene receded, until its beauties were lost in the soft southern sky.

No one in Blantyre advised us to attempt the river route in consequence of the numerous reports of dangers and disturbances. With not a little diversion we heard the utterance of various opinions respecting the probability of our being able to procure canoes. Even if we succeeded in overcoming this difficulty, much doubt was expressed as to whether we would be successful in reaching the Zambesi. The general impression seemed to be that we would reappear in Blantyre; the next entry, however, being from the south instead of the north.

The mission station had been reached and left behind. Singularly enough I was not, at the time, curious with regard to the meaning of the names *Ilala* (the name of the rescuing steamer) and Blantyre, the excitement of the surroundings possibly distracting my attention. Since those stirring days, however, and with very different thoughts, it was my lot to saunter quietly through the solemn and storied aisles of Westminster Abbey, gazing upon the tombs of the mighty departed. One especially attracted my attention. At my feet I saw the life-kindling words which told that David Livingstone was born at Blantyre, Lanarkshire, Scotland, and died at Ilala, Central Africa.

Strange feelings thrilled my heart when I read the simple inscription; and, as if through the touch of a magician's wand, distant but never-to-be-forgotten scenes flitted rapidly across my mental view. In an instant I was in far-off Africa. The word *Ilala* was burning through the deepening mists of retrospect. Every incident of that dark and dreary night, illumined by the recollection of rescue, arose before me as I stood over the grave of the departed hero.

There, in vision, were the silent sombre rocks, the baobab-tree, and Livingstonias' deserted street, all shrouded in the blackness of night! Methought I once more listened to a music which even excelled the rapturous richness of cathedral harmonies: it was the joyous shouts of boys, the throb of the *Ilala's* restless engine echoing through the gloom of the great lake, the whispered sound of voices speaking from the darkness—the voices of friends at last!—and the sighing song of the waves that gleamed red in the light of our beacon fires!

Then came to my mind the rescue: and the grasp of the sympathetic hands of men, of white men long isolated like myself from intercourse with country and kindred. Last of all I thought of the tranquil days in the African highland home, and I blessed Blantyre, and passed with a grateful heart from the honoured tomb of its founder.

But I am anticipating. We are yet far up the Shiré river, in the midst of difficulties of which many will have to be overcome ere we again feel the pulse of civilisation.

A glance at the long and narrow canoe floating close under the bank of the river, and almost covered with the bending reeds, was sufficient to show that her carrying capacity was very inadequate. Six men, at least, would be required to propel her, and the narrowness of the craft gave her a very cranky appearance. She was far from being a Clasper. M. Giraud's fancy evidently lay in the direction of a bigger but somewhat old and waterlogged boat which was moored close by.

Inquiring of Mr. Morrison, the engineer in charge of the repairs on the steamer *Lady Nyassa*, regarding the men who had been promised, he gave us the information that there was some doubt whether the chief Malalima would allow the canoe to start. The said chief had now made an imperative demand for a suit of black overalls; being in all likelihood under the impression that black clothes had something to do with missionary medicine. Surely a suit of this description was bound to become a fetish of marvellous efficacy when it graced the body of an expert!

Where could we get a black suit? The arrangement made by Mr. Moir with the chief was that each man was to receive eight *fathoms* of calico, but by some oversight only eight *yards* per head had been sent. Black men are in no way different from white men in the counting of payment or of change; which as a matter of course, in this instance, fell short of the mark. Malalima at once protested that the white man wanted to cheat and not to pay what had been promised. Mishaps of this description are always very unfortunate with Kaffirs, who in the circumstances cannot think of anything short of premeditated imposition.

Now we swore at the delay; not at the Kaffir. Negotiations had to be begun anew. The messages from the chief became more and more unsatisfactory, the latest being that unless all the calico he demanded, over and above that which he had already received, was handed over along with a suit of black clothes, he would immediately send back the canoe!

Not another canoe could be had; so we were forced to accede to every request. Bargaining and bartering about men took up a long time; but at length the canoe, with a crew of six of the Manganja tribe, was ready for the voyage. On loading up we found that our doubts as to the smallness of the craft were well founded. At the same time we were perfectly confident that any further delay might give a chance for the suspicious chief to harden his heart again, so there was nothing for it but to bail out the old waterlogged boat, and man her with Giraud's Wangwana boys. I did not like the look of the old coffin, but we had resolved upon making a start against all hazards.

At this point the incorrigible Fred must be introduced to my friends. Joseph would have been a more appropriate christening for him, if such matters went by appearance, for truly his robe was one of many colours. A small straw hat covered his head, the woolly hair being decorated by the insertion of a small comb jewelled with beads. Reserved and silent in disposition, Fred was nevertheless sharp, shrewd, and intelligent. A thoroughbred Ajawa, he had been under Christian instruction since he was, so to speak, a green sapling, his yearnings all lay towards the fetish of his fathers, and he wished to live in the land where they had lived and died. We see in Fred's case the force of fate. Many years ago he had been a thing of trade, to be bought and sold. But while a slave caravan to which he belonged was wending its way to the east coast, Livingstone crossed its track. A stampede at once took place. Some ran in one direction, and some in another. Fred was among the fortunate few who by fear fell into the white man's hands, and was thus snatched from the yoke and chain misery of his unfortunate brothers and sisters.

Mr. Moir advised that Fred with his knowledge of the river and the language should accompany me in the leading canoe, should it be found necessary to take two. M. Giraud he thought should keep out of sight as much as possible, because his dark complexion might lead to his being mistaken by the Mazinjiri for an enemy in disguise. So far as my knowledge of the Portuguese language went, it might be of signal service; while my general appearance in no way resembled that of a son of Portugal.

A quiet stroll about the outskirts of Katunga's in the evening was most refreshing, particularly when the burning heat of day had passed. Surmounting a pole in the main pathway leading into the village was the large skull of a male lion.

"That skull must go to England!" said I. "It must have a history."

Chief Katunga was away; but in his absence I worked diligently upon the elastic conscience of his sub; who told me that the lion had killed two men close to the town, and near the spot where its naked skull was now posted, as a sign and a warning to its kind.

Offering cloth for the trophy, I held the coveted and alluring sheet stretched between each hand so temptingly that an Oxford Street draper would have had no chance. Inch by inch I kept on increasing the quantity, remarking all the while upon my exceeding liberality and the enormous price he was demanding. Slowly the conscience and expression relaxed and expanded. Away went the cloth, while I collared the skull and hid it immediately, guessing from hard-earned experience the character of the seller; and rightly too, for sure enough there he stood, long after dark, close to the place where I had lain to snatch forty winks of sleep, protesting impetuously that he had received too little. Prepared to give in eventually, I commenced a long palaver with the man.

He said he did not know what the chief would say on his return, for it was "Katunga who placed the skull on the pole." Dubious to the last, the man paid me two other visits, receiving cloth upon both occasions; the result being that the lion's skull is now in London, its fleshless jaws clasping the chronometer which went with me through so many dark and hidden ways.

Relating this curious story of the skull-crowned pole at Katunga affords an opportunity of illustrating vividly the superstitious natures of the Ajawa and Manganja races, especially their extraordinary convictions with regard to witchcraft.

The people at Katunga's supposed that before the lion could have acquired a taste for human flesh it must have been bewitched by some one in the village. Suspicion is soon fixed in such cases, therefore two men were accused immediately. The Singanga, or witch doctors, were called in to perform their functions as mediums of second sight. *Ula* is the name bestowed upon the ceremony gone through by the witch doctors in their efforts to detect guilt. Metaphorically it may be termed a bridge between the known and the unknown; a jury elect whose truth is beyond human doubt.

The essentials of *Ula* consist of a mixture of Hecate-like quality, including strips of leather, small sticks and stones, bones, and bits of tortoise-shell. This assortment is thrown upon the ground, just as dice is thrown upon a table. In the special trial of which I am speaking, the witch doctors—Singanga—betook themselves to the mountains, and cast the fateful dice, changing ground three times, to places at distant intervals. Ultimately *Ula* returned a verdict of guilty against both defendants.

The chief and the headman were then advised as to the result, and gave judgment that the fetish *muave* should be imbibed by both. *Muave* is the name of a poisonous concoction administered to those who are supposed by the witch doctors to be guilty of witchcraft, theft, murder, or any other crime common to frail humanity.

All the inhabitants of Katunga's village assembled to witness the oft-repeated ceremony. To prepare the fetish fluid the witch doctors took up their position in the centre of the throng. As they pounded to dust the roots and herbs, they continued to mutter—

"Muave tell the truth. If these men have done wrong, kill them; if not, make them vomit."

The men drank from the cup of mystery, of relief or death; and then walked rapidly to and fro, until the perspiration profusely ran from every pore. Writhing spasms followed, and then they disgorged the fetish muave. This acquitted them before the supreme court, and they were borne away triumphantly by their friends. An equivalent for our process of false imprisonment followed, in the form of a claim for damages being advanced by the brothers of the accused against the accusers; the case being ultimately settled by the cession of a number of male and female slaves.

A few nights afterwards the lion again approached, but was soon pierced with the spears of the infuriated villagers, who now clearly saw that muave had spoken the truth. The lion had been bewitched by some one else. Muave never lied. Thus accident supported superstition.

All the tribes which I came across in the basin of the Zambesi, north and south, have the same ceremony with regard to muave drinking and its assumed detection of guilt. Death among them does not appear to be considered as a natural event, but is due to the subtle influence of an enemy. The so-called brothers, or next of kin, are invariably the principals, who jealously watch the encroachments of strangers upon the rights of their family. When a man dies, he is left untouched in his hut until his brothers come to bury him. No one else dares to approach the body, which sometimes lies until decomposition sets in, after which the people throw the house down over the remains. I particularly noticed this among the Mtande people in the Zambesi valley.

Death may be accounted for in various ways. For example, the infidelity of a wife may be declared a cause. Should the accusation be proved, a payment in slaves is taken from the brothers of the faithless one.

Another instance may be selected for illustration. In the event of a number of people dying in a kraal, and there happens to be a Methuselah among the residents, the unfortunate veteran is immediately accused of having caused the death of some one. The Ajawa boy who told me of this remarked that the brothers of the deceased go to the chief, and say:

"This man eats the dead at night. He must drink muave."

First, however, they may give an initial test to the truth of the accusation by administering muave to a pair of fowls; if they die, the man is beyond doubt guilty. There is no appeal.

Friends may at once offer to pay the number of slaves required; but in such cases often may be found the fearless trust in the infallibility of the muave, for the accused, almost on every occasion, will affirm his consciousness of innocence, and that he knows he will vomit muave. In the event of his actually feeling the sting of guilt, he may go and eat his best goat or sheep, believing implicitly that on the following day muave will kill him.

The ordeal is watched by suspicious enemies and anxious friends. The victim quaffs the mystic potion, and is immediately writhing in agony at the feet of the "doctors," until, in a last spasm of excruciating torment, he springs upward and falls to the earth dead.

Kinsmen and friends then run from the corpse, leaving it to callous enemies, who rush on, shouting aloud, "He killed our brother," while they belabour the inanimate body with sticks and clubs. Then the darkness of suspicion vanishes for a time, the sorcerer being dead. A day of festivity dawns, and pombe is prepared in honour of the occasion. The brothers of the dead evil-doer must pay in slaves, and if they have not a sufficient number they must themselves forfeit their freedom, and so ends the double tragedy of every death.

Superstitions extend to every branch of work, and to every event, whether it is in love or in war, in hunting, in travelling, in accidents, sickness, or death. Good or bad luck rules everything.

If any of them begins a journey, and a snake happens to cross the track in front, the traveller will immediately retrace his steps, and a case of inquiry is commenced.

If they are hunting, and a buffalo runs after one of the party, he will go home and begin an investigation, in order to find out who has been speaking evil of him, or what his wife has been about.

If they should be elephant hunting, and the beasts all hold their trunks upwards, the hunters will not shoot. Provided the trunks are hanging, all is peace, so they may blaze away.

If any of the hunting party is chased a formidable palaver takes place, and in the event of the fugitive having been killed, a still bigger talk is the result, the termination of the affair usually being another death.

Of marriage customs I heard very little. A man wishing to marry must ask the brothers of the girl; the father has no voice in such matters. The young aspirant woos from a distance, and will not approach close to the hut in which his sweetheart resides. He stands in the open, and the lady comes forth from the hut, looks at him, and at once makes up her mind, "I will have him," or "I will not have him."

Should this brief love affair be satisfactorily settled, the young couple spend a honeymoon of three days in a hut by themselves, after which the husband builds a hut. Much pombe is made, and the marriage ceremony is cemented by the brothers on both sides, who hold the sole right to consent and fault-finding.

The Ajawa custom at childbirth is that the expectant mother betakes herself to the woods, where a temporary shelter is erected. Should the child come into the world with an ugly face, seeming to resemble a monkey, my

Ajawa informant said that the mother hides it away, or, in truer words, she kills it. On the other hand, if it be fair to her eyes, she takes it to the hut of a friend, where she remains for ten days, before returning to her own hut.

Should the infant die during that period, suspicion arises, not regarding the death of the little one, but with regard to the conduct of the father. The friends and relatives of the wife set about examining the past life of the husband, and the nature of the company he has been keeping. Any discovery of an act of infidelity subjects him to a fine of a fixed number of slaves, which must be paid to his wife. Provided he has no slaves, he will have to draw from his brothers and sisters, so as to satisfy the demand. The death of the woman at childbirth, followed by a discovery of infidelity on the part of the husband, subjects him to heavier penalties, and may possibly cost him his freedom.

If a man travels, leaving his wife pregnant, wherever he goes he must never sit upon any mat excepting his own; his actions, it is supposed, influencing the expected child. While the husband is absent the wives dare not shave their heads or go to dances. Their occupations during his absence must be confined to the garden until his return, when they may shave and anoint the head with grease.

On the arrival of the man, if he has been untrue, he will stand far off, and say to his head wife—

"I cannot look upon your face."

After this declaration he must not go into his house until the doctor has given medicine to him and his wives. A chief who hears that one of his wives is with child to some one other than himself, forces her to point to the culprit, who is immediately killed.

Where there is a plurality of wives, it is customary for the husband to live for three days with one wife, and three with another, and so throughout the lot. This custom prevails among the tribes on the plateau of Angoni-land.

The Ajawa women do the decorating and tattooing. The women do all the work of cultivation, the men helping only if they choose to do so, giving so many days' help to each wife. Quantities of pombe are prepared if more aid is required, and men are then invited to come and assist in the field, work being concluded by a surfeit of the favourite beverage.

The Ajawa man has complete power over his wife, even to the most extreme limits. They are unlike the Manganja in this respect, the latter being a very jealous race.

CHAPTER XXIII.

DESCENDING THE SHIRÉ RIVER.

An erratic boat—Mbewe—Chiputula's burial services—The home of the deceased chief—Xopeta people—A rollicking uproar—The *Leviathan*—Canoeing more tiring than walking—Collecting palm wine—Among the water-buck — A good bag — Glad reception — Wet and fever — Approaching the seat of war—Separation of the canoes—Elephant spoor—Enormous ant heaps—Recoil and a tumble—Exciting hunt—The bull charges—Bearing down upon us—A good hollow bullet this time—Hippo attacks—Dangerous moments—Narrow escape of the *Leviathan*—Our new pilot—A welcome supper—News of the death of a chief's wife—Even mourning has a comical side—Ivory laws—Chiroma, Chiputula's town—The story of his quarrel with Fenwick and the tragedy of Chiromo—The sinking of the *Lady Nyassa*—A too well educated savage—Ransom for the steamer—Palm shelters on the *Leviathan*—Scenery on the river—A marvellous scene of the feathered world.

WHILE floating down upon the waters of the Shiré river I looked back and saw in the distance the old water-logged boat which M. Giraud had selected for himself and his men. The crew were evidently struggling to prevent their craft from being playful in her tendency to waltz in the middle of the stream. To keep her nose steadily down to work seemed to be an impossibility. Laden down to the gunwale, she looked in the distance like a small raft, on which the erect Wangwana, robed in blue and white, worked strenuously with long bamboo, like the veriest tyros in the art of propulsion.

Once upon a time the boat had oars, but they had gone

the way of all things useful—lost when wanted. A man fell overboard when the boat was close beside us.

Opposite the village of Mbewe, belonging to a son of the defunct Chiputula, were a number of small canoes. We resolved to land and make overtures to the young chief for the hire of one of them, as a substitute for the awkward boat. At this village we found a Mr. Miller, an employé of the African Lakes Company, who wished to go to the Zambesi, so that it was arranged he should accompany us.

A talk, too tedious to repeat, was entered into with the young chief, the end being that we were permitted the use of a canoe and of such men as we wanted upon payment of a large quantity of calico.

The time of our arrival at Mbewe was momentous; for it occurred during the final heat of the beer-drinking in connection with the conclusion of Chiputula's burial services. All the familiar forms of festivity were to be observed on this occasion.

Evening fell quickly upon us, for time had been well occupied. The edifice in which the departed chief's remains lay was certainly unusually large for a Kaffir's house. Chiputula's royal house, now his mausoleum, was an oblong building, the walls being constructed with poles from thirty-five to forty feet in height. In the grass roof at each end of the ridge pole were stuck small white flags. All his other houses had been dismantled. Nothing save the bare poles which supported the roof remained.

For three days large quantities of pombè in gourds had been carried into the house, and during that time the people abstained from tasting, in order that the spirit of the dead chief should be appeased by a copious regalement of the beverage which to the Kaffir is sometimes the only thing that makes life worth living.

Supper over and we walked through the town. While we were partaking of food we were robbed of several small articles; my hat, which lay close beside me, being among the other appropriations. A very inconvenient loss it was, too; and I never recovered it. This I may say was the first time I had to suffer from deliberate pilfering during the whole journey. Cynical people may say that we were dangerously near the white settlers' stations. Thieves are said to abound in such vicinities, and at Blantyre I heard they were as rife as rats.

Mbewe teemed with human life. Immense fires were encompassed by groups of merry mourners, the lively tongues of flame frolicking as if full of the spirit of the convivialities of the wake. A wild dance was proceeding, and sounds of jubilant song rose from the curious assemblage. The dance differed from all those I had seen in the earlier stages of travel.

We pushed and jostled our way through the swarm of mingled tribes, consisting of representatives of many ages and classes, brought together, as I have said before, by the distributing influence of slavery and internecine war; the result being often attributable to the exchanges between one chief and another. A young girl, for example, may be exchanged for a certain amount of ivory, which in turn is bought by Arabs.

Conspicuous among the crowd were the Xopeta. They were headed by six drummers, one after the other, winding like the figure 8, all the while singing in stentorian tones the wild chants of their race, accompanied by violent beating upon the drums which hung in front of their bodies, being suspended from the neck.*

The Manganja had hollow calabashes, in which small

---

* Those were the only people I saw who carried drums in this fashion.

stones rattled as they shook them with might and main. The Ajawa wore rattles on their legs, and clustered together they vigorously shook castanets of fruit-shells and stones.

Every one joined in the rollicking uproar, and threw off superfluous energy in song and dance. Joy was not the cause, but custom. Upon that night the whole town was in grand confusion; in a state of noisy and wild but harmless disturbance.

Nine o'clock had passed on the following morning before we were fairly off. Giraud and myself each had a canoe. Mine was so cranky that Miller had to go with Giraud, who now had a craft with greater beam. My vessel was singularly picturesque in appearance, being manned by a line of black men, who stood erect, each holding a bamboo of about fourteen feet in length.

Poling was the only method of propulsion, and when the crew would all punt at once, each alternate man swaying right and left as he bent his body to the task, the sight was peculiarly novel and striking.

The craft which I had was quite the leviathan of the Shiré, and so I will term it in this narrative. A small weather-worn Union Jack which had been borrowed at Blantyre waved from a somewhat slender staff, and with my battery of rifles, and Fred, wearing the coat of many colours, as flag-captain, I felt as proud of my command as I could have done in charge of a wooden-wall seventy-four in the days of old.

A small sunshade made of palm leaves formed my protection, and was set well forward, so as to leave room for working the poles further aft. Sitting in a cramped posture under this shade soon proved to be pretty stiff trouble, and as a rule I preferred to stand up in the sun, although its scorching heat was most trying. It was quite a relief when the day's journey was over, and we moored the canoes for the night.

M. Giraud and I both found the inaction of canoeing more trying to the system than marching. My head felt as if it would fall to pieces.

The men were all anxious to get some meat, saying that the poling was hard work; and as I was equally anxious to have a good shaking, during a doubtful two hours of evening light, I shouldered C.L.K., and calling upon Fred and a stranger, who said there were elephants hard by, away we went, sanguine hopes giving lightness to our steps. The elephants, we anticipated, would be found feeding near the great palm forests, which only lessened far away at the foot of the rough grey mountains.

"Shall we get to the palms at sundown, Fred?" I enquired.

"No," he replied; "the men say the elephants were on this side, but I see some people coming, so we will ask them."

Soon a number of natives came up, carrying pitchers of palm wine, off which the frothy foam was falling like soap lather to the ground. The people had been collecting the wine in the forest, and they reported a small herd of elephants, which, however, were at too great a distance to be reached that evening. A more encouraging piece of information which they gave was that a large troupe of water-buck (*Cobus Elipsiprymnus*) would be found close to the river.

Experience had given me many lessons regarding the marvels to be worked with meat, and as we had to start early, I resolved to put my best foot forward in the effort to make a big bag.

The grass had been partially burnt off the ground, and

the stiff coarse stalks which spiked upwards gave not a little pain to bare legs, even worse than wearing a kilt in a thorn thicket. On such occasions moments of excitement or anxiety make one indifferent to trivial torments.

We soon discovered the herd we were in search of, and a splendid lot they were, standing beside some dwarfed trees. They too had discovered our approach, and begun to move off at a slow canter. Being well warmed by the walk I felt myself to be as fleet as a greyhound, and testing the litheness of my limbs, was soon within range.

The first shot brought down a fine bull with a capital head, after which the fun was fairly afloat, the herd bounding off at ever increasing speed, pausing now and then to have a look at their pursuer. Advancing rapidly, I brought down a cow with two shots, after which they fell one by one to my pet rifle, until breathless and dead-beat I was distanced and gave up the chase.

There could be no cause for dissatisfaction with regard to the result. Five antelopes had fallen, the last two being badly wounded. The natives had followed the fourth and found him at some distance away. The three that I had killed at first, when fresh in pursuit, were quite close together.

The woods were obscured by the darkness of night when we were hurrying back, but in due time we were cheered by the sight of the camp fires' gleams. I shall not attempt to describe the delight of the Manganja people, who had heard the firing and had started out in the direction from which the reports had proceeded. As they met us on our return their joy knew no bounds. Jumping up they shook my hands with lively energy, all the time looking as though they had the immediate prospect of an earthly paradise.

Throughout the whole night the people made trips to

and fro between the canoe and the scene of the evening's successful hunt, returning laden with meat, which was stowed away in every available corner of the *Leviathan*.

The huts on shore were infested with bugs, so that we got little or no sleep. Rain came down in torrents, and prevented a movement to the open air. Sleeping in the open is always preferable, but at the same time it must not be forgotten that, no matter what may be the inconveniences under shelter, it is better to put up with them than to get wet: for fever is very prevalent upon the river, and deadly as well.

The very earliest gleam of eastern grey betokening the advent of morn was a signal for departure; for good headway would have to be made ere the parching day began.

Seeing that the river coursed in many crooked channels, and delay was occasioned by the numerous sandbanks, M. Giraud and myself agreed to proceed independently. We would try to get on as best we could, each regardless of the other. Should the different currents separate us, we would in any case make for the junction of the Ruo river that night. The seat of the Mazinjiri and Portuguese war, which we had heard so much about, would not be reached until we had passed that point, therefore sailing in consort was unnecessary. All the country on both sides, from Mbewe to the Ruo river, had been claimed by the defunct Chiputula.

A hard day's work was before the crew, but when braced by the coolness of the early morning, the atmosphere being moist through the midnight showers, they worked with right good will, so that the *Leviathan* sped swiftly past the reed-covered banks. The canoe over which the French flag floated was caught in a different current, and off she went as if darting through a trap-door in the solid bank. Giraud waved his hand, and in an instant was lost to sight.

Hours of hard work passed. We were constantly going aground and wading.

Suddenly it occurred to me that I had had nothing to eat since the previous night's supper.

"I say, Fred, where's that loaf that got all the flour we had before leaving Katunga?"

"Oh, that bread was lost. De boy bake it ter much; fire was ter strong, I tink. Other canoe has got all de grub!"

"Hillo! What's that bank all broken down there? It looks like elephant spoor."

"It is elephant spoor," said Fred; "and fresh too, I tink."

"Hold on, boys! This mustn't be passed."

Just as Fred and myself took up the spoor, I observed a strange black following.

"Who is that man, Fred?"

"He came with us from Mbewe. The young chief sent him : I tink to watch the master when he hear him speak about elephants."

The width of the tracks clearly indicated that a large herd had been drinking in the morning. The spoor led us through what is known as the great elephant marshes. At that time, just before the heavy rains, the grass was high, with belts of fierce spear cane interspersed, its far expanded surface being withered with the blaze of many hundreds of flaming suns, such as that which then flashed its strength upon us, and occasioned the atmosphere of frightful heat over the baked earth where rents and gaping cracks, like the hardened lips of an earthquake's fracture, abounded.

The soles of my shoes, which were like polished pebble, got no hold on the dry and slippery grass. Between the sliding and the earth-cracks pedestrianism was excessively hard work.

Ant heaps were numerous, the wide-spreading plain being dotted with their pyramid forms, some being twelve feet high. For a hunter they are unsurpassed as spying stations. Ascending one of the heaps, we distinguished a monster troupe of elephants, larger than any I had seen, for it must have numbered at least a hundred.

The wind, being shifty and light, was bad for stalking. We were almost blinded by the glare, but waded along sturdily until we were close up to the herd. The grass was so high at this point that, for the matter of outlook, we might as well have been in a thick bush.

However, I could just discern the tops of the heads of the immense beasts, and, listening, I could hear the tramp of their huge feet clipping the grass like a sickle. Now and again a cough, or mayhap a low bugle note, would come from some tough old trumpet as the herd swept irresistibly and majestically along. Those were exciting moments. The keenest eye and steadiest nerves were necessary.

Beckoning to Fred—who did not seem to relish the position very much—to be ready with the second gun, I seized the eight-bore, a good opportunity having occurred, for the grass was somewhat shorter, and at no distance off two fine bulls were moving along. With the object of seeing more distinctly, and yet knowing well what the result would be, I drew my feet together.

A flash, a crash, and away went three ounces of lead to lodge in the massive body of the nearest bull, whilst I fell violently to the ground in the opposite direction. Immediately regaining my feet, I discharged the other barrel in elephant number two, an ancient and splendid tusker of gigantic proportions.

ON THE GREAT ELEPHANT MARSHES, SHIRÉ VALLEY.

Down I went again, having been standing on tiptoe. The kick of the rifle was not heavy when an ordinary position was possible; but at that time it could only be compared to a stiff match with the gloves against some adept in the noble art. The second recoil resulted in a cut cheek and a black eye.

Both the bulls, however, fell when I fell. The rest of the herd with uplifted trunks broke away in all directions. The wind being weak they were uncertain which course to strike, which doubled our by no means improbable chance of being run over. As usual the empty cases stuck in the big gun, and for the life of me I could not extract more than one of them, although in less time than it takes to write this both the bulls were again on their legs, trumpeting wildly as they broke impetuously through the high grass. I managed to replace one cartridge, and after a hot chase succeeded in finishing off elephant number one.

At the sound of the rifle's report, number two—the biggest bull, and badly wounded—instantly wheeled and faced me, his trumpet tones shrieking in the air, while his ears, spread out in anger, flapped like a foresail in a shifting wind. The formidable beast was in the act of charging, and a thrill went through my nerves when I felt how weak I was without the big gun. Not a moment was to be lost, so I fired both barrels of C.L.K. right into his temple, which made him shake his old grey head and, with piercing screams, beat a rapid retreat towards the gloomy shades of the great palms.

"Confound those cartridges!"

"Look out!" shouted Fred at the top notes of his voice, "dere is elephants coming."

I had nothing but C.L.K., and sure enough a number of

cows were seen advancing with thundering strides, until I thought they were on the top of us.

"Look out! look out!" was the warning which again and again came from Fred's lusty lungs.

A rapid glance towards the right gave the alarming view of a grey mass of heads breaking through the high grass, and bearing down upon us like a cohort in mad alarm. Expecting to turn their course, I yelled as loudly as possible, and when they came within a few yards was relieved to see them swerve to one side and sweep past.

Not caring to lose another chance, I tried C.L.K. again. Knowing the lightness of my bullets I aimed for the ear shot, and let fly right and left, bringing down, wonderful to say, a fine cow stone dead with the first shot, and the bullets half-hollowed!

Sport on many occasions was utterly spoiled by the sticking of the empty cases; but the disappointment in this case was excessively annoying, for the lost bull was the finest African elephant I had seen. The tusks appeared to be very long.

"Master can't get to Chiromo on the Ruo river to-night. It is very far," quoth Fred.

"We must, Fred; for I promised M. Giraud I would be there to-night."

The hottest hour of the day was upon us, and we were at least two miles from the canoe. I had no fear of the Manganja people, who had shown much appreciation of my efforts on their behalf during the previous night. A little cloth to each would urge them to do wonders. But not a moment was to be lost. Hurrying on under indescribable heat we reached the river, with our bodies bathed in perspiration.

All plans were matured by this time. The Manganja people worked well. By four o'clock in the afternoon the tusks and trunk of the elephant were on board the *Leviathan*, and we were again skimming down in the run of the silver stream.

The day's adventures, however, were not yet over. We found the hippos in a defiant and daring humour. Passing through herd after herd, some of the monsters would rise half out of the water close to us, and facing the canoe would plunge as though bent upon swimming under the fragile craft. Right and left, front and rear, the threatening animals surged and dived.

All at once a crashing noise was heard among the reeds which fringed the river's banks, past which we were slowly gliding.

I heard Fred shouting: "Shoot, master, shoot!" and at the same moment there came plunging with furious force, from amidst the yielding dark green walls, one of the biggest of the mighty monsters of the river.

The boys braced their long bamboos simultaneously to stop our "way," but the depth of water defeated their efforts. As I fired, the hippo nearly struck the bow. Then quick as lightning he dived, the canoe passing over him, so that for a moment I felt as though we were passing over a torpedo. Little more than a second elapsed before he was up again, this time alongside, erecting his ugly head high out of the water.

Another shot, with better direction than the first, was followed by a tremendous splashing of water, which frothed and seethed as though it was in a boiling cauldron, and amidst the trembling confusion we saw the last of the formidable brute.

This herd consisted of about ten hippos, all playing and

romping in blissful contentment whilst this exciting bother was in progress.

The incident was nearly the cause of the total wreck of the *Leviathan*; for during the strenuous endeavours of the boys to stop her, the stern swung out, and now the canoe lay athwart the stream, a most unmanageable position, considering her great length.

Down we went. The poles could find no bottom. A promontory jutted out from the bank in front, forming the whirl of a strong eddy, the two currents flowing in opposing directions with equal velocity.

"Thunder and lightning, Fred! This will break us up."

The backwater, running like a mill race, caught the *Leviathan's* nose, while the strong central current swept her stern in the opposite direction. Round she spun like a top, and came into violent collision with the abutting bank, which met her like the ram of an ironclad. The cranky craft struck with a heavy thud, and heeled over, threatening to discharge both crew and cargo without further ceremony. We clung to the long reeds which inclined invitingly towards our eager hands, and managed to get a hold just in time to prevent a repetition of the pirouette movement, and the certainty of the craft going to the bottom.

Considerable delay resulted from this unforeseen mischance. Water, which had been shipped, had to be bailed, and the saturated cargo righted. As soon as this was over we shoved off once more, rejoicing at the two very narrow escapes we had had within a few minutes.

Towards evening the hippos became more playful, being about to enter their feeding grounds. They appeared on every hand, and we no sooner passed one herd of eight or ten than we ran into another, while difficulties and dilemmas were increased by the fall of darkness, the moun-

RUNNING THE GAUNTLET.

tains in the far west helping to shut out the light. Laying to the south-east was the village of Chiromo, where M. Giraud and I had arranged to meet.

Pitchy darkness was the chief characteristic of the night, rendered more gloomy by occasional thunder showers coming down heavily, and increasing discomforts that were already bad enough. Not a dry rag nor a dry stick could now be found in the canoe.

We were quite lost in the misleading currents, which threw us carelessly from one sand bank to another, until at last we grounded hard upon a hidden reef, and there firmly stuck. Busy boys were at once at work endeavouring to launch the old log again, when we heard a splash in the water as of something passing down in the safety of the deep current.

Could it be Giraud in the other canoe? We shouted, and needle-like from the gloom shot a tiny dug-out, propelled by a solitary Manganja, who in answer to our inquiries said that he had not seen the other large canoe. He agreed to pilot us, and at the close of that stage of the journey the troubles and vicissitudes of the day were over; the relief excusing a general sigh of satisfaction as we walked along the village street, Chiromo on the Ruo river.

The day had been weary through incessant work. Not a morsel of food had been touched for four-and-twenty hours. We found the other canoe moored at the bank.

"Ah!" exclaimed Giraud, "you have arrived at last: we have been waiting here and wondering what had become of you."

"I heard a good deal of firing after you left in the morning," I remarked.

"Yes," was the reply; "we were among hippos, and succeeded in killing an old bull. It was hot work; but we landed him. He had fine tusks. We bagged a monster crocodile too."

Exchanging stories of our hunting experiences, we sat down to supper, which had been receiving the attention of the Wangwana people for about a couple of hours. The viands were served in tin plates, placed on a split reed mat. Absolute silence ensued. Considering our protracted fast we were to be pardoned for devoting assiduous attention to the repast, and while I was engrossed with the attractions of the feast my small tea kettle was appropriated by some appreciative native.

By this time we had come to the conclusion that there was nothing like travelling quickly through this country; that is to say if we meant to reach the coast with some clothes on our backs. Already my hat was adorning some invisible descendant of Shem or Ham.

Revenons à nos moutons. The first course at the feast (chicken with *fillet d'éléphant*, the latter remarkable through its ashes, not its bread-crumbs) was hardly over when a man rushed through the cane-walled enclosure, as though he had just made a final spurt for a "best on record." He breathlessly inquired for the headman of the kraal.

The first thoughts we had were of stirring news from the front. We must make the messenger a captive after he has told his exciting story to the enduna.

Fred, however, immediately enlightened us regarding the real cause of the man's abrupt appearance. He was not a courier from the fighting front, but a simple messenger from the village of Mbewe, through which we had passed, charged with the news of the demise of one of the wives of the old enduna. The deceased had lived at the village; and not only had she been a stranger to the enduna for a considerable period, but had also been dead for some time, having been shot by some jealous and illegal lover.

Noting the results of the melancholy intelligence upon the bereaved one, we had a fresh example of the different modes of· showing sorrow. The aged enduna took little time to fuss himself into a state of confusion, if not of grief, as he ran in and out of the huts of his various wives, uttering plaintive cries. Then seizing his antiquated flint-lock, without ceasing to wail, he ran outside, loading and firing shot after shot into the air; his wives aiding him powerfully in the howling and crying. The sight was delightfully funny; for the old man's attire was far from being of a character to inspire solemnity or command veneration, consisting of a variegated cloth shirt which reached to his loins, his legs being wholly bare, while his feet were encased in a bright pair of English slippers (once perhaps the property of some luxurious traveller) tied with two thongs of bark: on his head was a very diminutive straw hat, bound with red and white calico.

The hypocritical old buffer kept us awake, until the early hours were doubling, by his efforts to make all believe in his great sorrow for the loss of a wife, or, correctly interpreted, the disappearance of a valuable lump of living property.

All next day was spent in attempting to dry the contents of the canoes, and in palavering with the headmen about the precious ivory I had shot, some having to be returned; because since the death of Chiputula some white man had killed an elephant on the river bank and given one tusk to the son, who it is supposed will succeed the father, although an older chief—Kasisé, or Ramakukan—has more power.

This concession created a precedent, and the young chief —an exceedingly insignificant-looking man—now claims half the ivory, or, as he puts it, "all the tusks that touch the ground." Had the chief himself been on the spot I might have arranged the matter of payment for the ivory; but under the odd conditions I preferred to leave the question to the kind offices of Mr. Moir, to whom I wrote, asking the favour that he would send to Mbewe and try to procure the tusks.

All the war news we heard could easily be boiled down to the bare statement that the Portuguese were victorious; some big chiefs had been captured, and the routed Mazinjiri were flying before the conquerors.

We were now in the town where the tragedy between white and black had occurred. I walked through all the old pole-walled buildings of the dead chief Chiputula, which without exception bore evidences of his emulative spirit and taste in house-building, a feature that was manifested on a very grand and lofty scale, considering the place and people. Remains of his spacious windowless buildings were as numerous in this neighbourhood as they were at Mbewe, where he was buried. Inhabitants of the district say that the height of Chiputula's ambition was to live in a large house like the white chief Mandala—namely, Mr. Moir.

Numbers of the slain chief's young wives were to be seen about the town, and, being in mourning, they allowed their hair to grow and become matted. Upon the whole they seemed cheerful enough in spite of their bereavement, for they were awaiting the day when they would be distributed among the friends of the new ruler, Kasisó, or Ramakukan, the old chief whose possessions lay higher up the river. He had the power to give or take these young women, whose heads would be shaved ere the new honeymoon began.

Unlike the other edifices, the house in which the chief had fallen was not dismantled; but it was closed, the door being barricaded with poles.

I heard many versions of the death story; but few kind words, or even the benefit of a doubt, were expressed with regard to Mr. Fenwick. The old adage, *De mortuis nil nisi bonum,* was a blank in that quarter.

The most comprehensible story ran thus. Chiputula had commissioned Fenwick, who traded and hunted in the vicinity, to take some ivory to Quillimane, to purchase cloth and bring it back with him on his return. Fenwick sold the ivory and brought back the goods to the town, along with a canoe-load of goods belonging to himself. Chiputula, Kaffir like, doubted the truth and the honesty of Fenwick, and demanded some of the latter's goods, which lay in the other canoe, saying that until the quantity he required was delivered up, he would not allow the trader to proceed on his journey up river.

Upon the third day of detention Fenwick lost patience, after repeatedly asking the chief to let him go, assuring him that he had delivered every yard of cloth that the ivory had fetched. Stubborn refusal resulted in a quarrel of words.

Fenwick, who remained in his canoe, was accosted by Chiputula from the bank, whose final remark (so the Ajawa boy told me) was, "I will go and fetch my gun. I will try you to-day."

When the chief went away with this threat on his lips Fenwick armed himself, and repaired to Chiputula's hut and killed him on the spot.

Quite aware that he was doomed to death as soon as the natives heard the news, he crossed the Ruo river. The people were soon in hot pursuit. Fenwick took to the reeds, from whence he fired at his pursuers, killing one only. After that he was soon captured, overpowered and slain. The body was decapitated, the trunk being thrown into the river, while the head was taken to Mbewe, close to the mission station at Blantyre, where it was stuck upon a high pole. Mr. Moir requested that it might be given to him, but the desire was not acceded to, and finally the head was taken down and thrown into the river. Thus ended the black and white tragedy of Chiromo.

Out of the strife sprang the difficulties which resulted in the sinking of the steamer *Lady Nyassa*, while on her voyage up the Shiré. The engineer—a Scotchman—having heard before he reached the Ruo river that something was wrong, sent two boys overland with a letter to Mr. Moir at Blantyre, to learn what course he should pursue.

Before I proceed further I must not omit to say that young Chikuse, the son of Chiputula, when a boy had been educated at Blantyre along with a companion who had proved an especially apt scholar, but, as is almost invariably the case, had left the mission after he had learned to read and write, returning with the young chief to Mbewe.

On the messengers from the *Lady Nyassa's* engineer passing through Mbewe, *en route* to Blantyre, the letter was intercepted and read by the young companion of the heir apparent, who wrote an answer with extraordinary skill. One of the messenger-boys was killed and the fear of death impressed upon the other, who was sent back to deliver the sham reply, and to say if questioned that he had handed the letter to Mr. Moir, and had come straight from Blantyre.

The engineer detecting discrepancies in the handwriting of the messenger, which told him to "come up to Katunga; that it was all right," questioned the boy, and, although somewhat dubious, started on the journey up stream. He little thought that the penmanship which had been so carefully taught in the mission school was being used as a lure to bring those who gave it to grief, if not destruction.

Nothing suspicious occurred during the voyage up stream, until the *Lady Nyassa* was approaching Mbewe. Close to that town a flotilla of canoes, manned by a horde of maddened fiends, surrounded the steamer, which was boarded, run ashore, and sunk.

All the goods were abstracted, while at the same time the engineer and his comrade were stripped of every stitch of clothes, and then sent adrift to find their way as best they could to Blantyre.

Mr. Moir had a friend in Kasisé, or Ramakukan, the old chief to whom reference has been made, and after payment to him of powder and goods, the white men were permitted to take their steamer away. When I passed Mbewe I saw on the beach a small collapsible boat, painted red, which had been unclaimed, and belonged to the steamer. It lay there as a memento of this shameful affair, which showed in telling contrast the white man's weakness against the strength of the black man in his own home. Does it not appear a weak sign that these Kaffirs should have been *coaxed* to give up the steamer? A more significant weakness is the existence of an English consulate at Blantyre, in the face of the incontestable fact that if steamers were to be looted and sunk every voyage, our official would be powerless to interfere : his threats would be wasted upon the wind ; he could neither rescue nor chastise.

But it is time to leave the tragic circle of Chiromo. The canoes are ready, and their contents at length dried. I had procured strong stems of the palm frond which were to be used as paddles, while the broad leaf was utilised as a shelter from the sun. The sun was hardly a quarter high when we were sweeping past the changing views of the shore.

The *Leviathan* looked like a ship that had been docked; the palm shelter being new, while a grass hoop-like cover had been improvised and thrown over the baggage as a protection against the rain. The soaring sun doubled and redoubled the intensity of its power, so that the meat we carried soon began to germinate into new life. The wind was aft, and the canoes had a sort of dead-horse smell. Oh, for a head wind! M. Giraud ruefully prophesied a pestilence, cholera, or something of that kind, before we reached the Zambesi.

And yet, although the heat was indescribable, the inaction depressing, and the effluvium something more than strong, there was an undoubted charm about this canoe life. Points of view were ever changing. New landscapes arose and rolled before us, to be quickly supplanted by others, owing to our rapid and erratic course. Distant hills on the left serrated the blue horizon, and nearer a peculiar luxuriance of verdure refreshed and charmed the eye as it rested upon the richly clothed banks of the river.

The tortuous run of the stream was like the fickle course of a fish, and every turn brought its changing scene, either of bare and bold rock mountains, vast palm forests, or boundless plains clad in yellow and green. These glimpses of ever-changing aspects of colour and contour were too enchanting to be easily described.

As the *Leviathan* skimmed along the men stood motionless, leaving the rapid current to bear us onward. We brushed swiftly past the long bending cane, causing it to spring back and whip the water into foam.

Small families of yellow and green birds, resembling

canaries, flew across the water, and as we swept onward round the curving shores, the breathless air was suddenly alive with affrighted flocks of other members of the feathery world. The birds were in immense variety. Disturbed from their perches amidst the branches of trees which spread far out over the river, casting crooked shadows on the glistening stream, they rose in clouds. "African darters" and "long-tailed cormorants" were seen among them.

On our right great white pelicans were pouting in crowding flocks, agitated by the advent of the rude intruders upon their solemn privacy. The older birds, with sedate and measured tread, moved proudly along the golden sands, their snow-white plumage glistening brightly in the sun —they might have been sentries robed in white. Close to the water's edge the white-breasted sand-plover ran with arrow-like rapidity, all the while uttering its low and plaintive cry.

It was a marvellous scene of bird-life. Winged creatures are so varied and so numerous here, that I question much if any quarter of the world could, in that respect, show sights equal to those which enliven the lovely banks of the Shiré.

CHAPTER XXIV.

THE PORTUGUESE AND MAZINJIRI WAR.

A scare—Flying natives—Fright of the *Leviathan's* crew—Black Senators in Congress—Bararika, the chief—Anxiety and misfortunes of the people—Expected attack by Portuguese—" Eat and grow fat; we want you next year"—The man with the gun—The challenge and the plunge—A sickening immersion—Hailing the enemy—In the Portuguese camp—Govea, or Don Manuel Antonio de Souza—War at an end—A hostage—" The Mazinjiri will be sure to kill him"—Bararika is enraged—" Why have you brought this man? he is a traitor"—Danger for the hostage—" I want to be killed at once"—A brave fellow—Parrying an arrow thrust—The *Tricolour's* crew rebels—Guarding the hostage—No provisions again—The Portuguese army—Easy discipline—Don Manuel again—He is hospitable—The cause and progress of the war—Example of Portuguese colonisation—An officious official—The scourge of war—Mercenaries of the Portuguese—Defeat of the Mazinjiri—Another horror of the Shiré—The gainers by war—How the mercenaries are rewarded—Under two flags—A fearful storm—Our soaking sleep—Results of the storm—Floating pumpkins, the spoils of war.

"AH, master, there's the Mazinjiri now! Look at them running. They must take us for Portuguese."

So said Fred, and following his indication, I saw a number of canoes, all propelled as though the lives of the occupants depended upon gaining the further side of the river. Without a moment's delay, after landing, they clambered out of their canoes, seized their bundles, and darted off with hot haste, so that they were soon hidden among the reeds.

We shouted and asked them why they ran; but the question was vain. Farther down the river we noticed that great numbers of people had detected our approach.

The flags clung closely to the slender bamboo staffs which stood up in the canoes, and were easily seen, as the current irresistibly hastened us nearer and nearer to the banks, from which panic-stricken crowds receded fast.

Fred shouted and waved to them, and at last they evidently understood him, for as we ran the nose of the canoe upon the shore, big crowds flocked to the margin of the water. The men were armed with bows and arrows, besides which they had short, barbed, stabbing assegais.

They wanted to know if there were more canoes coming, or any Portuguese on board ours. Fred assured them that there were none. Had a single Portuguese been with us, he would have had a bad time of it. Continuing our journey, we noticed that the banks here and there were blackened with refugees, who repeatedly asked if there were Portuguese on board; but we invariably replied that we were the white men from Nyanja.

We were now within a short distance of a village; and it was manifest that the lines of the contending armies were being approached. As the boys were frightened to proceed, we determined to stop and go ashore at the village, so that the situation might be explained, and our position stated.

The village lay on the skirt of a forest at a little distance from the river bank, on the west side of the stream. It was the late Chiputula's furthest outlying kraal.

Intimation was sent to the chief, or rather enduna, to the effect that we were approaching. As we trended towards the village, we observed on every hand, at every bend, and under every tree, large groups of Mazinjiri fugitives. Beneath an immense forest tree, which could afford shelter for a hundred, was a large gathering of aged men. The black senators were in congress assembled. On their venerable heads was the frost of long and dismal years.

These old masters of wisdom were the sons of the blood-stained valley through which the teeming Shiré winds like a silver cord.

Bararika, the chief, appeared; he was a remarkably handsome Kaffir, being tall and well-proportioned, with an erect carriage, altogether a noteworthy specimen of muscular humanity. First impressions gave the idea, too, that he was a man with some force of character, and was by no means devoid of intellect.

Our chief curiosity lay in the way of learning the condition of affairs in the neighbourhood, especially what might be expected as the next move of the aggressive army; but some time passed before the meeting resolved itself into a *milandu*, comparatively great deliberation, so that we might speak. One thing was very clear, and that was, that the Mazinjiri chiefs were much concerned about the condition of their people. And well they might. For the wretched creatures were on the verge of starvation. Many of the fugitives had not had time even to snatch a little food from their huts when they were forced to fly for their lives.

On landing we had heard that the Portuguese were close by, and were going to attack the village. This we could not quite understand nor believe, for the war had been against the Mazinjiri, and to have attacked this place and people would be the opening of hostilities with the Manganja, and the people supposed to be under the wing of Mandala at Blantyre.

Communications had been received a few months before this by the Portuguese governors of the Zambesi district, fixing the Ruo river as the line of demarcation between their possessions on the Shiré and those assumed to be under British protection.

Bararika's words were: "The Portuguese are camped on the other side of the river, not far off. You had better not go on yet." Continuing his remarks, he informed us that the day before he had sent an old man, "who had talked" across the river to them, and they had said: "We will not fight you now; but eat and grow fat, we want you next year."

Neither M. Giraud nor myself thought it necessary or desirable to linger; in fact, we had already agreed that I should go ahead to speak with the Portuguese, and there and then we told the chief that such would be our course.

I took Fred with me, also the patriarch "who had talked" and had been the ambassador of the previous day. Starting on our mission, we trudged over the dusty foot-worn lanes that led to the river. Ere long the path was lost in the thick belts of water-cane and other rank vegetation which fringe the river's brink.

A loud noise of many voices in the rear made me look backward. I was followed by a small army! Not without great difficulty could the people be persuaded to return and leave me to make my way in peace, for I was nearing the river, and did not know what the state of hostilities might be. I also remembered that no white man was expected by the Portuguese outposts.

I kept a sharp look-out; but no sooner had I got into the reeds than down I went, deep into the false mud. Immediately before this involuntary plunge I saw a man with a gun dodging about, with the evident intention of hiding from me. Just as I sank into the first pit I challenged the man; but he was off. I was nearly choked by the vile miasma that thickened the suffocating air, for the heat of the blazing sun was slowly and surely making the rotting reeds exhale the foulest gases that ever poisoned man. It was enough to stifle the strongest. Scrambling and struggling, I succeeded in getting out of the polluted mire, and reached the water's edge alone.

Then I discovered that the suspicious-looking man I had just seen was a Manganja, who among others was watching the movements of the Portuguese.

As soon as I reached the banks there was no difficulty in seeing the enemy's lines on the opposite side. The force seemed to be pretty strong. A great number were seen walking about under the shade of a large clump of trees. Considerable activity was apparent, evidently in preparation for something, although I could not guess what it might be. A fleet of canoes lay moored by the bank, also a number of large keel-boats, with the after portion covered by awnings.

The river at this point was just wide enough to make shouts from side to side indistinct. I sent a few yells of my very best Portuguese across, intimating that I wanted them to send a boat for me, for I wished to have a conference. An answer came echoing back to the effect that they could not send a boat over. Apparently they did not know what to make of the sudden arrival of a white man.

Perseverance, however, finally triumphed, for in time I saw a boat, manned by black men, wearing red caps, and a European soldier sitting in the stern, putting off from the shore. The work of ferrying occupied but a few minutes.

On landing at the other side, I soon introduced myself to the only three men who looked in any way different from the general gathering of blacks swarming in the camp. This was the most advanced post of the Portuguese army. Portuguese army, forsooth! The man whom I had seen in the boat was the only Portuguese I had noticed in the whole camp.

I inquired for the commander-in-chief, and was informed

that I had the honour of addressing the Capitao mor of the forces, no less notable a person than Govea, whose name I had heard uttered in tones of awe by the natives. The real name of the soldier was Don Manuel Antonio de Souza. He was evidently a half-caste, exceedingly dark in complexion, and portly in body. His clothes were a suit of pyjamas. He was accompanied by two young men, who were introduced as Portuguese officers.

They said that the assembled force was only a part of the army which had taken a part in the war; the rest were on the march to the Zambesi, as it was not intended to push the conquest any further. In short, the war was at an end!

Preparations were going on with a view to the immediate departure of the entire force. Purposely I had not as yet made any mention of my mission, because I wished to hear as much accurate information as possible regarding the position of affairs. For the same reason I wished to cause a little conjecture. I am tolerably sure that their first impressions were that I had come down the river from Blantyre in order to have a big palaver.

Ultimately I explained our position as travellers, and that our canoes were manned by Manganja people, who were afraid to pass down the river. Only one plan seemed feasible in order to convey security to the minds of the Manganja, and that was, that we should have a hostage. A request which I made in this connection was courteously granted. The hostage (a Senna man), in company with the old patriarch and Fred, were soon hastening back with me to the village, and as we went we heard the clamour of a thousand voices mingling with the roll of drums, which called the conquering army to embark for the south in their primitive fleet.

Singularly eventful are the footsteps of travellers in little-known lands, and very startling are the freaks of fortune and misfortune, which are, metaphorically, the milestones of their progress. In the present instance it was passing strange that after all the ups and downs of the journey from Cape Town to Nyassa I should, while on the way southwards again to the sea, find myself between the lines of contending armies on the very day, and almost at the very hour, when it was determined to restore peace.

Now there would be some satisfaction in being able to tell the miserable Mazinjiri that their warlike enemies were retiring, so that they were free to return to their own country.

"Ah! Fred," I remarked, "they'll be glad to hear that it's all over. Our boys will go nicely now that we can show we have been given a man."*

"The man wants to speak," replied Fred, dubiously. "Master, I think we have made a mistake."

Like lightning's flash the position was at once before me. By all the suns and stars what had I done? What foolish act was this?

"The man," continued Fred, "says that the Mazinjiri will be sure to kill him!"

"And here they are coming, Fred. It is too late to do anything. We must face them. Tell the man to stick closely to us; then go and find Bararika."

I approached with the hostage towards the senatorial tree, but the old men had left, and the chief also. I saw the latter making hastily for his hut. M. Giraud, however, was waiting; also Miller. They had observed from the attitude of the people that something was radically wrong.

---

* To be given a man amongst these people means that he is your property. You can kill him if you like with impunity.

"Never mind," was my response to their inquiries. "We must stick to the man now we have got him. The mistake is mine."

The news seemed to spread like wildfire, far and near. From tree, ant-heap, bush and hut, came the throng of Mazinjiri, talking as only agitated Kaffirs can talk. As if by magic, the living crowd bristled with the iron points of countless spears and arrow-heads, amidst which could be seen protruding old and rather rusty Tower muskets. The air resounded with the wildest threats and imprecations, and the scene every moment was gaining in excitement.

Coolness was the only bearing that promised safety—not exactly *sang-froid*, but, so to speak, wide-awake indifference, for the threatening people were now pressing dangerously near.

From among the mass came Fred, along with the chief, and the latter, I could easily see, had taken my well-meant but ill-judged action as a gross insult to himself and his people. He now carried his gun.

The unfortunate hostage seemed to have but a poor chance, and naturally all my anxiety was on his account.

"Don't speak much, master," said Fred; "the people may ask you for the man. The chief say he want to hear the white man speak, and tell why he brought this man here."

"Let the chief speak first, Fred. We wish him to tell *his* grievance."

An irate Mazinjiri here leaped among us and seized the hostage's red turban, which he shied to the wolfish herd, at the same time shaking his arrows over the man's head, and never ceasing to threaten and make signs of hate and of thirst for blood. The object of execration and enmity sat upon his rifle with an air of complete indifference, which was much to be admired; but this is a trait more common in Pagandom than in Christendom.

"Why have you brought this man into my town?" demanded Bararika. "He is a traitor. He has betrayed the villages to the Portuguese. Yesterday it was he who told my messenger that I should fatten my people for the time they should come."

"Tell him, Fred, that I brought this man to show my boys that the Portuguese would not harm them, and for no other reason. I alone am responsible; not the man. To touch him is to touch me, *his owner*. The chief must assist in protecting the man. I have nothing more to say, except that we will go to a hut, which will be paid for."

The situation was becoming graver every moment. We rose, and telling the man to follow close to me, M. Giraud and Miller looking out that he should not be attacked behind, we moved towards the huts.

Behind, before, and around us the crowd could only be likened to a porcupine armed with spikes of steel. The people had lashed themselves into a state of fury, and ever and anon some of them would make lunges at our black captive, or attempt to snatch away the gun he carried.

We three, however, kept close order for his protection; although, just as we were about to reach the hut, a rush was made from behind, one of the savage demons seizing the man's gun, while another plunged a barbed assegai at him, which M. Giraud, with the quickness of lightning, happily warded off.

In another moment we had the unlucky hostage stowed in the hut. He had stuck firmly to his gun.

I was truly a great deal more anxious about the safety of this fellow than he was himself, for only half an hour had elapsed, the people being still in a condition of feverish

PROTECTING A HOSTAGE.

passion, when he came out of the hut, saying to me in Portuguese:

"If I am going to die, I want to be killed at once. I do not want to stop inside!"

"There need be no fear," I said. "Sit down; we will not leave you. Only do as you are told."

Heedless of this advice, however, he shouted aloud:

"If you think I have betrayed you, give me muave. Muave will speak the truth!"

He had hardly got out these words when another thrust was made at him by a Mazinjiri with three arrows; but the attempt was parried by Bararika, who stood on the man's right side. The chief, who now seemed thoroughly roused to action, then gave vent to some harsh words, emphasised by still harsher looks. By main force the man was again forced under the thatch, where Giraud and myself kept watch and ward for the remainder of the day, never leaving him alone, even for an instant.

Other troubles, which had been brewing, had now to be tasted. Although my men belonging to the *Leviathan* were all right, and said they would go on in the morning, the men of the *Tricolour* said they would go no further, notwithstanding that they had been paid.

Certain it was that we would have to be off betimes in the morning, for we could not stop where we were any longer, owing to provisions running rather short. Considering the number of boys we had there was very little meal, and food was not to be had at the villages on account of the war. Of meat we still had enough for the boys, but could not use it ourselves.

By the time the sun went down that night, it was beyond doubt that the crew of the *Tricolour* would not go on. Three, in fact, had already decamped; therefore nothing could be done except to start short-handed, making the Wangwana do all the work.

The huts were small, and we three whites occupied separate shelters for the night. It was with no little relief that I stowed away the hostage and stretched myself across the narrow doorway, only to find a waking, restless sort of sleep, all night long. I watched with eager eyes for the silver streak of dawn, and no sooner did it thread across the brightening sky than we were all at the water's edge.

A number of Mazinjiri were moving about, but before any crowd gathered on the banks the two ensigns were floating in the whispering winds of early morn. Out in the stream we bade farewell to Bararika and his turbulent town, with its throng of wild, adversity-stricken, and much-to-be-pitied Mazinjiri refugees.

Gliding down the river the canoes almost touched, so that it was possible to maintain a conversation, in which the position of affairs was fully discussed. Speaking of what could be done, Fred declared that it would take some days to reach Mazaro on the Zambesi. The men in the boats worked hard, and now there was no meal left—an awkward deprivation, when it is remembered that the country on both sides had been deserted and laid waste. Assuredly no provisions could be expected from the Mazinjiri people.

We had almost given up hope of being able to replenish the commissariat when a sudden bend in the river revealed, at some distance down stream, a great concourse of people upon the bank, with a flag floating from a high bamboo. It was a detachment of the victorious army! A foraging party was immediately decided upon, the post of interpreter falling to me.

Immediately after landing we witnessed an amusing scene, which afforded an opportunity of noting the mode of military discipline maintained in the ebony army, whose uniform was "nothing before, nothing behind, and sleeves of the same." All seemed to be interested in our appearance, and hundreds flocked around as we made our way to a small marquee. Much to our amazement the crowd suddenly broke away, as though panic-stricken, and we had little difficulty in seeing the distributing power in the shape of a very tall man, of a devilish type, armed with a long cane, which he wielded with the most nimble agility, bringing it down, every now and then, with a ringing whack across the shrinking shoulders of some flying file, in a way that would have delighted the heart of an old British admiral.

The camp stood in a grass plain at the foot of Mount Malawe, and formed three sides of a square abutting the river. Nearing the scene, I can scarcely say I was astonished to see the same man whom I had met before, namely, Don Manuel Antonio de Souza, alias the dreaded Govea. We shook hands as if we had been friends of long ago, and introducing my friends we soon were seated in the shade of a small bushy tree. Directly in front sat the hostage Don Manuel had given me, and on being asked he recounted his experiences, while I expressed astonishment that the commander had not thought of the risk I was incurring for the whole party by the action. As it was useless to speak of the past, however, we soon let the matter drop.

Don Manuel's army was well encamped, and all the troops seemed to feel happy over the successful result of the campaign, they being now on their way homewards to the Manika country, eight or ten days' march southward across the Zambesi. The commander was evidently "somebody," for he assured us that he had 4,000 men of his own, and that all the men, 2,200, which constituted his half of the army in the field belonged to him solely. He generously extended his hospitality, so that we got a very good breakfast of such as he had, that is to say, rice, chicken and tomatoes, and coffee. Every mouthful I took reminded me that I was eating that which should have gone to sustain some unfortunate Mazinjiri.

Rice, which we were so much in need of, was supplied here; but at the same time Don Manuel informed us that provisions with him were not very plentiful, in spite of the fact that the army had the free run of the country. He pulled out his treasure-box—a characteristic act of these uncrowned kings or semi-monarchs—to show us his treasures, which consisted of trinkets, medals, and chains. The principal possession, or rather that which tickled his fancy most, was a very pretty English gold stop-watch, which attracted his most admiring glances like those of an impressionable æsthete considering the lily.

What I was anxious to hear about was the war. How did it arise? By whom was it waged? Who benefited by it?

The story I heard and now repeat was verified by officers whom I afterwards met, and who had participated in the hostilities.

It seems that when a native of Portugal marries a black woman, the Portuguese Government gives, or rather lends him, a large piece of territory for three generations. At his death this property again falls to the Government, and the people who have gathered round the standard of the deceased are claimed as soldiers, who receive some slight present now and again, so that there may be some right to demand their services should they be required.

At posts where beneficiaries die there is usually placed one Portuguese *commandante militar* and thirty or forty black paid soldiers, who are presumed to look after the interests of the Portuguese Government, interests which in this case it would be quite impossible to define.

The case in question, resulting in the war, involved the name of a man Matakeña, a very formidable half-caste, in fact a savage king, at whose death the usual rules were enforced. Death in such cases is not, as I have before explained, considered a natural or inevitable event, being ascribed to the influence of an evil spirit dwelling in some corporeal frame, the owner of which must be found out by the usual ceremonies of trial. When discovered the victim must drink the god muave, or die any death that the witch doctors decree. It does not matter whether the lot falls upon father, mother, or any other of the nearest of kin. Their belief is so strong that death is welcome.

The officer who had been placed in command over the property, but not over the functions of tribal ceremonies, forbade the carrying into effect of the common custom. Owing to his actions and interference, he had incurred the grave displeasure of chiefs, especially the two greatest, whose names were Repoza and Bzingwe. These the officer arrested, and despatched to Quillimane on the coast; but they managed to effect their escape on the way, and rapidly assembled forces among the tribes of the Mazinjiri, the report spreading far and wide that the Portuguese were interfering with their customs, and wanted to put the people in prison and take their country.

Thus another scourge began to sweep this valley of dread. The uprising expanded; the medicine of war was mixed; the war drum (ngoma) rolled; and over the magic tail of the buffalo* the people leaped from their homes to face the foe.

* Before going to war the chiefs who carry the tail of some wild animal of the larger species, have it well doctored by some competent medicine man. Then it is laid across the path where all the regiment from the

The post at Matakeña was attacked, and the officer killed with fourteen of his men, one Portuguese being taken prisoner. And so the fire of strife was kindled.

News was sent to the Governor at Mozambique, who requested our friend Don Manuel Antonio de Souza, of Gurrungosa, in the Manika country (annexed by the Portuguese in 1884), to take 2,000 of his men to assist in making war against the Mazinjiri. For the men and service in fighting the battles of the Lisbon Government he would receive a stated allowance. Likewise the rank of colonel was conferred upon him, and henceforth he would draw the pay of a colonel.

Along with others like himself he pressed the war to its conclusion, driving everything before them until they reached the country claimed by the heirs of Chiputula, where we met. The unfortunate Mazinjiri had shown a good front on three separate occasions, heroically carrying off their dead during the retreat. After the last battle, however, twenty-five of the slain were left upon the field. The Portuguese losses were inconsiderable. They sent one hundred and fifty prisoners, including thirty-seven chiefs, to Mozambique, from whence they were exiled for life to Loando, on the west coast of Africa.

Let us draw a veil over the horror, which only fills another line in the blood-marked scroll of traditions, telling of human life and struggles in the long valley of the Shiré.

---

kraal must pass. After finishing their final meal, the men spring up and one by one jump over the enchanted tail, and bound away without saying good-bye to or even looking at their wives. Should they by any chance look back the fates are against them; they must not go. All who leap over the tail and clear straight away will be invulnerable against bullets, and their lives will be saved. With this belief firmly implanted in their brave breasts they go forth to war fearlessly. In the event of defeat, the medicine simply must have been bad.

Before losing sight of the subject altogether, however, let me refer to one or two of its diplomatic aspects. Three important facts should be noted. In the first place, the cause of the war was the action of an over-zealous officer. Actuated by ill-timed motives he stepped beyond the pale of wisdom. The barbarian is as sensitive regarding his creed as the Christian. Secondly, the war was waged in the interest of parties.

The wires that work all warfare move in gyrating circles from a common centre. In this instance Lisbon gets the outer ring, and sees a phantom map of boundless acres in Eastern Africa. In the third place it is seen that the beneficiaries are not far off, for they are the isolated rulers in the Zambesi basin. Petty potentates there are year by year becoming powerful chiefs. They draw the spoil and wear the glories of war, while their coffers are filled with gold from far-off Lisbon. Our friend with the gold stop-watch is very near the centre of the assumed circle.

"Are you paid by the Government, and also armed by the Government?" I asked Don Manuel.

"Oh, yes. Before a regular Portuguese army could reach the Shiré river half of them would be dead!"

Men like this know full well the strength of their position.

He entrusted me with a Winchester repeating rifle, with silver-plated barrels, which was in need of repairs. I was to take it all the way to Cape Town if necessary, and have it put thoroughly in order. A new case was to be made, on which he wished his name engraved in full. He also wanted a few thousand rounds of cartridges included among the other commissions, which in the course of a few months were duly attended to.

We then said good-bye to this king of the mysterious Manika country. On the eve of our final departure he sent us a man for each canoe, also Portuguese colours, suspecting that some of the troops which might be encountered during the journey would fire on us, not knowing who we were.

Now the *Leviathan* was under two flags, the tattered and torn old Jack making one think of a Waterloo veteran, while the bright Portuguese ensign was a raw recruit.

" It looks as though we are in for it to-night, Fred."

" Yes; will be plenty rain this night."

On the right bank of the river we saw what appeared to be a deserted village or camp, over which a few carrion vultures hovered, giving an additional wildness to the general desolation. The position was far from desirable for occupation, but as we wanted shelter we landed, running the canoes into a small creek, which afforded protection from the high wind, by this time lashing the waters into waves.

Evidently the spot had been a temporary camp of Mazinjiri fugitives, and had subsequently been occupied by their enemies. Everything was in a wrecked condition. The only shelter that could be found were hastily formed grass huts, structures composed of forked sticks, with heaps of long rank grass thrown over the cross poles.

Morambala mountain, shutting out the southern sky, was clearly visible. Its old granite head towers 4,000 feet above the river which it skirts.

Each of the company quickly made his choice of a shelter; and not too soon; for now the threats of the storm king were vividly signalled in the lurid heavens. Out in the far distance sped the fragments of broken clouds, holding in their watery nucleus the forces of the fiercest power of fire, and closing together in dense unity ready for the rising tempest; their deepening darkness covering the heavens, eclipsing the sun, and anticipating night.

Stray sunbeams occasionally darted from breaks in the mass of closing gloom, flitting swiftly over the boundless expanse of reeds, and then vanishing from the scene of desolation, over which the wind howled its old tune, the wild weird notes of countless ages and endless time. All the offspring of the earth seemed to yield to aerial anger; the swamp was swept into deep green waves, while wildly impetuous gusts tore our rude shelters ruthlessly, and scattered their coverings like chaff.

As night drew near small clouds of grey mottled turtle doves shot past, and we could hear the harsh cry of spur-winged geese high up in rapid flight crossing to and fro. We also saw the last flock of flamingoes, returning to their roosts, flying low, being driven by the wild wind, and uttering that loud croaking sound which is so strangely uncanny as it dies away in the distance.

Then came night, dark as the deepest dungeon. A roar that might have filled the universe told that the demon spirit of the storm rode on. Brightest day and blackest night followed in instantaneous succession. The stately palms, which tossed their feathery fronds to the maddened gale, stood out in relief clear against a glowing electric curtain; the light, in a thousand fiery forks, flashing from the brow of blackened Morambala, and the vivid inconstant glare shone upon the winding course of the mountain torrent, until it seemed as though the deadly enemies of fire and water ran in currents side by side.

Above in the murky gloom a star might now and then be seen, to twinkle for an instant, and be lost.

On sped the tempest. The wind shrieked over the yielding reeds, and above the clinging thatch that remained hanging on our hurdle roofs. Then the floodgates opened and down came the deluge, the clouds discharging their liquid loads in heavy bodies. Streams soon coursed through the camp. All about was in darkness, inundation, and misery.

By midnight the strength of the storm was spent. The power of the angry heavens had passed away, and the wind whispered lower and lower until its voice was stilled to breathless repose.

Tired out and well soaked we all sank to sleep amidst the saturated grass and blankets, awaking now and then as the water would trickle to some yet undiscovered spot. Under the gleam of the sheets of lightning which still blazed in the wake of the running storm we could see each other at times. How uncomfortable, but how comical! Miller moved beneath a small hayrick of his own. M. Giraud marched on the brink of the river, his clothes clinging to his body so closely that he might have had none from all appearances. Mosquitoes followed him in myriads, for now they held the camp. As for myself I was sitting over my journal like a brood hen; holding up an old parasol of brown holland which had been brought from Tette, and which I tried to imagine was of some use in alleviating distress. Beneath its cover the tiny winged tormentors played and sung, drawing me involuntarily into their little game.

My eyes, however, were fixed on the east, and my thoughts dwelt upon sunshine. Time soon ran off with another night. At length aurora rose and dispelled the darkness. Over the vast tract a snow-white mist was hanging, resembling great volumes of escaping steam. It smothered the little camp with its wet embrace. This soft white veil soon began to rise, clearer and clearer grew the eastern horizon, until the break of the glad day brought the long-looked-for sunlight.

"Come along, Fred," said I; "we must be off soon."

All the boys needed stirring to life, for they had crept into their palm sleeping-bags (*fumba*), which look like wide flat sacks of plaited leaves, at once affording shelter from rain, mist, and mosquitoes. Once the boys were on their feet the work of bailing out the canoes was begun.

"Hillo, some things overboard during the night! Where are those elephants' and other tails that lay on the top?"

"I tink the wind take away everyting in the night," answers the shrewd Fred.

My trophies were few before, but now they were reduced still further.

"Where is the rice given us by Govea?"

"Here." We open the two palm bags, and much to our amazement and chagrin find that it is unhusked, and therefore useless until we could reach some village where it could be cleaned. Here was a mischievous mistake!

We tried to get something to warm us, but not a dry stick was to be found. Any of us would have made Faust's bargain, in order to get a bit of firewood.

More pain, more misery! The only consolation was that we would soon have the poor man's blanket, as the Mexicans call the sun. Some of the boys dived off the banks, heedless of crocodiles, in order to fetch floating pumpkins. Supplies which the victorious army had not wanted had been thrown into the river, which was thus bearing away the harvest of the Mazinjiri gardens. To us it was as the manna from heaven. The canoes were bailed, loaded with the unusual spoils of war, and were soon under weigh, southwards.

CHAPTER XXV.

TO THE INDIAN OCEAN, AND HOME.

Devastated shores—Heathen and Christian slavery—Village in flames—Portuguese in our wake—The merry conquerors—Dysentery—The dreaded Morambala—A fusilade—"We thought you were Mazinjiri"—Story of Hooft, the Dutch trader—Scruples of the Wangwana—Putrefying wastes—A heated silent scene—The *Leviathan* becomes unmanageable—An early start—Livingstone's headquarters in 1862—Mrs. Livingstone's grave—Mazaro—Mr. Lindsay—Preparing for the journey to Quillimane—The Kwakwa river—Excellent boatmen—Lovely evening views—Winged tormentors—Malarial atmosphere—Escape from a snake—Piracy on the Kwakwa—Unfortunate fishermen—The river meets the sea—Quillimane—Its appearance—"Oh! you're not the man"—Hospitality at Quillimane—Fever at the last moment!—On board the S.S. *Dunkeld*—M. Giraud's adieu—Retrospect—Home—The past is sad: is there a bright future?

As we moved down the winding river we saw that it washed deserted shores, upon which the most common sights were the fields of battles that had been waged and won. Morambala, which had frowned upon us during the previous night, was approached.

Stark scenes of devastation expanded from the river's brink. Over the land the skull and crossbones might have fitly waved.

It would be impossible to exaggerate the untold wretchedness which has made the Shiré valley a vale of blood and of tears. Sad indeed has been the fate of its persecuted people. The ruthless work of fire and sword has driven them hither and thither. Slavery and war here found a congenial soil; and even to-day may be seen on the river's banks the white-robed prince of slaves.

Close upon the heels of heathen slavers, more excusable, perhaps, than any, advanced the bristling phalanx, paid by Christian gold, to strengthen the power of the harsh half-caste chief, and so rid the land—*where no other people can sow or reap*—of its struggling but natural sons of toil! Thus fields are fertilised by the bodies of the slain, and the mocking sun looks down and bakes the bare bones until they return to their original dust.

The boats speed on, and we see gardens laid waste while the river runs green with their despoiled produce. Village after village is passed, all devastated by fire, showing rows of roofless huts, like heaps of smouldering straw. Far away we see leaping into happy daylight, seething flames that danced over the ruin of some luckless inland village. Fire, the soldier's only constant friend, is here left to complete the wreck that man began.

Could these poor sufferers be worse if civilisation had never approached their land? Of course, we must not forget that there are two tellings for every story. I, perhaps, have experienced that which enables me to speak only of one, which, unhappily, is on the side of sorrow.

A rough noise has followed us down stream. We look upwards and see that the water is black with a fleet of canoes, from which comes the merry beating of many drums. It is the Portuguese flotilla, carrying the triumphant army homeward. Borne along at the rate of four knots an hour they rapidly approach, and louder and louder becomes the heavy thud of many paddles and the babbling of a thousand tongues.

The larger boats soon sweep past, being well manned by Mazara boatmen (noted as expert watermen), with red caps brilliant on their black heads. They bend their bodies to the stroke as they plunge their paddles deftly in the stream. At the stern of some of the boats we see the luxury-loving young officer, reclining on a soft mattress enjoying a siesta, or smoking the soothing cigarette. A happy crowd truly to pass through a scene so gruesome!

That Portuguese flotilla was a novel sight. The army was the queerest assemblage that could well be imagined. No particular rule or order existed about anything, for the only anxiety that was evident was the desire to hasten helter-skelter home. None of the canoes were large; few contained more than eight men, and some with only two men were no bigger than long bath tubs. The large keel-boats might have about fifteen or twenty on board, and were propelled by paddles, the men facing the bow. No oars were used. There was a great abundance of drums, many of which were taken from the Mazinjiri.

One of the keel-boats, we were informed, had the Governor of Quillimane on board, very ill with fever. A hail came from another as it passed. A Senhor Leal was on board, and he told us that there was still war lower down the river.

Two days passed, and we were beginning to hope that the confluence of the river would be reached before long.

Dysentery broke out among the crew. One man who went ashore disappeared altogether.

Further down the stream the marshes were observed to be becoming more extensive, until they stretched as far as the blue horizon. By that time we had reached the foot of the Morambala mountain, which from north to south rises like a pyramid. The natives dare not call the mountain by its name, but speak of it as Salumbidwa, which literally signifies "I cannot call you by your name." At times, when great floods prevail in the Zambesi delta, all the land here, as far as the eye can reach, becomes an immense sea.

Salumbidwa's influence instils awe into the poor black who voyages in his rude dug-out, and sees the towering pyramid rising in solitary grandeur from the vast sheet of water stretching from horizon to horizon. Sometimes the voyager may encounter a floating island, for whole banks, often acres in extent, break away from the reed-covered swamps, to drift under the careless whims of wind and current. With strained and anxious eyes he looks out for the crescent moon to gild the western skies; and full of fearful awe he watches the cloud-omens which hang over the misty crest of Salumbidwa. If perchance the dreaded deity frowns and thunders, flashing the transient but deadly fire from its beetling brows, he will turn away in terror, and with all his might hasten to the distant shore, there to await the pleasure of the mountain spirit, when the wild winds shall be stilled and the angry waves subdued.

A camp was formed at the foot of the mountain, but we were soon again on the way. The moon shone brightly, lighting up the scene. Passing a large camp of the Portuguese army they challenged us, but we answered that we were Govea's men. They warned us to keep a good look-out below, for we might be fired on.

The canoes parted at this point; the Wangwana working so well in the coolness of the morning that the *Leviathan* was beaten. My men had worked so hard that I had not the heart to press them. The canoe was an old one, very heavy, and so unwieldy at times that the work of navigating was doubly difficult.

Without the slightest appearance or sound of anything to warn us, firing all at once was opened on the left bank. We happened to be keeping in the deep stream on the right, and before I could even protest, the canoe was ashore and the men jumping out of her.

"Come, master," shouted Fred. "We must get out. They are Mazinjiri, and will fire on us."

The Portuguese guide, too, ran in hot haste up the bank, calling out, "Quick, quick! Mazinjiri, Mazinjiri!"

A great deal of shouting was indulged in, during which I heartily eulogised all hands for their effective funk. Some time after, the words in native tongue came echoing across the water, "We are Frau's men, and thought you were Mazinjiri." This adventure made us challenge every one we saw. Even numbers of the Portuguese flotilla we roared at as they passed, our shouts astonishing the natives very much.

The canoes met near a burning village. Pumpkins by the score were found, so that our stores were replenished. We skirted the left bank, passing a deserted French station, and finally reaching a post occupied by a Dutch trader (Mr. Hooft), who had been a great favourite among the natives; so much so, that they had given him timely warning to leave during the earlier stages of the war. On hearing of the close of hostilities Mr. Hooft had returned, only to find that there was nothing left in the house. Through sheer want he was about to leave directly overland to Quillimane.

While we were here some soldiers arrived bearing a message from Portuguese officers, begging Mr. Hooft to let them have some provisions, from which request it was evident that the country had been pretty well drained of supplies.

From this point both M. Giraud and myself concluded that it would be useless to attempt to hold together, seeing that no one knew the channels, which, near the junction of the rivers, break away in all directions. The Portuguese guides, with their banners, bag and baggage, had left in order to join their friends on the homeward march.

Once again we had run out of provisions, and the men were devouring raw pumpkins.

If the *Tricolour* and the *Leviathan* kept together, unnecessary delay would arise, so that the best plan would be to divide what trifling supplies were left, and each find the course as well and as quickly as possible to Mazaro. My share in the grand division was a tin of pea-soup.

Giraud's Wangwana men, poor creatures, suffered most, owing to their religious scruples forbidding them to eat that which they had not themselves killed, or to dip in a dish with others not of their own kin.

Each canoe strikes out on its own account, and before two miles had been covered they part.

Ahead is the false mirage drawn across the southern sky like a landscape curtain. Such views dissolve suddenly. The optical illusion dies before the eyes. The current changes. It now flows from west to east, and for the second time I find myself buoyed along on the strong bosom of the Zambesi.

Astern, far away, stretches the peaceful savannah, cut by the silvery and sinuous lines of the converging streams. From these putrefying wastes rises the deadly malaria, invisible, and yet invincible as the mightiest forces of the dread unknown. These vast tracts defy the puny skill and strength of man; no mortal power can subdue or remove the poison of their miasma.

I remember well the wild fierceness of the heat upon that memorable day when we floated into the wide Zambesi. Under the terrible rage of the noonday sun all vegetation withered and wasted, as quickly as though cast into a scorching furnace, while a white, blinding glare was reflected from the glistening sands.

Not a sound was heard. Not a tremor moved the heat-charged atmosphere. There was nothing to hear, and not a living thing to be seen. The mud-bank became pale, and curled its blistering face into crisp rounds of baked clay. Cane-crowned islands, which turned conflicting currents, faded to faintest yellow. On both sides in the wide basin we saw the banks tossed up into hillocks armed with spear grass sharp as the keenest arrow-head. At the point we drifted there stood, in ages past, forests and grassy plains, for the fickle stream breaks its banks, building up great mounds where its waters formerly ran. Away in deserted spots may be discovered the stretching arms of some forest monarch, whose trunk lies deep in the settling sands, bleached and whitened by the merciless sun. A sermon in wood is that old tree. In long forgotten years it stood proudly rivalling thousands of its kind. Now it is bare, alone, a landmark in a desert ages ago swept by furious floods.

Our weary first day on the big river was spent in getting on sand-banks and pulling off again, and night found us still striving hard to reach Mazaro. Evening, however, had brought a strong head-wind, which, as it swept up-stream, nearly, on more than one occasion, caused the loss of the *Leviathan*. Water and air were at war, through the easterly wind and the westerly stream, so that our heavy craft became unmanageable. The wide surface of the river was roused to fury, the waves becoming much too high to be safe.

Looming in the dusk was seen a small promontory, seeming to offer a haven, which we struggled to reach, although the spray splashed on every side in our battle against wind and wave. Fred urged the men on, and, poor fellows! they seemed thoroughly exhausted through the contest with the elements. But we continued to bail; the bamboo poles were plied with a will, until at last, when we were worn out and tired with the fight, our craft bumped ashore, half full of water, on the northern banks.

All of us landed, and wayworn limbs were soon extended in rest. My tattered old blankets were again in use, in a room true to the wildest state of nature; its walls being of spear grass, and its roof the arch of the blue-black sky, glittering with its myriad golden worlds.

"Fred, what's all that noise about?"

"Mazaro men going up river, master. I have got some rice for you."

"Good! Supper at once: boiled rice and nuts."

The tin of pea-soup I spoke of had been a complete failure. When mixed it looked like cement for mending china, and tasted just as I imagine Thames mud would taste.

"To-morrow," continued Fred, "we shall get plenty to eat."

In order to avoid being cooked, done, as it were, "to a turn," which had been our experience on the previous day, we were up and away long before daylight, and at sunrise were passing Shupanga, catching a fleeting glimpse of the old deserted house, which is now a crumbling monument to Livingstone, for it had been his headquarters in 1862. The house was almost covered with the tropical vegetation, which climbed and hung on every tree and branch with a luxuriance such as I had never seen before. Nature seemed to droop and weep sadly over the relic of the departed great.

The gigantic baobab tree beneath which Mrs. Livingstone was buried stood up bravely above the netted mass of fern and fig tree, screw palm, twining plants and creepers of every description.

A few more reaches and sweeping curves were passed, and then over the tops of houses and huts we could see the British flag waving. We had reached the village of Mazaro.

First thoughts inclined to speculations as to the chances there would be to get down to the coast, and there get a steamer to South Africa. The *Leviathan* had now finished her long journey; her crew were paid off. Contented in mind, and full inside, they basked in the sunshine.

I explained the circumstances of my case to Mr. Lindsay, the agent of the African Lakes Company.

"Where is my friend, M. Giraud?" I inquired; "has he not arrived?"

"No," was the answer. "We have seen no one but yourself for a long time."

I wondered what could have happened, but came to the conclusion that he had been caught, and mayhap damaged in the big storm.

"I think you had better hurry on to Quillimane," was Mr. Lindsay's advice, "if you wish to catch a steamer for Natal."

He kindly informed me that the *Dunkeld* was due very soon, and that a steamer for Zanzibar touched at Quillimane, and would go north in about three weeks. Mr. Lindsay further stated that it would take five days, good going, to reach Quillimane; that he had a good keel boat on the Kwakwa river, about eight miles off, and that I could have her next day if I wished. No time was to be lost.

M. Giraud and Miller turned up in the afternoon.

Every attention was given us by Mr. Lindsay, who at once set about making preparations for our boats, of which fortunately there were two, so that each of us could be suited. My time was the most precious, for should I miss the steamer, a whole month must elapse before another chance would be offered.

The messenger who had been sent to the Kwakwa, to prepare the boat and muster the crew, returned; and it was at once arranged that under the circumstances it would be wise for me, at least, to depart early on the following morning.

Giraud, with thoughtful kindness, lent me the "blue man"—one of his Wangwana, who was always robed in blue—who had been "Through the Dark Continent" with the famous H. M. Stanley. With this man and with Fred, the slave child of Livingstone, I felt quite distinguished.

There was a novelty in the circumstances which had a marvellous charm, for in grim Africa the winds of chance are fickle. I had been thrown among many sorts and conditions of men, in many curious scenes and vicissitudes, to be at last picked up by one who had come straight from the last discovered lake of Livingstone, and now in company with two followers of the two mightiest travellers of the world I was to complete my journey to the sea! Eleven moons had grown old and died during the course of my wanderings.

Mandama, the boatmen's village on the Kwakwa, was reached soon after noon next day. There we lost an hour in repairing the rudder.

The Kwakwa was very low, and the banks littered with vegetable deposits rose high upon each side of the narrow, alley-like waterway, which at some points was not a boat's length in breadth.

Work during the first two days was very tedious and very hard upon the men, for the boat was grounding incessantly, and all hands had to get out, so that with united effort they might lift her along over the silt and shingle.

The crew consisted of seven men and a captain-coxswain, the latter standing aft steering with his foot, and with a loud shrill voice leading and enlivening the boatmen's chorus.

Mazaro men are admirably adapted for their work, being excellent river men in every respect. They can swim; and seem as happy in the water as in the boat, being quite an amphibious race. The mode of life is exceedingly hard, their bodies bearing out the truth of this by showing signs of arduous exertion, every muscle being strained to its utmost tension, the sinews swelling in response to the effort with paddle and pole. No better models for the painter or sculptor could be found.

The atmosphere on this portion of the river was exceedingly sultry, close, and damp, the feeling being as if we were passing through a heated drain.

Evening effects in scenery were lovely. At intervals we coursed through lakelets fringed with brilliant flora, and anon glided past banks richly clad with palms and great green trees. Matted wreaths and clusters of creeping plants and weeds hung in heavy folds over the shores, obscuring the mellow light of evening, which gleamed over our heads and made the tiny stream a mirror of gold.

Limited as the view was, it was singularly picturesque and full of life, with its schools of chattering monkeys swinging from branches and bending boughs. Flocks of lively greenfinches clung to the long waving reeds. When the shades of night fell upon the earth, the luxuriant foliage was lit with fire-flies darting like living sparks through the sylvan shades.

> "Like winged stars the fire-flies flash and glance,
> Pale in the open moonshine; but each one
> Under the dark trees seems a little sun,
> A meteor tamed; a fixed star gone astray
> From the silver regions of the milky way."

At night-time we climbed to the tops of the banks to seek repose, for the air was thick with winged life. The insect world was awake in the darkness, and sweeping round our ears were clouds of harassing pests—mosquitoes, gnats, and larger winged tormentors. The camp fires were kept blazing, their heat and smoke being bad, but bearable, so long as they kept the air free from the flying plagues.

The men about me were born and inured in the roughest of rough life, especially in the matter of food; for a rude pot is put on the fire, and no sooner does the water boil than they tumble the meal in, not allowing it to seethe, but keeping on pouring, stirring the while with the handle of a paddle which has been used all day long, and invariably burning their fingers as they dump out the thick half-cooked stuffing on to the palm leaves which they use as plates.

Under the mangroves, even in bright daytime, the shade is almost as black as the blackest night, and in such positions is felt the clammy damp of the malarial atmosphere, while mosquitoes are so bad that it would be impossible to linger among them for a few minutes without a chance of madness. Mangrove swamps are a breeding ground of the mosquito. Marshes are the hot-beds of the deadly fever so common to this country.

I have observed snakes in the open high grass, but not under the nightly shade of the river's banks, where the ground is excessively damp. Once I had a narrow escape from being bitten by a black *mamba*, whose long thick body, with a broad flat head, lay in the footway leading to the boat. Happily I noticed the brute just as I was about to tread on its body, and springing to one side avoided it. I got a good start, but was safe. One of the Mazaro boys who was close at my heels got a tremendous fright, as for him the appearance of the snake was an omen of events unborn.

The last day of our journey on the Kwakwa had dawned, the river beginning to widen as we floated swiftly down the stream. Every now and then the vigour of the paddles would subside into absolute inaction and silence, as the boat swept onwards, borne by the resistless current.

The revolting crocodile was frequently seen, large and loathsome.

Sometimes I would shoot a bird, and then my merry watermen would plunge to the banks and, up to their knees in soft mud, give chase. This seemed to afford great amusement.

The spirit of piracy, however, had by this time contaminated the breasts of the men, for whenever a fishing canoe passed they indulged in a little buccaneering, which I could not prevent until quite a number of craft had been looted. I asked the skipper why he had taken the fish, and his reply was that "the Portuguese always do so," a statement that I cannot endorse as being true. Some of the poor fishermen would throw their catch overboard among the reeds in the hope of the store being missed, so that they might again recover it. From this it would appear that the custom of robbery is common.

The fish in the Kwakwa are very good, much better than the birds which are so lively upon its banks. The boys indulged in the latter, and relished them thoroughly as delicacies. One of the birds they called *Nanchengwe*; it was a kind of fish-eagle. Hook-billed divers were called *Nondwe*.

In such observations as these the days, nights, weeks, and months of 1884 had passed away, and now that I was rapidly nearing the end of my long journey, thoughts of its close were somewhat sad, even with all the troubles and woes which had been contended against.

Without a stop we continued to glide along. The boat's helm is put "hard down" as we near the sharp bend of the river, and swinging round we head E.S.E.

New scenes now burst upon the view as the tideway expands on every hand, smooth and calm, like a vast sheet of burnished silver, framed by the dark savannahs. The water becomes brackish, for it is mingling with the sea. Mangroves still roll past upon the marshy mud-banks, deep green foliage without a break—an emerald cloak for the passing land. The leaf-laden boughs incline downwards in graceful arches, and over the flowing tide they kiss the waters of the sea!

The sea at last! We inhale the refreshing breath of old Neptune, who whispers of home, and welcomes us out to the great Indian Ocean! The Dark Continent has been traversed for nearly a thousand leagues; from where the waters of the vast Atlantic break upon the rock-bound shores of Table Bay!

As we survey the view behind, we see the great marshes sinking under sand and sea. Tall palms and the twin cupolas of a church arise before us, and on the bosom of the ebbing tide we direct our course swiftly to Quillimane. The Mazaro men sing in gleeful tones their happy boatman's song; the captain's loud and long-drawn notes giving the lead—

Wo-oh! ai! oh!

in which with spontaneous impulse every one joins heart and soul, swelling with joyous will the cheering chant.

The boat darts forward at every bend of the primitive paddles, which strike the water with pulse-like thuds, keeping time to the spirited song, and throwing the spray high in the air. Merrily we move, singing to the sea, and with the noonday sun land on the white stone pier of Quillimane.

The boys shoulder the baggage, and we march in straggling file through the street in the middle of an avenue of acacias, whose deep ruby blossoms contrast pleasantly against the houses glistening with ochre and neutral tints.

Flags of all nations float over the light-walled dwellings. The dome-topped spires of the whitened church now rear high above our heads. We pass unconcernedly the standards of the Dutch, the Germans, and the French, until on our left we see the meteor flag of old England, and to the house over which it waves we direct our steps.

I handed to Mr. Shearer, the agent of the African Lakes Company, the letter I carried from Mr. Moir of Blantyre. After reading it he welcomed me heartily, but remarked—
"Ah! you're not the man. There's no reward for us with you."

"What man?" was my natural question.

"Well, we have received communications from London offering a large reward for the capture of some individual who is supposed to have obscured himself in Central Africa. We thought the mysterious man for whom so many letters have come could be none other than the "treasure" travelling under a convenient alias."

The steamer was expected in a few days. M. Giraud arrived on the following morning, just in time to participate in a good French breakfast with M. Rosier of the French house and myself, a repast so long unknown, that the occasion has left a lasting impression of our host's hospitality.

At Quillimane we made many acquaintances, accepting with pleasure the hearty good-fellowship of the various mer-

"WO, OH! AI OH!" SINGING TO THE SEA. (QUILLIMANE).

chants. Strolls through the town in the evening were agreeably refreshing after the heat of the day had passed and the gentle winds swept up from the sea. We wandered in the groves of the tall palm forest which covered the landward expanse, and back again to the church, where the military band played, and the social circles of the town revolved.

Congratulations were freely bestowed upon us when it became known where we had been, from whence we had come, and—*mirabile dictu!*—that neither of us had suffered a day's illness from fever.

Five days passed and then, sure enough, the S.S. *Dunkeld*, Captain Broadfoot, came to an anchor in the estuary.

Reclining in an easy chair I read the latest news. Cholera at Marseilles and details of the black Soudan business. To me a newspaper was like food to a hungry man. Ease was not my lot, however. A burning sensation came over me, and I felt as though I would be consumed with the heat of the body. I was fairly caught. At the very last moment here was the fever! Oddly enough its attack began on the very day, and within a few hours of embarkation. I cannot further tax the reader's patience with an account of the long and lingering illness which followed.

"Come along; pull yourself together; the boat is at the quay!" were the words with which young Mr. Miller of the African Lakes Company encouraged my departure.

But a brief time elapsed, and I found myself lying on a sofa in a deck cabin of the *Dunkeld*, where Captain Broadfoot gave me every kind attention he could, and continued to do so during the trip.

While reposing here there fell upon my ears many sounds of other days, such as the jingle of knives, forks, and spoons, and the whirling of plates and dishes, varied by a continuous shuffling of hurried feet passing to and fro along the deck. A strong odour of coffee pervaded everywhere.

Numbers of Portuguese residents crowded into the cabin to see their friends off, and high above the din of many voices rose the doleful strains of a tuneless man trying to warble about something that was going to happen, "Some day, some day!" Who but an Englishman would have the boldness to attempt such an infliction?

My friend M. Giraud was about the last to leave for the shore. He still had some weeks to wait for a steamer to Zanzibar. In bidding him good-bye I could not help thinking of how admirably we had agreed, and how glad I would be at any time to meet such a companion again. For in Giraud I found all the attributes that link a friendship fast—a bright companion, an unselfish sportsman, and a trusty comrade.

The wind twanged the chords of the rigging, which sighed the old Æolian tune, soon to be overcome by the harsh roar of steam coming from the funnel. Signal-bells rang from the bridge to the engine-room. Then I heard cracking sounds, as link after link of the cable was taken in by the rattling capstan. At last the anchor was weighed, and we were outward bound.

With such sounds and scenes of the modern world in my ears, the charms and reverses of the wandering life became the treasures of memory. Farewell to the rough roving in the home of the black man! Farewell, land of the equatorial sun! Thy scenes have vanished, but their picture is indelible on my memory, intertwined amidst the leaves of sadness and the flowers of hope. Often again will I think of thee when in cloudy climes the sun's face is veiled by filmy fogs which rise from heated cities in the white man's home! The fascination of thy woods and thy mountains will then re-awaken to vivify my veins. I will forget all troubles with thy people, and wander once more, like them, a free son of Nature. Thy forest plains of stately palms will be before me, and thy wealth of animal life. Thine are beauteous adornments of a saddened face, which I will ever think of as I linger on the memories of eventful days.

Perils and adventures, mental and physical suffering, doubts and apprehensions are past, and these troubles are troubles no more.

So in spite of the maze of dilemmas through which it has been my lot to emerge successfully, I look back upon the past, as a whole, with not a little pleasure, for the retrospect brings something more than the mere satisfaction of having made the journey I intended to make, and I am confident that whoever follows my wandering footsteps in Africa will find that the tribes among whom I moved, and the chiefs with whom I dealt, will not treat them worse through my having been before them.

This narrative may show what difficulties a single European without reliable followers has to encounter while travelling in the remote central regions of Africa. Does it not, however, say much for the negro that such a journey was possible? I have heard many bad things said of him, but I found out that he has a vast deal of good in his composition. True he has deserted me frequently, and left me in awkward dilemmas, but he has treated me kindly as well. I say, with the sincerest satisfaction, that from the time I left the Cape of Good Hope until I reached the shores of Lake Nyassa I was never robbed of a single bead nor a yard of cloth, although the goods bank as well as the banker were entirely at his mercy. I never barricaded a door, preferring to show absolute indifference to evil influences. Every night afforded opportunities for attack.

The black man might have poisoned me had he wished to to do so, for when in villages or towns I gladly drank the water given by the people.

In so far as my own dealing with the natives is concerned, I found that kindness, firmness, and justice were the best and surest roads to success.

Tribes may differ in their customs, but there is a characteristic similarity of disposition among them all.

Let us hope that Africa will be for the Africans. They are the people best adapted for the climate, and they are contented with the products of their land. Every endeavour, however, to help them to alleviate their miseries and to give them comfort must be applauded—whether the effort is that of the missionary, the trader, or the explorer. We see what may be done in a single lifetime. The untiring exertions of Mr. H. M. Stanley, and his indomitable pluck and perseverance in the giant effort to found in Africa a new state, which shall be open to the commerce of the world, form one of the brilliant episodes of the century. Its lustre is heightened by the generous and philanthropic aid which has been so freely accorded by King Leopold II. of Belgium.

With the swifts, the swallows, and other birds of passage, I was home in the summer of 1885. For the first time in thirteen years I again sauntered in the lovely green groves and glades of old England during the month of May.

The air was sweet with the fragrance of flowers, and merry with the music of warbling birds; for the nightingale sang its winsome song, that ever-changing melody of sadness and of joy; the chaffinch chirped cheerily mid the warm verdure of the spring-clad hedges; and the thrush trilled its liquid notes, making the while festoon-like curves in the air, as it swooped from branch and twig of tree and shrub.

Buds were forcing their variegated beauty through the close clasping, but yet yielding, coats. The young leaves rustled in the whispering winds of morning.

Nature rejoiced in its soft garments of tender verdure, and as the mingling melodies and views touched the senses of sight and hearing, they roused again the slumbering thoughts of the past, as the strains of some familiar air often inspires happy dreams of days gone by.

My dreams are now directed towards the dark continent, and in fancy I soar high in the ethereal blue. From the centre of the sky, on the equatorial line, uninfluenced by worldly contact, let us look down with clearness upon the heart-shaped land of sorrow. On its outer edge, at all points of the compass, in every nook, on every strand, and in every bay and gulf, a blood-red margin skirting the land typifies the white man's dominion on its soil. This outer line is broken by the crested billows of the restless sighing sea, which bears to Afric's shores the white-winged butterflies of the coveting world, to feast on the misfortunes of her sons, and then to die.

A black impenetrable cloud obscures the centre of the heart, and from its gloom emerge the waving lines of great arterial streams. White lines in erratic courses of varying length mark the footsteps of explorers.

We are told of the stars that are born in the illimitable firmament, that years, yea ages, may elapse ere their light reaches our eyes. Perhaps through this darkened cloud the dim rays of what may prove a lustrous unquenchable light are beginning to break forth, as surely as the magnetic needle points to the northern star. The struggling light of Hope was kindled many years ago on the poisonous shores of Bangweolo.

Yet another line may pass across our fantastic vision,

fluctuating like the curves on a weather chart, and denoting, after centuries of fruitless strife, the ingress of the pale-faced marauders of the civilised world, whose footsteps have a hideous following of fleshless frames, showing the wake of the worshippers of the only God, whom they preach as the incarnation of justice, freedom, and mercy.

Our conclusions would be that all the efforts of the most indomitable and intrepid races of mankind to gain a lasting footing in this coveted land have, in the ages that are gone, been fruitless. There must be something stronger than war, something more potent than gunpowder, something more pregnant even than the Gospel, that has acted like a centrifugal force in throwing off and destroying every encroaching element.

Mayhap with the rise of an irresistible tide of progress the sun of prosperity may appear, dissolving the clouds of storm and strife from the face of this unhappy land, and shedding for ever a light of peace and joy, making the hitherto inaccessible home of the black man a World's Elysium.

FINIS.

INDEX.

"ABANTU!" ii. 70
Adansonia, ii. 18
Æpyceros Melampus, 29, 304
Africa, estimating travel in, ii. 17; Portuguese in East, 41; for the Africans, 300; white man's dominion in, 301; hopes of, 301, 302; fruitless efforts to colonise, 302
African Lakes Company, ii. 222
   ,, travellers, reckless statements of, 107
Agriculture, Ajawa, ii. 196
Ajawa or Nyanja tribe, ii. 194
   ,, at Mbewe, ii. 243
Alarm, a dangerous, ii. 177
Alcelaphus cauma. *See* Harte-beest.
   ,, *lunatis*, 114
Amaholi tribe, 73
Amandabeli, 67. *See* Matabeli.
Amazoe river, 145, 149, 168, 225, ii. 32, 49
Amazuiti, Mashona name for Matabeli, 151
American gold seekers, 20
Ammunition, 63, 121
Angoni and Makanga hostilities, ii. 122
Angoni carriers, danger of having, ii. 178; accusation by, 187; flight of, 190
Angoni corn stores, ii. 113
   ,, people, ii. 85, 86, 95; salutation of, 112; burial ceremonies, 114; witchcraft among, 118; slave kidnappers, 125; do not disfigure their faces, 122; not given to dancing, 123; arms of the, 153; clannishness of, 188'
Angoni villages, ii. 97, 98
Angoni-land, ii. 61, 83, 84; first town in, 86; cattle in, 111; slaves in, 224
Animal life on the Shiré, ii. 218
Animals, superstitions regarding, 19
Antelopes, 29, 47; Tsesesebe, 114; roan, 144, 241; sable, 171, 186; impala, 304; ii. 26, 169, 244, 245
Ants, black, 37, 175; at Tette, ii. 53; white, i. 276
Aqua ardiente, ii. 9, 36
Arab opposition to whites, ii. 159
Armies, contending, ii. 263
Army, strength of Khama's, 34
   ,, the Portuguese, ii. 267
   ,, Portuguese, mode of maintaining, ii. 276, 277
Arrows, poisoned, 29
Assegais, 227, 251
   ,, throwing, 227
   ,, neatness of Matabeli, ii. 153
Axe carried by Mashoma, 138

BABOONS, 235, 256; ii. 25
Baggage, weight of, 121
Bahurutsis tribe, 24
Baines, the late Mr. Thomas, 306

Bamangwato. *See* Khama's Town.
Bangweolo, lake, ii. 159
Bananas, 74
Banyai tribe, ii. 195
Baobab, ii. 18
Bararika, a chief, ii. 264; is incensed, 270
Bargaining with natives, 50
Bark blankets, 248; mode of making, 257, 258
Bark manufactures, 119
„ mats, 182
Barre, mountain pinnacle, 193, 257
Baskets, palm, ii. 20
Bath, digging for a, 297
Bathing habits of natives, 279
Battle at Chibinga, ii. 15.
Batuka (drum), 313
Bazurke tribe, 204
Beaconsfield, Lord, on the Zulus, ii. 125
Beads in request at Nyassa, ii. 192; in Angoni-land, 192
Beans, ii. 122
Bechuana people, laziness of, 33
Bechuana-land, 24, 28; its characteristics, 31; a worthless country, 37-39
Bed, comforts of a, ii. 223
Beds unknown, 52
Beer, maize, 247
„ native, effects of, ii. 90, 103, 122
Beer-drinking, 54, 56, 262
Bengula. *See* Lo-Bengula.
Benia river, ii. 18
Birds, absence of song, ii. 73, 77
Bird-life on the Shiré, ii. 216, 261
Black man, the, opinions respecting, ii. 299
Black suit, a, ii. 230
Blacksmithing, Mashona, 158, 159
Blankets of bark, 248; mode of making, 257, 258
Blantyre, ii. 194, 217, 228, 229; carriers from, 219, 221, 222;
scarcity of provisions, 225; a consul at, 226
Boar, good shot at a, 303
„ ii. 218
Boat upset by a hippo, ii. 219
Boatlanama, 29
Boatmen of Mazara, ii. 283, 292
Body-guard, the, 121
Boers, 23; aggression of, 25; religion of, 26; polygamy, 40; "christening," 85
Bonga, a chief, ii. 54
Bonumarungo mountain, ii. 73
Boots and sham bootmakers, 187
"Boys," old and young, 80
Braga, Senhor, Governor of Tette, ii. 44
Branches used for fording, 88
Broadfoot, Captain of the *Dunkeld*, ii. 297
Britons distinguished from Boers, 67
Buffaloes, ii. 84, 85, 115, 169-171, 173, 218
Bullets, hollow, 47, 79
Bultfontein Diamond Mine, 12
Buluwayo, 43, 45, 51
Burchell zebra, 78
Burial customs, ii. 105, 113, 133
„ service at Tette, ii. 50
Bush pig, 290; ii. 169
Bushman lost, 240
Bushmen, Masarwa, 29, 38

CALICO, 63
California, mining speculation at, 11
Camp, Portuguese, ii. 266, 273
„ troubles, 163
Camping places, native, 264
Cane mats used as couches, 52
Cannibalism, belief about English, ii. 75
Canoe, an awkward, ii. 240
„ life, charms of, ii. 260
Canoeing more trying than marching, ii. 244

INDEX.

Canoes on the Shiré, ii. 230
Cape cart, 10
" Town, 4, 6–8
"Cape smoke," 20
Captain, incident of the loss of H.M.S., 122
Caravans, slave, ii. 127
Caroeira mountains, 42, 62
Carriers, difficulties about, 107, 111, 112, 164; ii. 67, 171
Cartridge cases, bartering, ii. 34
Cartridges sticking in rifles, 91; ii. 249
Castor oil, ii. 122
Catoblepas Gorgon, 29
Cat-o'-nine-tails, 298, 299
Cattle in Angoni-land, ii. 111
" "lung sick," 38
" subject to lung sickness, 66
" Mashona, 118
Cattle-whips made from giraffe hides, 33
Cattle-whip signal in South Africa, 100
Cervicapra arundinacea, 145, 314
Chakundakoro, native name for the Governor of Tette, ii. 44, 68, 80
"Changing houses," diamond, 15
Charlatans, medical, ii. 116
Charms used by natives, ii. 116
Chibero, the chief, 105
" men threaten to loot the waggon, 240
Chibinga, 260, 285; the great dance, ii. 3; battle at, 15; elevation of, 17; vermin at, 13; farewell to, 23
Chickens, ii. 152
Chief, a sick, ii. 198
Chiefs, power of, 184, 204
Chikuse, King, appearance of, 108; first mention of, ii. 90; his demeanour, 101; suspects a spy, 107; wants to hear speech, 108, 109; cruelty of, 121; and tea-drinking, 130; kills his mother's lovers, VOL. II.

135; number of his wives, 132; sends spies to Livingstonia, 212
Chikuse's mother, ii. 109, 133–136
" sister, visits from, 103, 108
Chikuse's town, disagreeable reception at, ii. 100; mysteries and miseries at, 103–105; welcome appearance of da Costa, 106; slavery at, 126; departure from, 149
Childbirth, customs at, ii. 237, 238
Chimlolo, one of Livingstone's men, ii. 199
Chiputula, a Shiré chief, ii. 55, 215, 223, 241; country claimed by, 246, 255; the tragedy of, 256–258
Chiromo on the Shiré, ii. 253, 258
Chizæris concolor, 281
Chlorodyne, ii. 198
Chobe river, 64
Christianity in Bechuana-land, influence of, 31
"Christening," a rough ceremony, in, 85
Chronometer, 177; broken, ii. 82; destruction of the, 90; the final smash, 172
Chuwe people, ii. 65
Chuzu, a Makorikori chief, 191
Chuzu's, dangers at, 202–211
" vindictiveness, 234
Citrons, 225
Civilisation, comparison with, 251
Clanship, 162
Cleanliness unknown, 250
Cloth, Africans indifferent about coloured, 205
Cloth, curious opinion about, ii. 131
"C. L. K." rifle, 78; a good shot from, ii. 250
Coal, ii. 65
Cobus Elipsiprymnus, ii. 244
Coffee, 63
Cold, degrees of, 262
Colesberg, 10, 11

X

Companion, an affrighted, 241; longing for a, ii. 174
Conjugal infidelity, ii. 238
Conjurors of Msenga, ii. 10
Consul at Blantyre, uselessness of a, ii. 226, 259
Contentment of natives, 249-251, 271
Cooking, rough, ii. 88
Copper, 225
Corn-grinding, ii. 167
Corn stores of the Angoni, ii. 113
Costumes of Msenga minstrels, ii. 10
Cotton, ii. 19
Couches of cane mats, 52
Courage of Kaffir, ii. 198
Cows, Mashona, 182
Crane, crested, ii. 114, 150
Crocodiles, 39, 80; victims of, ii. 55; shooting, 113, 217; in Lake Nyassa, 202; traveller killed by, 213
Cruelty, instances of Kankune's, ii. 143-145
Cuculos Indicator (honey-bird), 94
Cynocephalus porcarius, 256
" *babuini*, ii. 25

DA COSTA, EUSTAQUIO, welcome appearance of, ii. 106; friendly assistance from, 142, 187
Daingi, town, ii. 20
Dake river, ii. 25, 29
Damp, dangers of, 99
Dance, the great Matabeli, 60
Dances, extraordinary, ii. 10, 12
Dancing, similarity of civilised and savage, ii. 12
Danube, steamer, 8, 10
Dartmouth, 3
Date palm, 197
Dawson, Mr. James, 30
Day, a lost, ii. 40
Dead, burial of the, 249; wailers for the, ii. 101; mourning over the, 137

Deare, Major, 9
Deaths, customs at, ii. 52, 53
De Beers Diamond Mine, 12, 15
De Souza, Don Manuel Antonio, ii. 267, 273
Delagoa Bay, game leaving, ii. 48
Delay, dangers of, ii. 81
Desertion, dangers of, ii. 81; by Landin, 83; by Maravi, 91, 92
Deuka's town, ii. 86
Dews, heavy, 130
Deza, Mount, ii. 150
Diamond Fields, 5, 6, 9, 11
" dealing restrictions, 15
" market, 14
" mining, 11, 12, 13, 14
Diet, 189
" of Angoni people, ii. 122
Digging for a bath, 297
Dingamombe mountain, 273
Dismemberment, a punishment, ii. 121
Dissel boom, a broken, 70
Divers, ii. 73
Doctoring a chief, ii. 199
Donkeys, absence of, 248; victims to tsetse fly, ii. 118
Dorah river, 264
Dove, stalking a, ii. 202
Draughts, ii. 33, 49
Drinking in the tropics, 279
Drummond Castle, steamer, 3
Drums of native make, 225; carried by Xopetta, ii. 242
Dry river beds, 289, 305, 310; ii. 18, 25, 32, 39, 63
Du Toit's Pan Diamond Mine, 12
Ducking, a, 80
Duiker, 39, 77, 265
Dunkeld, s.s., ii. 297
Dysentery, 245; ii. 194, 201, 284
" cure for, ii. 220

EARWIGS, 150
Eclipse of the sun, a puzzle to Lo Bengula, 67

Edwards, Mr. Sam, 41
Eland, 135, 144, 203, 235, 241, 259, 290; ii. 2
Elephants, 44, 77; trees uprooted by, 83, 89; an exciting hunt, 90-92; ii. 47, 106, 115, 170, 247-251
Elephant-fat, melting, 113
Elephant-hunter, Da Costa, the, ii. 106
Elephant tracks, ii. 169, 172
Elliot, Mr., missionary at Inyati, 75
Emigrants deceived, 37, 38
Encounter, an unexpected, ii. 93
Endurance of Matabeli, 189
England, return to, 300
English cannibals, belief about, ii. 75
English currency, Sakanii's, appreciation of, ii. 17
Entertainments, Mashona, 140, 143; at Chibinga, ii. 12
Equipment for the journey, 63
Etsatse river, 145, 148, 235
    „ valley, 214
Eucalyptus, 25; ii. 221
Euphorbia arborescens, 29
Europeans in Tette, ii. 47
Execution scenes, ii. 28, 137
Exercise, benefit of, ii. 64
Exodus of Mtavara, ii. 32, 33
Explorers, old, 2
Explosion, tremendous, 9

FAIRBAIRN, Mr. GEORGE, 51, 52, 54, 55, 57, 64, 67, 69, 70, 71
"Faithfuls," the, 68; paying off the, ii. 7; farewell to the, 8
Fat, how to get, ii. 195
Fatness, a Kaffir ambition, 35
Fauresmith, 11
Feast, a royal, 56
    „ at Chibinga, ii. 2, 3, 4
Feather head-dress, 49
Feathers, native liking for, 49
Feeders, gross, 189

Feet, torments of, 187, 192, 274; ii. 34
Fema mountains, ii. 36
Fenwick, a hunter, ii. 215, 223; kills Chiputula, 257; his own fate, 258
Festivals, similarity of civilised and savage, ii. 12
Fetichism at Tette, ii. 44
Ferry for slave traffic, ii. 214
Fever, African, 41; at Tati, 41; in Matabeli-land, 51, 62; produced by damp, 99; ii. 49; marshes the hotbeds of, 293; attacked by, 297
Findlay, Mr., 8
Fire, mode of defeating grass, 101
Firearms, result of familiarity of natives with, 44
Fire water of civilisation, ii. 9
Fires essential to Mashona, 134.
Fires, prairie, 70; pursued by prairie; 101; an immense, 128; prairie, ii. 77
Firmness with natives, ii. 300
Fish, ii. 73
    „ and fishermen on the Kwakwa, ii. 294.
Fish hawks, ii. 190
Fishermen of Lake Nyassa, ii. 197
Fishing on Lake Nyassa, mode of, ii. 170
Fit, curing a, 223
Flies, 36; in myriads, 293
Flint-locks, 225; in Angoni-land, ii. 89
Floods, ii. 49
"Fly," country, 145. *See* Tsetse fly.
Fonseca, Vincente Rubero de, 312. *See* Sakanii.
Food, native, 251; bad, ii. 99; half-cooked, 122
Foote, Captain, death of, ii. 225
Forest, cutting through, 83
Forests, ii. 63

INDEX.

Forge, a primitive, 158, 159
Francolins, 300; ii. 34
Frasincho, an unlooked-for friend, ii. 94
Fred, Livingstone's boy, ii. 231
Fredericks, Captain of the *Ilala*, ii. 210, 221
Free State, Orange, 11
Freebooters of the Transvaal, 23
Fumigating for small-pox, 24, 25, 26
Funeral feasts, ii. 57
„ services, Chiputula's, ii. 241
Furnaces, iron smelting, ii. 158

GARDENS, Matabeli, 49
Gill, Dr., 8
Giraffes, 29, 30; slaughter of, 33; 39, 44
Giraud, Lieutenant V., ii. 210, 217, 219, 220, 222, 223, 226, 240, 243, 244, 246, 253, 260, 265, 268, 270, 286, 287, 290, 291, 296, 298
Girls, bartering, ii. 242
„ of Angoni-land, ii. 139, 140
Goat, eccentricities of a, 147; left behind, 275
Goats, ii. 152; in the "Fly" country, 33; killed by leopards, 225
Gobuluwayo. *See* Buluwayo.
God, no Idea of, 249
God, natives have no conception of a, ii. 132
Gold, 149; in the Rusaka mountains, 218, 219, 184, 225, 233, 264, ii. 18, 19, 49
Gold-dealing, ii. 9
Gold-dust, mode of carrying, 147
Gold-fields, the Tati, 40, 41
Gold mining at Tati, 42, 43
Gold ornaments, absence of, 230
Gold-producing rivers, 218
Gold seekers, American, 20
Gold-washing, 225; ii. 18

Gonté trees, 197
Goque river, 79
Gorilla dance, ii. 11
Govea, a Portuguese commander, ii. 267, 273
Grass fires, ii. 77
"Greenhorn" gold, 184
Greite, Mr., 24
Grumapudzi river, 144, 218, 225
Gubuluwayo. *See* Buluwayo.
Guinea-fowl, 39, 300; ii. 26
Gun accident, a fatal, ii. 213
Gunpowder, native, 233
Gwailo river, 80
Gwigwi river, 138

HALF-CASTE kings, ii. 46
Hanyane river, 80, 94, 100, 108, 126
Harkess, Mr. W., of the *Ilala*, ii. 210, 219, 221
Harris, Mr. (London Missionary Society), ii. 220
Hartebeest, 81, 144, 168
Headrings of headmen, ii. 110, 111
Head-shaving, ii. 21; among women, 124
Hemp-smoking, 152, 230; ii. 65
Henry express rifle, 78
Hens, Misiri and the, ii. 88
Hermansberg Mission, 25
Hippopotamus, 19, ii. 55, 112, 113, 175, 217, 218, 219; charged by, 250; trenches of, 96
Hippotragus niger, 171
Hive-shaped huts, 53
Hlonipa, the law of, 65
Hollow bullets, disappointing, 47, 79
Holub, Dr., 7, 8
Honey, 93
Honey-birds warning elephants, 90
Hooft, Mr., a Dutch trader, ii. 286
Hope Fountain mission station, 52
Hopes of Africa, ii. 301, 302

Horse sickness, 46
Horses, absence of, 248
    „   "salted," 21
Hostage from the Portuguese, ii. 267; his dangerous position, 268-272
Hot springs of the Zambesi, ii. 58
Hottentot liking for the name of John, 43
Houses of missionaries at Livingstonia, ii. 193
Houses on stilts, 276
Hungry followers, ii. 79
Hunters, Maravi, ii. 115
    „   native, at Tette, ii. 47
Hunting, 29, 30, 84, 90, 91, 92, 114, 145, 203, 241, 267, 303, 304; ii. 26, 170, 171, 217, 244, 245, 247, 248, 249, 250, 251
Hunting-medicine, ii. 116
Huts of Matabeli Queens, 53, 55
    „   form of, 148
    „   filthy, 291
Hyenas, 270; ii. 141

IGNORANCE, native, 250
Igova, a Mashona town, 169, 182
Igrezi, native name for English, ii. 75, 79
Ikalafing, a chief, 24, 25
Ilala, The, mission steamer, ii. 209, 210; 217, 221, 229
Impisi, a name for leopards, 93
Implements, the manufacture of, 230
Incursions by Matabeli, 33
Indecency of Landin, ii. 74
Indifference to danger, a pagan characteristic, ii. 270
Industry not a prominent trait of the blacks, 74
Industries, 119; at Tette, ii. 48
Infidelity, conjugal, ii. 238
Inhamessinga, a chief, ii. 54, 55
Inkwezi river, 43, 44, 45
Insanity unknown, 252

Interpreters, doubts about, 216
Inthlathlangela village, 51
Inyati mission station, 75
Inyota, a Makorikori town, 237; departure from, 203
Inyota-men paid off, ii. 6
Inxwala, a great dance, 60
Iron, 225
    „   bows, 230
    „   ore, signs of working, 257
    „   smelting furnaces, ii. 158
Ironstone, 160
Ironworking, 159
Irrigation, 35
Ivory, half claimed by chiefs, ii. 255, 256

JA-JA, or lip rings, ii. 195
Jacobsdaal, 24
Jandani mountain, ii. 78
Jansen, Mr., of Hermansberg, 25
Jesuit Fathers at Tati, 41; at Tette, ii. 42, 50
John, a name liked by Hottentots, 43
John, the Korana hunter, 43, 68; his drunken freak, 69, 71; 76
"Johnny," the old British tar, 54, 67
Jumbe, a slave ferryman, ii. 214
Jumbe's, slaves at, ii. 155
Justice towards natives, ii. 300

KAFFIR diamond workers, 15
Kaffir pluck, ii. 198
    „   superstitions, 45
Kaffirs, voracious, 93
Kafua mountains, ii. 24
Kalahari desert, 33
Kameo river, ii. 95
Kanga Tore, a native name for guinea-fowl, 304
Kankune, King of Makanga, ii. 66, 142; a bloodthirsty tyrant, 143
Kanyemba, a slave boy, 36
    „   a Zumbo chief, ii. 46
Kapinja river, ii. 38

Kapirizange mountains, ii. 72, 75
Karemba, the Mashona "Faithful," 21, 68, 78, 79; his stories at Chibinga, ii. 5; his history, 7
Karemwe river, 94
Karonga on Nyassa, ii. 210
Karue river, 197
Kasisé, a chief, ii. 255, 256, 259
Katunga, a Shiré chief, ii. 224, 228
Kebrabasa rapids, ii. 54
Khama, a chief, 31, 32, 33, 39
Khama's army, strength of, 34
,, town, 30, 31, 32, 35
,, wife, 35
Kidnappers, slave, ii. 90
Kimberley, 11, 12, 14, 15, 18, 20
Kindness to natives, ii. 300
Kings, half-caste, ii. 46
Kingfishers, ii. 73
Kirton, Mr. Argent, 25, 27, 30, 35
Klerksdorp, 5, 17, 20, 21, 22
"Klipspringer," the, 104
Knobkerry, the, ii. 154
Koodoo, 290
"Kooes-cop" elephant, meaning of, 90
Kopjies, 10
Korana, John. *See* John.
Kota-Kota, slaves at, ii. 155; a slave ferry, 214
Kraal, Lo Bengula's, 53, 57, 60
,, a miserable, ii. 153
Kunyungwi, native name for Tette (which see), 106
Kuruman, Lo Bengula's rival, 64, 65
Kwakwa river, ii. 291, 292, 294

Labour, native, at Tette, ii. 45
Land, a worthless, 37
,, cultivated at Shilo, 74
,, moving from bad to good, ii. 33
Landeen. *See* Landin.
Landin tribe (*see also* Angoni), ii. 59
,, grievances, ii. 68; alarm of, 70, 71; indecency of, 74; deserted by, 83
Lane, Mr., 23
Lapanose, M. Comte de, 63
Law of Hlonipa, 65
Leask, Mr. James, 5, 17, 18
Lemon trees, 74
Lemons, 225
Leopards, 93; killing goats, ii. 225
Leopold II., King of the Belgians, ii. 300
Letters, native objections to carry, ii. 188
Leviathan, the, canoe, ii. 243, 246; attacked by a hippo, 251; nearly wrecked, 252; fired upon, 286 end of her journey, 290
Lichtenberg, 22
Lightning, a deadly flash of, 45
Limbo, trading name for cloth, 50
Limpopo river, 50, 80
Lindsay, Mr., African Lakes Co., ii. 290
Linekana town, 24, 25
Lioness, adventure with a, 269
Lion adventure on the Mkumbura river, 305
Lion ceremony at Chibinga, ii. 9
,, woman attacked by a, ii. 14
Lions, 30, 81, 94, 189, 259, 265, 266, 270
Lions, night attacks by, 86, 87
,, at Chibinga, number of persons killed by, ii. 14
Lion's skull, incident of the, ii. 232, 233
Livingstone, David, ii. 159, 199, 229, 291
Livingstonia, unknown at Chikuse's, ii. 133, 148, 163, 175; arrived at, 183; alone at, 185; foraging at, 186; missionaries' houses, 193; fruitless labours of missionaries, 204; life sacrifice at, 205; a light on the lake, 207; rescue at, 208; 229

INDEX. 311

Livingstone's boy Fred, ii. 231
" deserted house at Shupanga, ii. 289
Livingstone's, Mrs., grave, ii. 289
Lo-Bengula the Matabeli King, 19, 33, 39, 45, 46, 49; interview with, 53; 56, 57, 61; description of, 64; and the eclipse, 67; and Captain Paterson's Mission, 72; his regiment, 74
Lobo, a chief, ii. 46
London Missionary Society, 75; ii. 220
Looking-glass, astonishment caused by a, 244
Lost, a day, ii. 40
Lubola mountains, 257, 272
Lung sickness of cattle, 66
Lupata gorge, ii. 64

MABADE river, 64
McEwan, Mr., engineer, ii. 214
Machabele forest, 78; ii. 84
" tree, 115, 159, 182
Macheangombe, a chief, 133
Machilla, a conveyance, 313
Machilleiros, bearers, 315
Madeira, 3, 4; chest affections at, 4
Magnetism surprises the natives, ii. 32
Magombegombe mountains, 255
Magubuduani, a kraal, 50
Mahalapse river, 36
Maize beer, 247
" fields, Matabeli, 49
Makalaka people, 33, 42
Makanga tribe, ii. 53, 55, 63, 65, 69; camp of the, 71, 72; 121
Makhobo hills, 45
Makinjira and Mpemba, battle between, ii. 214
Makoka, ii. 228
Makololo people, error about, ii. 91, 199
Makololo war, ii 215
Makomwe mountains, 273; ii. 17, 22

Makorikori country, 190, 278
" tribe, 183, 200, 224; live in detached bodies, 233; 225; murder unknown, 251; attack on Chibinga, ii. 16
Makorikori women, 229
Makomwe mountains, 276
Malalima, the chief, ii. 230
Malawe, Mount, ii. 273
Mandala. *See* Blantyre.
Manganja mountains, ii. 77, 78, 95, 105, 161
Mangoni. *See* Angoni or Landin.
Mangue river, 46
Manufactures, no progress in, 251
Maps, study of, 7
Mara, a Maravi guide, ii. 151; his obese ambition, 194; good-bye to, 211
Maravi people, ii. 43; desertion by, 91, 92
Maravi hunters, ii. 115
" traveller, a noted, ii. 74
Marching under difficulties, 187, 188
Market, diamond, 14
Marketing, boisterous, 110
Marriage customs, ii. 51, 52, 237
Marshes the hotbeds of fever, ii. 293
Martinez, Senhor, merchant at Tette, ii. 56
Masarwa bushmen, 29, 38
Maseeha, scenes at, ii. 30, 31, 32
Mashona-land, 53, 80
Mashona tribe, 42, 101; citadels of the, 104; mode of hunting, 115; appearance, customs, and condition, 115-119; hunters, 102; physique of the, 103; wooden pillows, 133; voracity, 137; music of, 140; entertainments, 140, 143
Massacre of Usikuana, 61; of sepulchre watchers, 61, 62; of Captain Paterson's party, 72
Matabeli-land, 7, 39, 40; fever in, 51, 62; the plateau of, 51

312　INDEX.

Matabeli tribe, superstition of, 19, 32, 33, 34, 45; a warrior of the, 49; queens of the, 53, 54; morals of the, 62; raids by, 102; mode of warfare, 104; endurance of, 189
Matebi, King, 25
Matope on the Shiré, ii. 217
Mats of bark, 182
Mauni river, ii. 78
Muvuba, a garden, 49
Mazara boatmen, ii. 283, 289, 292
Mazaro village, ii. 290
Mazinjiri people, ii. 55; in flight, 262; fugitives, 263; enraged by the appearance of a hostage, 269; Portuguese defeat of the, 276
Mazinjiri and Portuguese war, ii. 223
Muzua, native name of a fruit tree, ii. 33
Mbewe village, ii. 241, 242, 246
Mboma mountain, ii. 90
Mchesa, the Vulcan of Mashonaland, 144, 155–160
Meal not regularly carried, 181
Measles, 36
Meat, a fierce squabble about, 135
Medical charlatans, ii. 116
Medicine chest, a hunter's, 36
　„　　for hunting, ii. 116
Mexican peone, 298
Military system of the Portuguese, ii. 46
Milk and honey, missionary promise of, 67
Milk, queer-looking, ii. 196
Mill, diamond, 13
　„　a Syenitic, ii. 167
Miller, Mr., of the African Lakes Company, ii. 241, 243, 268, 270, 290, 297
Mining, diamond, 11, 12
Minstrels of Msenga, ii. 10
Mission stations, Hermansberg, 25; Hope Fountain, 52; Inyati, 75; Livingstonia, ii. 184; Blantyre, 219

Mission steamer at Nyassa, ii. 191
Missionaries, native idea about, 66
　„　　away from Livingstonia, ii. 186
Missionary, a persecuted, 52
Missionary Society (London), ii. 220
Missionary effort, ii. 43; misdirected, 205
Mjela, a chief, 259, 260, 263
Mjobva river, ii. 64
Mkoma river, ii. 18
Mkoudozi river, ii. 78
Mkumbura river, 305, 310
Moghose's station, 25, 27
Moir, Mr., of Blantyre, ii. 219, 222–225, 227, 230, 256, 258, 259, 296
Molepololi river, 27
Money, precaution about, 208; as a medium of exchange, ii. 48
Monkeys, ii. 203
Montgomery, Colonel, 5
Mopani bush, 43
Mopani trees, 78
Morals, Matabeli, 62; Mashona, 116
Morambala mountain, ii. 278, 282
　„　　superstitions, regarding, ii. 284, 285
Morrison, Mr., engineer, ii. 230
Mortars for millet and rice, ii. 20
Mount Deza, ii. 150
　„　Malawe, ii. 273
Mountain scenes, 193, 194
Mountains. *See* under names:—
Bonumarungo, Caroeira, Fema, Jandani, Kafua, Kapirizange, Lubola, Magombegombe, Manganja, Makomwe, Mboma, Morambala, Rusaka, Umvukwe, Vunga.
Mourners, hypocrisy of, ii. 137, 256
Mpanga village, ii. 181, 193
Mponda, warning about, ii. 169
Msenga slave women, 302

Msenga, a town, 310
  „ minstrels and conjurers, ii. 10, 11
Msenga women, lip-ring of, ii. 20
Msingua, river, 281, 284, 285, 289, 297; ii. 18
Mtande, tribe, ii. 19
Mtavanda, tribe, ii. 19
Mtavara, tribe, ii. 31
Muave, a superstitious compound, ii. 234; custom of using, 234, 235, 275
Mudzi river, ii. 30
Mufa river, ii. 35
Muliliti, chief of Igova, 182
Murder, unknown among Makorikori, 251
Music, Mashona, 140; native, 249; of the Chibinga dance, ii. 3
Musical instruments, 232, 249
Mutua river, 272
Muzimba people, ii. 53, 65
Mvudzi river, ii. 73
Mvurezi river, ii. 169
Mwendapezi people, ii. 65
Mzungo (meaning Portuguese, or white man), 208, 286

NAMAQUA partridges, 39
Nanchengwe, a bird, ii. 294
Native customs, danger of interfering with, ii. 275
Native labour at Tette, ii. 45
  „ shrewdness, 137
Nations, vicissitudes of, ii. 53
Nazaras, or slave agents, ii. 126
Neanda, a town, 138
N'gami lake, 10 (note).
Negomo, a Makorikori chief, 216, 239
Nets used in hunting, 115
"New Valhalla," the, 51, 59, 67; the final farewell, 71
New Zealand mine at Tati, 41
Nondwe, native name for diver bird, ii. 294

N'tumbani, a king's grave, 61
Numida Pucherani, ii. 26
Nuts (Arachis), 118
Nyanja (see also Nyassa), ii. 174, 189, 191
Nyanja, or Ajawa, tribe, ii. 194
Nyansanga river, ii. 35
Nyassa, road between Tanyanyika and, ii. 214
Nyassa Lady, steamer, ii. 220; sinking of the, 259
Nyassa, lake, 7; ii. 173, 174, 180; tribes on, 192; its extent and depth, 199; slave dhows on, 203; emerging from, 216; first glimpse of, 161

OIL, not used for light, ii. 167
Orange Free State, 11
  „ river, 11
  „ trees, 74
Orators, Mashona, 167
Ordeals of superstition, ii. 233, 234
Orcas canna, 135
Ostriches, 143
Ox, mode of securing an, 261
  „ driving, 81, 82
Oxen, killed by lightning, 45; difficulty about, 71, 75; stubborn, 80
Oyengweni, town, 73

PALM baskets, ii. 20
  „ sleeping bags, ii. 281
  „ wells, ii. 64, 65, 66
Palmero, the infliction of the, 298; ii. 58
Pamalombe lake, ii. 216
Panama, isthmus of, railway, ii. 215
Pantumbo's village, mischief at, ii. 165; its poverty, 167
Partridges, ii. 69
Paterson (Captain), massacre of his party, 72, 73
Pauw, 47

Panw feathers, native liking for, 49
Payment in advance, 182; ii. 27
Pembe river, 187
Pereira, Senhor, merchant at Tette, ii. 56
Pereira, Cipriano Gaetano (see Kankune), ii. 65
Perfume used by Matabeli Queens, 53
Persecution of a missionary, 52
Physic sent for by a chief, ii. 198
Piebald Kaffir, a, ii. 31
Pigeons, trading for, ii. 28
" Piner !" a, ii. 35
Pipe, the wild hemp, 152
Piracy on the Kwa-kwa river, ii. 294
Pillows, wooden, of Mashona, 133; in Angoni-land, ii. 124
Plantain-eaters, 281
Podophyllin powder, 245
Poetical expressions of the Matabeli, 58, 59
Poison on arrows, 29
Poisoned water, 73
Polygamy, 62
Pombe, name for beer, ii. 31, 104, 119, 120, 122, 141, 164, 181, 194, 239, 241
Port Elizabeth, 6, 8, 9
Portuguese and Mazinjiri war, ii. 223
Portuguese possessions in Eastern Africa, ii. 41
Portuguese military system, ii. 46
„ forces on the Shiré, ii. 265
Portuguese camp, ii. 266, 273
„ army, mode of maintaining, ii. 276, 277
Potatoes, sweet, 225, 226
Pottery, native, 248
Power of chiefs, 184, 204
Prairie fire, pursued by, 101; an immense, 128; ii. 77

Preëmption law, ii. 34
Presents, 120
„ from natives, 224, 226, 261; ii. 29, 196
Presents indispensable, 112
„ not pay, 137
Prestage, Father, 41
Pretoria, 20
Prospecting for gold, 148, 219; ii. 49
Provisions exhausted, ii. 74, 76, 287
Pumpkins, 97
„ on the Shiré, ii. 281, 286
Punishment, dismemberment a, ii. 121

QUEENS, appearance of Matabeli, 53, 54, 55; huts of Matabeli, 53
Quillimane, ii. 223, 295, 296
Quills used for gold dust, 225

RAINY season, 310; ii. 19, 49
Ramakukan, a chief. See Kasisé.
Ramotsa, a chief, 25
Rat-hunting, boys, ii. 114
Rats, ii. 6, 13, 98
Recruiting carriers, 111
Reed bucks, 145, 314
Regiment, Lo Bengula's, 74
Religion among the Boers, 26
Retreat from Chuzu's, 211
Revubwe river. See Revuqwe.
Revuqwe river, ii. 61, 62, 96, 113, 155
Rhinoceros, 102, 259, 280, 290
Rice, ii. 19
Rifles, 63; Henry express, 78; cartridges sticking in, 91; exhibitions before natives, 225, 244
Rings for head-dress, ii. 110, 111
Rivers. See under names:—Amazoe; Benia; Chobe; Dake; Dorah; Etsatse; Goque; Grumapudzi; Gwailo; Gwigwi; Hanyane; Inkwezi; Kameo; Kapinja; Karemwe; Karue; Kwa-Kwa;

Limpopo; Mababe; Mahalapse; Mangue; Mauni; Mjobva; Mkoma; Mkondozi; Mkumbura; Molepololi; Msingua; Mufa; Mutua; Mvudzi; Mvurezi; Nyansanga; Pembe; Revuqwe; Ruia; Ruiana; Rumabiri; Ruo; Sabia; Sarue; Sepaque; Shashi; Shikambe; Shiré; Simbo; Umkhosi; Umquadzi; Umtenge; Umvuli; Umzengaizi; Umzwezwe; Vaal; Vilange; Waynge; Zambezi.
River beds, dry, 37, 289, 305, 310; ii. 18, 25, 32, 39, 63.
Roan antelopes, 168, 241
Robberies, ii. 254
Robbery of a trader, ii. 227
„ ii. 242
"Rock of Wisdom" at Inyota, 246
Rocks, towns amidst, 104, 117, 118
Roll-call, native amusement at, 192
Rosier, M., of Quillimane, ii. 296
Rubero. *See* Sakanii.
Ruia river, 165, 168, 186, 254
Ruiana river, 272
Rumabiri river, 187
Ruo river, ii. 246, 253, 264
Rusaka mountains, 144, 218

SABIA river, 50, 80
Sable antelope, 171
Sagwam, a "faithful," 68
St. Helena, 4
Sakakaka. *See* Kankune.
Sakanii, King, 282; his mother, 296, 301; his parentage, 312; meeting with, 311; bargaining with, ii. 9; payment of, 17
Sal volatile, ii. 182
Salt carriers, ii. 162, 166
Salt water, a majesty-making medicine, 65
"Salted" horses, 46
Salumbidwa, native name for Morambala mountain, ii. 285

Salutation, mode of, 120
Sandani, Old, 185; negotiating with, 215; his numerous wives, 219, 242; sings the white man's praises, 243
Sarue river, 94
Scott, Dr. and Mrs., at Blantyre, ii. 225
Sebaii, the guide, 133
Secheli, King, 27
Sechuana language, 24
Selous, Mr. F. C., 5, 9, 16, 18-20, 24, 30, 35, 49, 52, 53; attacked by fever, 62, 63, 79, 80; his furthest N.E. camp, 94
Sentinel, the mysterious, ii. 99
Sepaque river, 82
Sergeant, Mr., 72, 73
Sewing karosses, 32
Shashi river, 39
Shearer, Mr., African Lakes Company, ii. 296
Shepstone, Sir Theophilus, 72
Sheep, loss of, 126
Shidim, ii. 35
Shikambe river, ii. 64
Shiloh, a station, 72; cultivated land at, 74
Shiré, Upper, river, ii. 216
„ river, animal life on the, ii. 218; birds on the, 218, 223, 261, slave kidnapping on the, 224; sad war scenes, 278, 282
Shiré valley, slave captain in the, ii. 125; slavery in the, 283
Shoshong. *See* Khama's Town.
Shoshong infantry, humours of the, 33, 34
Shot, the mysterious, ii. 102
Shupanga, Livingstone's deserted house at, ii. 289
Silence enforced, ii. 92, 95
„ an advantage with savages, 106
Simbo river, 92
Singanga or witch-doctors, ii. 233

Skern, meaning of, 138
Skin diseases, ii. 33
,, of Mashona people, 132
Slag at iron-furnaces, ii. 158
Slave agents, ii. 159
,, dhows on Lake Nyassa, ii. 203
,, ferry on Nyassa, ii. 214
,, kidnappers, ii. 90, 125, 224
,, scene, a, ii. 156, 157
,, traffic, danger of interference, ii. 214
Slave women, Msenga, 302
,, yokes, ii. 155
Slavery at Tette, ii. 47; at Chikuse's, 126; aspects of, 127-129; in the Shiré valley, 283
Sleeping bags, palm, ii. 281
,, in the open, ii. 246
Small-pox in the Transvaal, 24-26
Smyth, General Sir L., 5
Snake dance, ii. 11
Snakes, ii. 293
Snuff-boxes, calabash, 169
Soil near Tette, ii. 48, 49
Soldiers, Portuguese, at Tette, ii. 45
Song-birds, absence of, ii. 73, 77
Spies in Livingstonia, Chikuse's, ii. 212
Spinning-wheels, ii. 20
Spoonbills, ii. 73
Sport in Africa, 77
Spy, suspected as a, 210; ii. 107
Squirrels, ground, 29
Stanley, Henry M., ii. 291, 300
Statistics of diamond-mining, 12
Steamer, suitable for the Zambesi, ii. 54
Steamer, mission, at Nyassa, ii. 191
,, Ilala. See Ilala.
,, Lady Nyassa, ii. 220
Stella-land, 23
Steinbuck, 39
Stewart, Mr., a trader, 64, 65, 67, 70
,, Mr., engineer, ii. 214
Stomach, the sensitive governor of the world, ii. 202

Stores, amount carried, 120, 121
Storks, ii. 37
Storm on the Shiré, ii. 278, 279
Storms, M., a Belgian, ii. 210
Strepsiceros Kudu, 290
Sugar, Madeira, 4
Superstitions, 19, 45; about teeth, 66; about a future state, 66, 238; about baboons, ii. 25; suppression hopeless, 117, 233-237
Supplies for the journey, 63

TABLE Bay, 8
,, mountain, 4
Tanganyika, lake, Giraud deserted at, ii. 210; the road to, 214, 220
Taroman, a "faithful," 68; sets the prairie on fire, 101
Tati gold fields, 40, 41
Tattoo marks, Makorikori, 229
Tchakani Vlei, 37
Tea, 63; the best tropical drink, 279; Chikuse drinks, ii. 130
Teeth, bad, 230
Teeth-filing, ii. 20, 195
Teteiros, natives of Tette, ii. 43
Tette, Portuguese town on the Zambesi, 106; ii. 41; in Livingstone's time, 42; its appearance, 41, 42, 45; decay of, 42; fetichism at, 43, 44; soldiers at, 45; native labour at, 45; its history, 47; slavery at, 47; native hunters at, 47; Europeans in, 47; soil near, 48, 49; industries at, 48; burial service at, 50; white ants at, 53; departure from, 58, 59
Thackeray on Africa, 1
Theft unknown, 153
,, Makorikori punishment of, 252
Thermometers smashed, ii. 90
"Thirst Land," the, 36
Thomas, Mr., an early settler in Matabeli-land, 24, 51
Thomas, Mr. D., of Shiloh, 72-75

INDEX.

Thomas, Mr. Morgan, 72, 73
"Three Brothers," the, 276
Time, natives, heedless of, 106, 250
Tobacco, 230; ii. 111
Toothache, curing the, ii. 27
Tower muskets, 225
Towns, Mashona, 117, 118
Trade, articles for, 121
Trader, a wily native, 185
Trading for pigeons, ii. 28
Tragedy of Chiputula, ii. 256, 257, 258
Travel in Africa, estimating, ii. 17
Transvaal, 22, 23; justice in the, 26
Tribes. *See* under names :—Ajawa; Amaholi; Bahurutsis; Banyai; Bazurke; Bechuana; Landin (*see also* Angoni); Makalaka; Makangu; Makorikori; Mashona, Matabeli; Mtande; Mtavanda; Mtavara; Wazezurus; Xopetta.
Trick in gold dealing, a, 184
Tricolour, the, canoe, desertion of the crew, ii. 271
Troughs, wooden, 248
Tsessebe antelope, 114
Tsetse fly, 145, 184, 256, 282, 293, 306, 307; ii. 24, 33, 48, 54, 63, 65, 75, 118, 193
Twins killed by Bechuana, 66

UAKANIA mountains. *See* Rusaka.
Ubenanzwa's country, 73
Ula, a superstitious, ii. 233, 234
Umganen village, 51, 64
Umhlangene station, 75, 102
Umbelo, a Matabeli, 74
Umkhosi river, 51, 62, 71
Umlugulu, a headman, 73
Umquadzi river, 144, 148
Umtenge river, 126
Umvukwe mountains, 94, 144, 186, 190, 192, 193, 310
Umvuli river, 85
Umzengaizi river, 310; ii. 18

Umzengezi river, 190
Umzilagazi, the conqueror, 42; his death, 61, 64, 66
Umzwezwe river, 83
Universities Mission, ii. 214
Unyamwenda, the chief, 130
 „ Little, 108
 „ people, threats of, 177
Urongwe, wells of, ii. 139
Usibigo, a Matabeli, 73
Usikuana and his people, massacre of, 61
Usinduana, a Matabeli, 73
Uxuala, i.e. beer, 59

VAAL river, 17
Vanity, a characteristic of African potentates, ii. 108
Vermin in the Chibinga hut, ii. 13
Victoria Falls, 41, 72, 107
Vilange river, ii. 82
Villages only makeshift affairs, ii. 33
Vitality of Zebra, 79
Vultures, hovering, 268
Vunga mountains, ii. 25

WAGGON, necessity for a, 70; abandoning the, 108, 109, 124
Waggon-life, pleasures of, 98
Wanhungwe, people, ii. 43
Wangwana men from Zanzibar, ii. 210
War, the Transvaal, 23; dread of, 33; on the Shiré river, ii. 55; rumours of, 91, 133, 148; Makololo, 215; Portuguese and Mazinjiri, 223, 246, 256, 262; end of the, 267; its origin, 274–277; war scenes on the Shiré, 278, 282
Warning, a woman's, 210
Wart-hog, 290
Water-buck, ii. 218, 244, 245
Water-bucks, ii. 173
Water-wells, 29
Waynge river, 156, 166, 220, 234
Wazezurus tribe, 312

Weapons, Mashona, 116
„ the manufacture of, 230
Weaving, ii. 19, 20
Wells, ii. 167
„ of Urongwe, ii. 139
Whata, 218
Whip signal in South Africa, 100
Whitaker, a Canadian traveller, 41; death of, 52
White man's dominion in Africa, the, ii. 301
Wild animals, spoor of, 305
Wildebeeste, 29, 30
Windvogel, a bushman, 69; shoots a companion, 84, 85; is lost, 240
Wine of Madeira, 3, 4
Witch doctors, ii. 233
Wives, a man of many, 219, 242
„ Chikuse's, ii. 132, 139
Wolf, adventure with a, 84
Wolves, 88; ferocity of, 291; ii. 13, 14
Woman attacked by a lion, ii. 14
Woman's warning about Chuzu, 210
Women, Mashona, 116; appearance of Makorikori, 229; gold-washers, ii. 18; slaves, 19; visitors at Chikuse's, 103, 119; shaving their heads, 124; native, behave better than men, 164; workers, 197

Wood stacks at Nyassa, ii. 191
Wooden pillows, of Mashona, 133; in Angoni-land, ii. 124
Wooden troughs, 248
Writing a mystery, 228
Wynberg, 5, 6

Xopetta tribe, ii. 112, 242

Yao porters, ii. 221
„ villages, ii. 227
Yokes of slaves, ii. 126, 128, 155

Zambesi river, 36, 53, 80; first sight of the, ii. 37; its navigable parts, 54; steamer suitable for the, 54; story of the, 56; hot springs, 58; crossing the, 59, 287
Zambesi basin, first sight of the, 277
Zambesi valley, races of the, ii. 57
Zanki, 73
Zebras, 39, 78; vitality of, 79, 168, ii. 64, 218
Zeerust, 24
Zingabila, a town of, 247, 257
Zulu conquests, ii. 112
Zulus, Lord Beaconsfield on the, ii. 125
Zumbo, a Portuguese station, ii. 41

www.ingramcontent.com/pod-product-compliance
Lightning Source LLC
Chambersburg PA
CBHW032358230426
43672CB00007B/744